PRAISE FOR *THE HATE NEXT DOOR*

"*The Hate Next Door* takes us on a wild and distressing ride through the white supremacist and extremist worlds where Former Detective Matt Browning was immersed for decades. Having seen the dangers firsthand, Browning's oft ignored prophetic warnings could have protected our democracy if they had been heeded. For anyone who wants to know how this country went from neo-Nazis on the fringes of our society to an insurrection by a massive extremist movement at the Capitol, this is the book to read."

—Dr. Heidi Beirich, former director of The Southern Poverty Law Center's Intelligence Project, *Intelligence Report* and *Hatewatch* blog-producer, and current co-founder of The Global Project Against Hate and Extremism.

"This book is riveting yet shocking even for a girl who grew up in a racial minded cult. The amount of hate is alarming, enlightening, and a must-read for anyone wanting to make a difference against injustice. Matt and Tawni's determined resolution to bring light to a growing institution of abhorrence, bitterness, and brutality is praiseworthy. The undercover journey they take us on shows the raw reality of where hatred takes one's soul as well as the danger and difficulty to bring about justice in an often all too hateful world. Professionally and personally, this couple is the real deal. A compulsory read."

—Rachel Jeffs, author of *Breaking Free*, activist, and FLDS polygamist cult survivor

"This book is an invaluable wake up call to all of us regarding the work that is still left to be accomplished in order to understand and effectively address racism and extremism in every facet of American culture. Matt and Tawni allow the reader to peer into the real cost that police officers, their significant other, and their families pay to keep us safe. *The Hate Next Door* should be required reading as part of training for mental health professionals working with law enforcement personnel to truly understand what is really required physically and emotionally for them to be a successful police officer. I would implore every police chief, academy training director, police officer, cadet, or individual considering a career in police work to read this book and consider the personal and professional implications of what this book represents."

—Joel Beckstead, PhD certified clinical psychologist, clinical director at the U.S. Federal Indian Health Services, and former post-9/11 psychologist to the Pentagon

"Matt Browning speaks in a voice that is conversational and his story-telling range is impressive. Yet underneath his easy manner, he conveys the grip that hate groups have on our society, right under our very noses. His book is a call to awaken to this truth and come together in unification for all. Matt spent his entire career risking his life for those marginalized and his expertise sheds a light on the darkness of hate, urging us all to victory."

—Jane Elizabeth Caplan, MD, Harvard-trained clinical psychiatrist whose therapeutic expertise includes PTSD treatment for veterans and first responders

"*The Hate Next Door* is a must-read for parents, teachers, politicians, and mental health professionals. In fact, this book is for anyone wanting to have an inside view of the warning signs and dangers of hate groups still at work in our country. Matt's heroic service and sacrifice is inspiring and brings to light the need for others to continue to stand against the modern hate movements of today. A fascinating read that you will not be able to put down."

—Brent Hatch, author of *How to Raise a G-Rated Family in an X Rated World*

"Matt's book, *The Hate Next Door*, provides a fascinating look into his undercover work in hate and militia organizations and teaches the importance of respect for all. I had the privilege of working with Matt during my days in the Arizona State Legislature. Matt has repeatedly risked his life to mitigate the effects of violence from hate groups and continues his work across our country to eliminate violent ideologies."

—Krysten Sinema, US Senator

"This book is more than an investigation of one man's experience infiltrating a dangerous world; it is at every page an honest, transparent, and challenging symphony of experience, success, grief, loss, endurance, and resilience. Matson Browning is the real deal and so is this book. Read it, absorb it and share it."

—Judy Saba, CF Churchill Fellow and clinical psychologist for the New South Wales Force

THE HATE
NEXT DOOR

Undercover within
the New Face of
White Supremacy

MATSON BROWNING
with TAWNI BROWNING

To our children, who taught us what love really means.

Copyright © 2023 by Matson Browning
Cover and internal design © 2023 by Sourcebooks
Cover design by Heather VanHuizen/Sourcebooks
Cover images © Daniella Fishburne/Arcangel, John Coletti/Getty Images
Internal design by Tara Jaggers/Sourcebooks

This publication is designed to provide accurate and authoritative information in regard to the subject matter covered. It is sold with the understanding that the publisher is not engaged in rendering legal, accounting, or other professional service. If legal advice or other expert assistance is required, the services of a competent professional person should be sought.—*From a Declaration of Principles Jointly Adopted by a Committee of the American Bar Association and a Committee of Publishers and Associations*

This book is a memoir. It reflects the author's present recollections of experiences over a period of time. Some names and characteristics have been changed, some events have been compressed, and some dialogue has been re-created.

Published by Sourcebooks
P.O. Box 4410, Naperville, Illinois 60567-4410
(630) 961-3900
sourcebooks.com

Cataloging-in-Publication Data is on file with the Library of Congress.

Printed and bound in the United States of America.
VP 10 9 8 7 6 5 4 3 2 1

INTRODUCTION

Six of them had driven 250 miles to start a war with Mexico.

They were mostly quiet and had been since the start of their long trip. No radio. No bragging about the "wetback" they'd recently sucker punched or some rant about keeping America pure. The only sound was the car's tires heading south quickly. There were empty McDonald's bags and soda bottles and cigarette butts on the car floor. In the trunk lay several hunting rifles with scopes, AR-style semi automatics, and one shotgun.

I was still an hour behind them as my truck rattled down I-10 at 90 miles per hour. My Glock pistol lay heavy, and admittedly consoling, on my hip. I'd also snatched my own shotgun, now loaded and resting beside me in the front seat.

I'd gotten the call that afternoon from a buddy in the Department of Public Safety. He'd asked in short breaths if I was familiar with anyone who owned a red four-door Nissan Sentra. I was, and my whole body clenched like a fist. *They were actually doing it.*

"You gotta get down here," the DPS guy said.

A red Sentra had been spotted loaded with a full crew of skin-heads heading south. I'd run back into the house to grab my guns, kiss my wife, Tawni, goodbye, and jumped in my truck.

I'd first heard of this road-trip possibility only days before at a downtown meeting of the Arizona branch of the National Alliance, a neo-Nazi organization whose conceptions of "White supremacy" marched in lockstep with its notions of "patriotism." The president of the group—Jerry Harbin, a guy I'd now known for years while working undercover—had been rallying his Mesa-area troops to help out the Minutemen Project, another anti-immigration, keep-things-White type of militia, down on the border. Harbin wanted a carpool to head to the border and help.

I'd gotten curious. Then, I got alarmed as Harbin added, "Some of our Unit 88 brothers are going." Unit 88 is the most violent strain of skinheads in the Southwest. They were generally hard for *other* hate groups to manage and only brought in for muscle and so-called "wet work," the spilling of blood. Their newest scheme offered plenty of opportunity for that.

I'd headed straight to my new office at the FBI and began writing a memo. I still have no idea what happened to it once submitted. The Phoenix FBI didn't have a great reputation for doing much with our intel. Ironically, I shared an office with the same agent who'd written the infamously ignored 9/11 Memo, which had advised the FBI of Bin Laden's flight plans before the attack.

Four days after I submitted *my* ignored memo, these six skinheads were heading south. Mathew, Brian, Billy, Cam, AJ, and Wes were not men to mess with. In the past few years working undercover, I'd gotten to know each of them—and I knew what they were capable of. Given any opportunity, these guys were prepared for a racial holy war—a RAHOWA, as they called it. In their minds, it was a prophesied crusade destined to put Whites forever atop the hierarchy of humanity. The U.S.-Mexico border, they also believed, was the perfect setting for such a crusade to begin.

The ranch they were likely heading to was seventy-some acres and owned by a "White brother" named Casey Nethercott. I knew Nethercott as your typical antigovernment racist. His property on the border was where many of the most influential and hard-core activists often gathered; the price of entry was only hate. If I had *any* hope of stopping these guys, I'd find them there. Every night, Nethercott's crew of volunteers went out with rifles with infrared scopes, loaded with expanding all-copper bullets designed for elk and wild boar but intended to shoot at Mexicans and Guatemalans.

Opposite one stretch of Nethercott's property, which lies directly across the border and marked only by a dirt road and a chain-link fence, was a small outpost of the Mexican Army composed of a dozen soldiers with German G3 assault rifles.

The plot of those in the red Nissan seemed simple enough—they'd meet up with others at the Nethercott ranch and then get one of those Mexican soldiers in their sights. BAM! If all went well, the soldiers would fire back. *How could they not?* And if one of the skinheads was killed, or even all of them, so be it. True patriots had died for America for three hundred years. And, if America was to have *another* three hundred years, blood would need to be spilled again. It'd be the biggest event since 9/11, when, they believed, America had finally woken to the wolves at its doors. Their ancestors had once hunted wolves and hung their heads from fortress walls. Now, they believed, America was too weak to even build a wall. The outcome of their attack—Americans murdered at the border by Mexican soldiers—would change all that. The American people would rage, unite, and finally be heard; the wall finally built; illegals rounded up, and then...

But first, they needed to get to the ranch.

I could well imagine Wes turning to Billy, no doubt checking his pistol for the tenth time. "God bless America," Wes would say.

———

I once thought I knew what hate looked like.

I could easily picture a handful of drunk bumpkins sneaking around at night with pointy hoods on their heads. Maybe some unformed teenage skinhead spray-painting a poorly drawn swastika on an overpass.

Nothing worse. Not in America. Not today.

(It *also* hadn't yet occurred to me that such "silly" actions were genuine threats to marginalized folk and an easy path to future physical violence.)

I was wrong.

Hate, and its particular rendering of White supremacy, has morphed over the past forty years. The pointy hats became shaved heads, bad tattoos, and shiny Doc Marten boots. Then the boots morphed into camouflage and the idea of "protecting our borders." Later the camouflage became guys in khakis and golf shirts carrying torches and shouting about "taking America back."

It's Volksfront, a notorious global White separatist organization, using government money to run a clinic for British veterans with PTSD returning from Afghanistan—a clinic they were using to indoctrinate and recruit young soldiers.

It's playfully shooting at targets of Black men down at the local gun range or driving down streets with historic Confederate flags while living in places like Arizona or New Jersey.

It's suburban high schoolers drawing swastikas on their cheeks before the big game "as a joke" or chanting "He can't read! He can't read!" from the student cheering section whenever the single Black student on the court gets the ball.

Or it's a single man in body armor covered in graffiti borrowed from the Crusades with two AR-15s entering a mosque in New Zealand.

For twenty years, I was an undercover cop with a front-row seat to all this hate. And even merely pretending to be part of this world almost killed me.

———

This book tells the history and hard realities of racial hatred and the many organizations and systems that advocate and support such thinking.

To tell such a huge story, it's been framed largely within an account of my own career as an undercover detective *within* these very organizations. With an invented identity, as a churchgoing, suburban father of five (I mistakenly believed at the time that such labels were some kind of counterpoint or antidote), I was able to infiltrate, study, and then even thwart hate groups from the KKK and Unit 88 skins to several of the various militia groups now flooding to our southern borders and state capitals in America's heartland.

I won't pretend it was always perfect. Far from it.

For example, one White supremacist, a man named JT Ready, remained the "one who got away." He'd begun as a racist, leaflet-passing loudmouth and become a violent militia member, an elected official, and ultimately a murderer. He'd already allegedly killed several Mexican Americans in "self-defense," organized local hate groups, was leading hunting parties on the U.S.-Mexico border, and, with the support of nationally known politicians, even ran for local and state office. He was always one step ahead of me.

If anything, *I* was the one being destroyed. As a direct result of my work against White supremacy, my entire family was threatened in public (years later, we learned our son slept with knives under his bed for "when the bad guys came"), our pet butchered with a shotgun, my hard-built reputation vilified in weeks by a methodical smear campaign. Eventually, they even took out contracts on my life while Ready and other local racists systemically dismantled my career. If only they'd known, I was already falling apart anyway.

Kurt Vonnegut once wrote, "We are what we pretend to be, so we must be very careful what we pretend to be." Damn, I wish I'd known that quote twenty years ago. Spending all that time with hate-filled men was like walking into a radioactive wasteland. You could only stay for a short time, and even then, the toxic stuff still got into your clothes and hair, eventually under your skin. My thoughts grew violent and filled with hate, and I eventually struggled to define who I was anymore. I even started looking at my Mexican American neighbors…differently. Eventually, for too many long nights, death seemed the only option out for me. I know that revelation may sound extreme, but the FBI won't let their crew stay undercover for more than two years to protect their mental health; as a Mesa, Arizona, detective, I did almost twenty.

Fortunately, I *also* had my wife of thirty years, Tawni, who kept me sane (mostly) while I worked undercover for decades and over time became a legitimate partner in gathering intel on these people, eventually going so far as to go undercover *with* me—all in the name of protecting our family and me.

While it was never easy on us—the threats from criminals *and*

even cops alike, the constant need for secrecy, the nonstop exposure to terrible violence, my own eventual suicidal thoughts—we
somehow got through it together.

Eventually, I quit the force and stopped—well, mostly
stopped—doing undercover work. If I was going to fight hate *and*
stay alive, I needed to do it out in the open with Tawni officially
beside me. Since then, she and I have built a global information-
sharing network for law enforcement called the Skinhead
Intelligence Network (SIN) to help educate law enforcement and
communities worldwide on White supremacy and become internationally sought-after experts on White supremacist groups and
border militias. Originally the Skinhead Intelligence Network, the
organization has now evolved in more than simply name to keep
up with the changing face of White supremacy.

Through SIN, we've lectured all over the U.S., the UK for
Scotland Yard, Australia and New Zealand, Germany, and Holland
as rhetoric, music, and a sense of belonging continue to lure young,
disaffected men—and plenty of women too—into these hate
movements across the globe. With worldwide economic strife
and an ongoing worldwide immigration crisis, each bringing new
waves of anti-immigrant hate, we find ourselves busier than ever.

It's time to "deputize" the rest of the world.

For too long, White supremacists were seen as a fringe
movement going largely ignored. But the racists are out again:
Confederate banners waving, rifles slung over camouflaged shoulders. Emboldened to emerge from the shadows. Marching in capitals across the Western world. And, with the world economy and
labor force recently shaken by a global pandemic, you can expect
an even greater surge in the years to come.

Quite recently, I got word that two American militias were

calling supporters to the southern U.S. border. "Bring everything you got," they bragged, referring to weaponry. "It's going to be a bloodbath." It wasn't the first or last time supremacists were hoping to start an actual war with Mexico.

Worse, these border militias are especially interested in recruiting me, a well-trained police officer, their ranks already swelling with ex-military and *active* police officers, as law enforcement seeks supporters wherever it can find them following the social consequences and rhetoric of 2020.

After the 2020 presidential election, I worked undercover again at a "rally for America" in Gilbert, Arizona, attended by the far-right Proud Boys standing side by side with a bunch of the same skinheads I'd known years before—now middle-aged men and women dressed up for suburban America, tattoos hidden. A similar scene played out earlier this year, as Tawni and I worked undercover at a pro-Trump "Protest the Vote" rally in Phoenix. Most people in attendance were merely disappointed and devoted conservatives, period; but *some* in the crowd were more than that— White supremacists legitimizing their radical views by joining a larger stage. And there are increasingly more of them every year.

This battle, we fear, is only beginning.

No more than a year ago, I discovered there was a new contract on my life for the recent work we've been doing—further proof this threat is escalating, growing more violent, and now morphing into mainstream thought and expression.

This story is written in first person, but in reality, it is told by both Tawni and me, sharing our words, memories, fears, and hopes through my singular narration. It chronicles our time undercover to fully expose these hate groups and the varied profiles of their members, and the geopolitical and psychological dynamics that make them tick, from the racists we locked away to those, like JT Ready, who evaded me, hiding openly within our increasingly fractured and contentious culture.

In telling our story, we hope to fully introduce readers to the dark and complicated world of White supremacy. The who, what, when, and WHY.

A world that, *now more than ever*, must be exposed.

The supremacists have persevered, and even flourished, for decades because most of us have no idea what a White supremacist looks like, let alone what they actually believe or do. What to look for in our friends, neighbors, and colleagues. I was a detective in an area of the country with a staggering White supremacy problem and, at first, even I didn't know it existed.

The importance of information and understanding cannot be overstated. It's everything. The rest—how to tackle the problem—becomes so much easier once you recognize the symptoms and see the issue for what it is: the evolution of racial hate remains an ever-growing threat that has brought us to a fundamental, and frightening, brink.

Maybe close enough now for us all to finally do something about it.

1

AMERICAN NAZIS

Initial Meeting

The first official White supremacist I ever met tried to kill me. It was a fitting start to the next twenty-plus years.

I say "official" because I suspect I'd encountered such people before in my life but was still oblivious to the fact. That's part of what helps this particular subculture persist and thrive. If you're not looking for it, it can exist, invisible, for decades.

Growing up in the suburbs of Phoenix, I had friends and teammates of every shape and color, and from what I could tell, we all got along. So, to me, the possibility that someone would hate another person solely because of their skin color or religion was something I might only see in an *After School Special*. Never in my own school or front yard.

I was raised a member of the Church of Jesus Christ of Latter-Day Saints, a Mormon in the common parlance. While serving my two-year mission in Oklahoma, I met a guy who'd—at least, this is what he told me—trained his dog to be "racist to Black folk." He'd taught it to bark violently anytime a Black person passed. I was twenty and couldn't fathom why anyone would do this. He might as well have told me that he'd taught his dog to bark at sneezes. I was a naive kid raised by parents who treated everyone the same and *honestly* believed we were all brothers. I guess this man was an unofficial supremacist. And those guys at school who sometimes told stupid jokes about Mexican, Jewish, or Black people…I wasn't sure yet how to categorize them.

I'd honestly forgotten all about the guy with the racist dog and the jokes until this skinhead almost ended my life.

At this point, I'd been a cop for about four years. It was late one night. My ten-hour shift was over, and I was maybe ten minutes from home. First, however, I'd rolled up to "shoot the breeze" beside a motorcycle officer I recognized. Tawni and the kids were in Montana with her mom, and I was stag for a few days, driving home to an empty house.

While talking, this officer and I both watched as a white Dodge Dakota ran a red light through Brown Road. My fellow officer smiled, shook his head, and chased after the truck. Staying put, I flicked on my police radio and listened along. I heard the motor officer call in a vehicle pursuit on the truck, almost immediately followed by a "foot pursuit of the White male driver." The driver had, apparently, already ditched his truck and was trying to escape by sprinting off into the night.

And, from my position, I could now see the guy running through some backyards. I quickly parked and got out of my car, then headed for a backyard *ahead* of the driver to see if I could scare him back out into the open. *Bingo!* As I came around the corner of the first house, he was running my way.

He was in his late teens or early twenties with a shaved head, white T-shirt, and blue jeans, donning big black boots.

My badge was draped around my neck, and I went to pull it free from under my shirt to identify myself as an officer. Even shouted, "Mesa Police!"

Everything slowed way down. *All I need to do is tackle him, turn him over, and handcuff him,* I thought. No problem; I'd done it hundreds of times.

But something was different this time, strange. This guy didn't have that typical look of fear in his eyes most folks get when scanning for any escape or finally realizing they're about to be arrested. Rather, *this* guy had the look of "I'm going to fuck you up." *This* guy wasn't afraid of my police declaration. At all. If anything, he looked *thrilled* to be encountering a cop and turned directly toward me.

Then, he lifted his shirt, reached into his waistband, and pulled free a gun.

Before I could even flinch, I felt the barrel of a semiautomatic pistol driven into the direct center of my chest as he racked the handgun's slide to chamber a round. With no time to pull my own gun, I went into total football mode and tackled him. On impact, the gun barrel jammed down from my chest and into my stomach. I couldn't believe this was happening. It had turned into one of those movie moments where two people are fighting over a gun.

Somehow, I was able to knock it from his hand and into the grass. After, I have no idea how many punches were thrown by either of us or even where they landed. Other officers arrived and had to pull me off the guy. He ended up face down in the dirt with his hands cuffed behind his back.

As I sat nearby catching my breath and replaying the incident in my mind, I realized the gravity of what'd just happened. I'd been in some scrapes those four years and couldn't count how many people I had taken to jail. The difference? This guy had been *trying* to kill me. He had no clue who I was, and vice versa, yet he had wanted to end my life—not to avoid arrest; he just wanted to kill a cop.

I drove home trying to figure it out. The adrenaline still coursing through my body, I grew angrier with each passing block and might have taken it out on my steering wheel a couple times. No one on scene had once asked how I was doing. *Pointless to get mad about, right?* This was my job. No one died. Why *should* they care? Still, it upset me.

I composed myself and called Tawni. Usually, I'd talk to her while driving home to decompress, and every time I called, she seemed genuinely excited to talk with me. This was no exception. But I wasn't sure where to start.

After a moment of silence, and a "Matt, are you OK?" I told her what happened. I'm not sure she truly understood it all, and I desperately needed her to. But I don't think I'd finished processing it enough yet myself. "You're obviously upset. But you're OK though, right?"

I wasn't.

"Do you need us to come home?" she asked.

"No, but I need you to stay close," I said. When I got home, I couldn't hang up. I didn't want to. I went to bed with the phone and Tawni's voice on the pillow right there beside me.

COPLAND

I'd first told Tawni I wanted to be a cop shortly *after* we had married.

She threatened annulment. So, I went to work in retail, miserable, for six months. Then, I tried to go back to school again before pleading my case to her. I genuinely knew what I wanted to do with my life—it was almost a calling. The notion of law enforcement had never conflicted with my faith-based upbringing; as corny as it might sound, I'd always seen it as an opportunity to help others. But I also wasn't going to do anything that affected our family at that level without her support.

Tawni's blessing came with two conditions: (1) I couldn't work for Phoenix PD and (2) I couldn't work narcotics. Both deemed too dangerous, she'd concluded. I, admittedly, ended up doing a little of both, but not in a way that—technically, with some serious leniency—ever broke my promise. I did, after all, understand her fears for my safety. Being the spouse of a cop ain't easy.

And nights with an almost fatal foot chase didn't help...

———

A couple of days after the incident with a gun jammed into my chest, a fellow cop stopped me outside work, a guy I'd known for years. "Heard you got into it with Jason Stafford," he said.

"Who?" I was honestly trying to sort out who he was talking about. Then, my brain finally pulled it together. "The guy who almost killed me..."

"Yeah." This cop was almost smiling about it; I couldn't get a read on what his point was. *Was he genuinely concerned about me? Was he just breaking my stones?* He'd brought Stafford up like we were talking about an old high school pal.

"Guess you can say we 'got into it,'" I said. "You know this guy?"

"I know people who know him," he replied. But that was all.

"He crazy or something?" I prodded. "What's the story?"

"He's a fresh-cut skin is what he is," he said. I had no idea yet what that meant, and my face must have shown it. "A skinhead. A new recruit trying to prove himself."

"Like 'Heil Hitler' and all that White power shit?" I confirmed.

I didn't even know that was still a thing, certainly not in Arizona. Made me think of Europe maybe and the early 1980s. Skinheads? Neo-Nazis? White power? I hadn't heard those words

in Mesa *once* in four years of police work. We'd spent all our training in the police academy on Latino gangs and learning about rap
music to understand the Black gangs better (seriously).

"Is this skinhead stuff really a thing here?" I asked.

The other cop shrugged. "Not a big deal. Mostly White guys
beating up other White guys." It was the first of many, *many* times
I would hear this same line.

"'Mostly?'" I said and got another shrug in reply. "You know
people who say Stafford got into this… stuff? Or, do…you know
actual skinheads?" There was no easy way to ask this question. I
didn't want it to sound like an accusation, yet…

"I'm glad you're OK," he replied and patted my arm as he
walked away.

Seems there was no easy way to *answer* the question either.

Two months later, Jason Stafford (back on the streets because
Maricopa County didn't have the money to prosecute) shot a Mesa
police officer in the back. This cop was a rookie, his sixth day on
the job. His bulletproof vest saved his life.

The night we'd tussled, I'd recognized that Stafford wanted to
kill a cop, and he'd gotten much closer this second time—as close
as you can. He was sentenced to twenty-four years in prison. (He'll
be a free man by the time this book comes out.)

I started asking around about this "skinhead scene" in Mesa
and Phoenix.

I got blank stares from everyone, including the first guy who'd
talked to me about Stafford. My then-sergeant wasn't any help
either; there were no state or federal grants or budget for "White-
boy gangs," so there wasn't much, in *his* world view, to talk about.
There was not one police whiteboard or chart or plan in the state
that included the word "skinhead" or "neo-Nazi" or "supremacist."

The guy who'd deliberately attacked two officers was, officially, just a violent dude who happened to be White with a shaved head. End of story.

And, having not once heard anything about a skinhead problem in town before, I almost believed it myself.

Almost.

———

Now, I gotta be completely honest here.

A thirty-year career combating White supremacy began, admittedly, with entirely selfish motives: *I wanted out of the van.*

After four years working my way up the ladder, I was a detective with the Mesa Gang Unit, a squad that focused almost exclusively on Black and Latino street gangs. As the sole White detective on our team, I wasn't—as you'd well imagine and understand—often chosen to go undercover among these particular gangs. I'm good at undercover work, but not *that* good.

Instead, I was usually assigned to sit in the surveillance van. We kept it a block or so away from the real action. My job was to listen to the audio coming in from the undercover guys' microphones, take some pictures, and provide backup if anything ever went wrong. Nothing ever did. Four years of training and wanting to be a detective had resulted in sitting alone in a van listening to scratchy AM radio and trying not to be seen while eating piles of sunflower seeds in 100-degree-plus Arizona weather sans AC because keeping the van running would be too suspicious. When things were slow, they'd let me pretend to be a john and solicit prostitutes, which whom the team would swoop in and arrest once discussions of this-for-that had been formalized. (Not that they always "swooped in"; a favorite prank of the guys was to delay the arrest long after the signal had been given, just to see the undercover officer squirm as he ran out of ways to stall the now-hired sex worker.)

Other than providing backup from the inside of a van and upping my improv skills with local streetwalkers, there wasn't much undercover work for me to do. I'd asked to get more involved in the gang scene, rife with drugs and violence, and they'd shrug, smile, and say, "Yeah… you're too white. *White* people think you're too white."

I'd even come up with simple storylines to explain why a guy who looked like me *might* be talking to these gangs of color— something involving a biker gang looking to make a partnership or gun purchase, for instance. But it was simply far easier for them to send in one of my Black or Latino counterparts to achieve the same ends.

But now… "White power skinheads." I surely wouldn't be too White for them. So, I continued to ask my fellow detectives and others around the office about the local skinhead scene. They all looked at me like I was nuts. Months went by. No one had a single shred of information on any White power movement in town.

Then, I found Lester.

LESTER

I was flipping through old police reports and discovered that months earlier some guy had been arrested for putting racist cassette tapes (yes, clearly an *early* story from my career) into the tape decks of local electronics stores and blaring the tunes for all to hear. He'd been cited and released. I asked around about the incident, but no one in the office remembered it.

Using a phone number on the police report, I called this man directly. The act started. "Lester?" I said. "I'm a reporter for the *New Times* and I'd like to talk to you."

He inquired about my interest in him of course, but there was genuine interest in his voice.

"I heard about your antics at the electronics store," I explained, "and thought it would make a good story. Tell your side of things. Some kind of message or whatever, you know. What do you think?" Lester, now unable to control the excitement in his voice, agreed, and we set up a meeting for the very next day.

Per policy, I went to my new sergeant, John Meza, and told him I wanted to talk to this Lester guy.

"Why?" Meza asked.

"Seeing if there's anything to this skinhead scene," I said.

"Why?" he said again.

I had no real answer yet.

"You going undercover?" Meza knew that's mostly all I wanted and was giving his blessing. Good boss.

"I'm going as a reporter. Told him I'm writing a story about his agenda or whatever."

Sergeant Meza laughed, a laugh I'd get used to over the years. "Fine," he said. "Just take backup."

Again, the other men on my squad were all Black or Latino, and I could only assume the guy with racist cassette tapes wouldn't talk to us if I brought one of them; I needed a White guy. Fortuitously, that week, we had a young patrol officer working with us. A cop named Kenny. White guy. Quiet, but a real good guy. (Ken happens to be Mesa's new chief of police as of the writing of this book.) I told him the plan for the next day and to get his best Jimmy Olsen ready.

Lester lived alone in a single-wide trailer out in east Mesa, a shabbier neighborhood affectionately called "Asshole Acres" by everyone, both cops and bad guys. It was a low-income, racially diverse neighborhood. We had a lot of issues with Latino gangs in that area. It was an interesting home base for a White racist. I wondered if this guy was merely lashing out at his neighbors from the safety of cassette tapes at the local Best Buy.

As we pulled up, I could tell Lester wasn't much of a landscaper. His yard was mostly dirt. He *did* manage, however, to have a Black lawn jockey statue standing just outside his trailer door.

"You gotta be kidding me," Kenny said as we approached the statue and trailer.

Lester was twentysomething with a shaved head, white T-shirt, and shiny black boots. He looked like a wimpier version of Jason Stafford, the guy who'd attacked me (if he'd dressed like Stafford for Halloween or a school project maybe).

After introductions were made, he invited us into a messy trailer with a small couch and chair to sit on. The kitchen counter behind him was cluttered with pans, dirty dishes, and mostly empty Heineken bottles. There was nothing else of note in his place. No guitar or cat food dish or fishing pole or anything. He was just a guy with a TV and piles of clothes and dishes.

I asked if he minded me recording our interview, as he seemed excited to talk to us. Once we started, it was like opening a dam and I couldn't get him to shut up. For the first time in heaven knows how long, someone was paying attention to this kid.

We quickly established he was unemployed. Didn't have family in town.

The guy was alone.

Maybe for good reasons, clearly. But maybe it was the other

way around. It was tough to tell which had come first: had he gone down this wannabe skinhead road hoping to find allies, a connection, in a world where he had none?

He first prattled on about the Jewish people "taking over" the banks, the media, the wars, and how Black people were "the muds," Mexicans were "invading" the country, "If you're not White, you're not right"—the same ole list of clichés, very stereotypical. Like a TV-show version of what you'd expect to hear from a racist skinhead. Then, he launched into how "Jesus was killed by the Jews" so "all the Jews must die." I'd heard more than enough and asked Lester what he'd played on the tapes.

He jumped out of his chair and ran back with an old-school boom box. He played us something called "Who Likes a Nigger?" by someone named Johnny Rebel. (Rebel is the stage name of Louisianan Clifford Trahan, who'd recorded the racist songs, he later claimed only for money, in the 1960s. The singles made it into Southern juke-boxes and, with the internet's help, have spread more easily throughout the White supremacy movement.) The song's lyrics lived up to the title. Just a simple country song with childish racist lyrics. I asked if we might have a copy, and he quickly handed over a tape.

We then talked about the local skinhead scene, and Lester told us it was growing every day. "How do you mean?" I asked.

"Just see more people into it," he claimed. He seemed more hopeful than anything. "You know, the boots and braces."

I asked him to explain; I had no idea what this meant yet.

He pointed to his boots. "Doc Martens," he said, as if that clarified everything.

"The red mean anything?" I asked, noticing his black boots were laced with red. You could tell he'd carefully rolled his jeans up like a 1950s teenybopper to make sure the shoelaces showed.

"You've shed blood for the movement," he explained. It was like a direct quote he'd heard somewhere fifty times.

"You've done that?" I asked, knowing from his reaction that he likely hadn't. And the boots looked like he'd never worn them outside of his own trailer. Without them, he was just a skinny kid with a shaved head in 501 button-up jeans. With them, he wasn't much more.

He avoided the question entirely. "You should check out The Nile," he said.

The Nile? It was a warehouse-type club downtown mostly used for heavy metal bands, ska, and sometimes more "provocative" bands whose stage shows involved XXX-rated theatrics. They brought in live bands from across the country; no one particularly famous, but at least it wasn't another local cover band playing Skynyrd badly. It was known across Arizona as the Valley's punk capital. And Friday nights would frequently be billed as "gangsta rap night" and brought in Black gangs from throughout the Valley. At the time, there wasn't much of a nightlife in Mesa. We had our typical bars, but The Nile Theater was as close as we got to special.

"Skinheads hang out at…The Nile," I confirmed. I tried to imagine such people there on gangsta rap night.

He nodded. "Sometimes, yeah. Saturdays, usually."

Didn't make sense. Multiple cops and detectives I knew sometimes moonlighted as security at The Nile, collecting cover charges, working the door and such. I'd *specifically* asked around about a "skinhead scene." How had this never trickled up before?

"*You* go down there?" I asked, suspecting he hadn't. "The Nile?"

"Sometimes, yeah." He was clearly lying.

This kid was so desperate for an identity. Perhaps, any he could find. Maybe becoming a skinhead was the path of least resistance—all it took was a $100 pair of boots and a severe hair-cut. Yet he still didn't have the confidence to pursue the next step. Maybe that was for the best. Maybe blasting these moronic tapes was as far as he'd ever go. In all cases, it was sad.

"You know a guy named Jason Stafford?" I asked.

He didn't.

"He's the skin who shot a cop," I said.

This kid just stared at me, not sure what to do with that info. We shook his hand, and I told him it was a pleasure to meet him. He asked when the story would be out, and after telling him it was "up to my editor," we exited the trailer.

In the car, Kenny and I let out a laugh we'd been holding in for almost an hour. Our first reaction wasn't that these guys were so dangerous but, rather, "what a joke" they were. I was, at first, also guilty of easily dismissing White supremacists.

For years, I would diminish their influence and power by call-ing them "morons," "clowns," and "trash." I still do when I slip up. It's easier than admitting what they really are. But it's a dangerous mistake.

"So," Kenny said. "What do you think?"

I'd stopped laughing and stared at the depressing trailer with the pathetic shaved-head guy in his red-laced boots inside.

"Think we're heading to The Nile," I said.

———

Dylann Roof, who was sentenced to death for the 2015 Charleston church shooting, had attended seven different schools in nine years. At nineteen, he had no job, driver's license, or romantic relationship and mostly just stayed in his room. There, he created a website, the

Last Rhodesian, a nod to the White settlers who'd both occupied and immigrated to modern-day Zimbabwe—featuring photos of himself posing with Old Glory (the American flag) and the apartheid-era South African flag. His online posts expressed disdain for Black people, specifically targeting Black-on-White crime, which he'd first learned about online. He'd never once met face-to-face with any supremacy group and so was later deemed "self-radicalized." Despite numerous minor run-ins with the police, he was able to buy a Glock 41 and eight magazines filled with hollow-point bullets. He walked into a church in Charleston, South Carolina—the oldest African Methodist Episcopal church in the South. And for an hour, he participated in a Bible study with twelve Black congregants. After he began shooting, he reloaded five times while shouting racial epithets. "I have to do it," he shouted. "You rape our women and you're taking over our country... And, you have to go!" One woman and her five-year-old granddaughter survived by pretending to be dead.

Later, Dylann admitted he'd almost called off the attack because the people in the Bible study were so nice to him.

INTO THE PIT

Kenny and I never made it to The Nile together.

His week with our Gang Unit was up, and he'd been called back to regular police duty. I'd have to go with someone else. First, though, I asked around town and confirmed White supremacist bands had started playing The Nile on Saturday nights. I found it interesting that this information had not been made available to me until I had enough knowledge to ask direct questions.

Honestly, I was still floundering. Until now, I hadn't even

*Dylann Roof: https://www.splcenter.org/files/miseducation-dylann-roof.

known there *were* White supremacist bands. But there were and are. Lots. Local and international. With names like Battlecry, Definite Hate, Blue Eyed Devils, Endless Pride, Broadsword, Freikorps, Kill Baby Kill!, Prussian Blue, Berserker, Skull Head, the Spear of Longinus, Hate Forest…you get the idea. The Southern Poverty Law Center (SPLC) keeps an ongoing list. There are scads of groups—far too many—that you can find online or even on Spotify in seconds.

My plan was to visit the club on a Saturday night and monitor the crowd. If only a handful of guys there with shiny black boots showed up, I'd move on. Everyone at work would be proven right. It would be a non-issue. If not, however…

My "ops plan" was approved through the chain of command with only one usual concern: *Who was going into the club with me as backup?* All of my coworkers were still Latino or Black.

Sergeant Meza laughed at me again and told me to figure it out. I called one of the few White undercover detectives I knew in the area, and arrangements were made. I'd found my new "pale-faced" partner.

———

The night arrived and I called to confirm final plans with my undercover backup. I reminded him it was some kind of skinhead show, so "boots and braces" would be fine. Though no one actually *had* to shave their head to be considered a skinhead, the boots and colored suspenders were still borderline requirements.

The boots are generally high, shiny black Doc Marten boots, preferably steel-toed—for decades, the standard-issue foot-wear of White supremacists across the world. They reinforce the movement's initial ties to the working-class man as steel was added to the boot's toes in the early 1950s for the world's coal miners and construction crews. (Perfect also for when needing to kick flesh and bone.) White laces are used in the boots to connote "racial purity" and "White pride," or red laces for those who have, as Lester explained, spilled blood in the name of White supremacy. The ties are always laced in a specific ladder style, which the skins call "straight laced." That the original boots were created and marketed by Klaus Märtens, who'd fought for the Nazis in World War II, is a skinhead bonus.

And then there are the "braces," the suspenders skinheads wear colored white or red, either up over the shoulder or hanging proudly at their sides.

Symbolism in the neo-Nazi/skinhead culture is particularly important. While all tribes and cliques (from countries to small social clubs) choose exclusive and specific colors, greetings, handshakes and phrases, this group pays particular attention devoted to the historical legacy of the icons and language established over the past six decades.

Skinheads trace their roots back to England. Late 1960s or even 1950s, depending which historians you ask. In either case, these original skins were known as the "boot boys" because of their fondness for the steel-toed boots and their working-class identities. They were proud of their proletarian origins, upholding "working-class values" and had great disdain for convention and authority. Though patriotic, they were initially mostly apolitical and primarily enjoyed sharing time and laughs and gripes over infinite pints of beer.

These early skins had a tendency of getting involved in brawling and hooliganism, particularly during soccer games. Typically, they directed their aggression toward students, gay people, and, only occasionally at first, people of other religions and cultures. Racism wasn't yet the agenda. In fact, Shane Meadows, a British director and ex-skin from this era, "argues skinheads were amongst Britain's first *anti*racists, mixing with newly arrived waves of West Indian immigrants with whom they indulged a mutual love of reggae and ska music."[i]

It wasn't until the end of the 1970s and early 1980s, when the British economy had fallen, that the skinhead subculture took a turn to full-on racism and neo-Nazism. These young men were feeling the pinch of a tightening job market and a diminishing empire—sound familiar?—which, following WWII, no longer "ruled the world," and they weren't going to "take it" quietly.

In a *Time* article on the history of skinheads, Meadows asserts it was only during the 1980s that the skinhead movement became infected by the Far Right. With the decline of British manufacturing and the onset of high unemployment, many working-class skins, whose communities bore the brunt of the new arrivals from abroad, became seduced by the promises of anti-immigrant politicians.[ii]

Immigrants have always made easy scapegoats for a myriad of problems. (Today's neo-Nazi skinheads are *especially* focused on immigration, and talking about it with them is like throwing gasoline on the hate fire.) Anti-Pakistani virulence and fights now erupted throughout the streets of Britain, resulting with many in the hospital or even dead. And these White young, unskilled ex-factory workers needed a more distinctive look to tell each other apart, so eventually they shaved their heads in defiance to go along with the boots and braces.

It is here the original "boot boys" split into two distinct groups: the anti-immigrant neo-Nazis and the SHARPs (Skinheads *Against* Racial Prejudice).

Yes, many skinheads have remained true to their *anti*-racist roots. There are also Redskins (leaning Marxist and Socialist) and anarchist skins, but these mostly align with the SHARP.

These two opposing groups—neo-Nazis and SHARPs—had now fought for almost fifty years. The only thing still connecting them was their working-class origin, boots, braces, shaved heads… and, as I would soon see firsthand, the music.

———

After eating dinner and somehow convincing our young sons to eat their peas and take a quick bath, I snuck into our bedroom to pull on the newly purchased Doc Marten boots Tawni had found for me at a second-hand thrift store and the white braces she'd picked up at some local head shop.

I'd already made it an early habit to bring Tawni into the things I was doing at work. She was always great to bounce ideas off, and it also kept her invested in me and what I was doing…or *trying* to do. Including her was the only way it worked for either of us. In any case, Tawni loved Halloween, and once I knew the skins had an actual "costume," I let her know. She'd handled her part of the mission perfectly; the rest of the night would be up to me.

I stood in front of the bedroom mirror. I looked just like Lester or Jason Stafford. For $50, I appeared to be a part of *something*. It was bizarre, and scary.

"Good luck," Tawni said. She knew I was nervous. Until that night, the totality of my undercover work had consisted mostly of picking up hookers, buying twenty-dollar rocks of crack, and sitting in vans while providing largely unused backup. Tonight, I was the lead detective and had no set script to work from. I'd been apprehensive all week. This was different from sitting in a car with a backup van of colleagues behind me, talking to a hundred-pound hooker.

I drove to The Nile and watched from afar before approaching.

The first thing I saw was that it wasn't just a few guys.

The club was packed.

I easily counted *twenty* guys in "boots and braces" heading *into* The Nile. Who knew how many were already inside, where you could already hear the distinct bass of live music rumbling. Just about every guy's head was shaved. I was nursing a short mullet then (in my defense, it *was* a perfect undercover cop look then *and* today), and there were just enough guys there with my same look to get away with it. It seemed you didn't have to be an official skinhead to still enjoy hate music and White Pride bands.

There were also plenty of women too—young girls, really—who moved among these guys like they'd all known each other for years.

While I watched from afar, there was one more thing I needed to check out. The club, as I said earlier, often employed off-duty cops as bouncers at the front door. The last thing I needed was to run into a colleague and get any questions that would ruin my undercover work before it even started. I didn't recognize the guys working the door, so I went inside.

Thankfully, my nerves vanished as soon as I passed through the narrow doors; it was game time. My first move—one I would use for the next twenty years—was to vanish into the background as quickly as possible, not to draw too much attention. You don't get any real training to be an undercover detective. You can either bluff your way into places, or you can't. I leaned back casually and surveyed the dim room while I waited for my partner to show up.

There were more than seventy people—mostly young men—crowded inside. Seventy. I couldn't believe it. *Where had all these guys come from? How had I never noticed them around town before?* Closer now, I could spot the "fresh cuts" right away—like the one who'd run at me with his gun. These neo-Nazis still had a sunburn around their newly shaved heads.

Just about everybody wore a "wifebeater" T-shirt. Some shirts had logos for bands like Skrewdriver (one of the most popular neo-Nazi groups) or a Hammerskin symbol (the crossed hammers you might recognize from the film *The Wall*).

I noted a lot of poorly done tattoos. Stick-and-poke tattoos from prison or home. Or just cheap ones done locally. Bold-lined swastikas, lightning bolts, or the words "White pride" or "White power" showed on skin or bled through the shirts' material. I started filing away tattoos in my memory, perfect for IDing these guys later if ever needed.

This is exactly the reason many neo-Nazi leaders now preach *against* getting tattoos, because they make it easier for law enforcement officers to spot racist extremists. But, for the proper skinhead, getting inked remains as popular now as ever. Typical tatts include special numbers, swastikas, WWII German military medals, Viking symbols, and portraits of past "martyrs to the cause."

Some popular symbols worth noting include the following:

14. Just the number. For White power groups, their unofficial, routinely quoted motto: "*We must secure the existence of our people and a future for White children.*" Fourteen words. Get it?

88. *Heil Hitler* as *H* is the 8th letter of the alphabet. Not so long ago, Target recalled baseball caps and shorts that displayed the number 88 from all of its stores.[iii]

311. The letter *K* is the 11th letter of the alphabet. KKK.

100%. 100 percent Aryan or White.

4/20. You might think it's a pot thing. To White racists, it's Hitler's birthday.

Any Norse stuff (from runes to Thor's hammer) *could* be White pride symbols. The Norse, White supremacists believe, were the "true" White Aryans. You have to see what else they've gotten tattooed to get the full story, as they may just enjoy comic books (also, there are *thousands* of practicing Norse pagans not connected to supremacy at all). Celtic crosses now also fall under this same category, though there are plenty out there with just such a cross proudly tattooed on their ankle who'd be mortified to learn this.

Most of the women at The Nile were just as tatted and some as fierce-looking as the guys. Those who identify as neo-Nazis, I soon learned, are called "skinbyrds." In the decades to come, I'd learn that these distinctive women can be as violent and indoctrinated as the men, if not more so.

Several women this night had the infamous Chelsea haircuts— variations of an extreme punk rock look with a shaved crown, keeping long hair on the sides and back of neck—now the "certified" skinbyrd haircut for thirty-some years. All, despite their real size, were wearing the same supersmall T-shirts and skirts to show as much ink and skin as possible. A lot of dark makeup and short denim. Bras seemed optional at best. I'd learn soon how easily and quickly these girls moved around between the Skins; one murderess I later caught had "dated" every guy in her crew—it was a badge of honor for both sides.

Now, to the music.

One of the primary driving aspects of this particular subculture is its music. Tom Metzger, a now-deceased major skinhead leader and former Ku Klux Klan Grand Dragon who founded the White Aryan Resistance *and* won the Democratic nomination for a seat in the U.S. House of Representatives in the 1980s (representing *California*??!) always believed that the way to any young man's heart… is through the music.

The bands' tunes are all fast, loud, and hard—rock-n-roll on steroids and filled with all the buzz words of ferocity, strength, and solidarity a young brain is all too often looking for. Today, a skinhead's playlist will include everything from hate-labeled bands like Skrewdriver, Max Resist, and Hate Breed alongside more commercial—and unconnected to the movement—groups, including Irish bands Flogging Molly and Dropkick Murphys, country superstar Johnny Cash, and the Reverend Horton Heat, a popular '40s-style swing band.

Genuine Skin music, however, is distinct, with a solid driving sound, filled with messages of hate and violence. Lyrics such as those in Skrewdriver's "Skinhead" are characteristic. (Copyright laws prevent printing the full lyrics here, but a lot of it's about pulling on boots and braces and "looking for a fight," smashing non-White faces, showing no mercy, until "the job is done.")

That's basically what the guys on stage now played.

The entire band performed in knee-high Doc Marten boots with red and white laces, with braces down. The music was what you might expect. Loud and obnoxious, the same muffled two chords over and over while some guy screamed in a garbled voice, more yelling than singing.

The crowd of young Whites—the *whole* room was White, almost statistically impossible in Arizona—cheered and yelled "Oi, oi, oi!!" (a skinhead salute of agreeance akin to saying, "amen" in a prayer) to the music while throwing up *sieg heil* salutes. British hooliganism and German Nazism somehow merged into one for dancing in some Arizona club.

I understood the real problem now: these young people who had all gathered for a single night had come from all over the Phoenix Valley. If I was looking for a Blood (primarily African Americans) or a Barrio Pobre (a new Latino gang in Mesa) we knew exactly where to go. There were specific blocks and parts of town they lived in and controlled.

However, *this* particular group of White kids who thought the Nazis expressed good ideas was spread over a hundred miles in every direction. Scattered throughout almost *every* neighborhood.

Then, during one of the songs, I noticed the whole band looking back over the crowd toward the doors. The crowd turned with them to see what was going on. I'd been to a lot of concerts in my day but never seen an audience turn in perfect unison like that. They'd stopped everything to see one guy walking in.

My guy. The undercover who was supposed to be my partner all night.

He'd strolled in wearing tight jeans akin to what the lead singer of an '80s hair band would wear, and a white wifebeater T-shirt. His day job was as a State Police officer, and his boots were black but looked exactly like the boots a motor officer would wear—because they were! Worse still, his pants were tucked *into* them. Meanwhile, the braces should match the boot laces in color and be no wider than one-quarter inch. My partner must have hit Home Depot on the way over because his "braces" were straight-up suspenders and about two inches wide. There should have been hammers and tape measures hanging from his hips. The inexplicable thing about it was that, clearly, *he* thought he looked good.

I avoided standing anywhere near him that night. As a matter of fact, I ignored him completely. I couldn't get outed before I even started this work. Danny was a good guy, but I never saw him again that night. He got bored and left about halfway through.

I'd made a mistake and was on my own. So it goes.

Being tall makes it easier to look over a crowd. I wandered around, taking it all in, nodding my head to the "music" and shouting out "Oi, oi, oi" whenever called upon. To fit in, I even hit the mosh pit for a short period of time.

A mosh pit is a big swirling circle of "masculine ferocity" in front of the stage with tons of swinging fists, and elbows and body slamming. Mostly harmless but brutal. It is a way to prove how tough you are in a world with few official rites of passage. But there are still plenty of dislocated shoulders, broken noses, etc., along the way. At six foot four, I was an immediate target in the churning circle as twenty-plus skinheads slammed into each other, and me, while the band raged on.

I eventually worked my way back around the club again and started picking out its leaders, the guys everyone looked up to. I sized up the ones who had that genuine look of hate, and those who were just there to meet some girls and get drunk in the parking lot.

Here, listening to the bragging, I first learned about "hunting trips." This is when guys went out, always in groups, looking for someone to beat up—ideally a "spic" or "nigger." I never once heard the words "Black" or "Hispanic."

So much for the notion of only "White guys beating up other White guys."

As the night went on, I could also tell who the posers were, the guys dressed like hard-core skins but who probably wouldn't ever go on a "hunting trip" or get in a fight if it came to it. Lester, the cassette guy, was not to be found.

I spoke with a lot of guys from all over the place that night—most notably five skins who'd driven out from Phoenix and two from California who had direct connection to a neo-Nazi crew in England. The White-pride scene was seemingly international and connected.

"What's up?" "Where you from, man?" "Hey, good band." Small talk. Soon enough, I was BSing with some guys in the club parking lot. A gray VW Beetle had just pulled up, and three giant guys, all three a good six-six and 320 pounds each, stepped out with shaved heads, wifebeater shirts, boosts, braces. Out of this little VW. I broke cover and chuckled.

"Kinda funny, huh?" the guy smoking next to me said.

"Hilarious," I admitted.

We started talking. He was one of the skins from California. He kept on about waiting for some call from pals in the UK: Combat 18, a UK hate group. I'd never heard of them before but made a mental note. He told me he and his buddy were starting their own group here in the United States but finding it hard to muster the "true believers." Everybody at this show "was posers," he told me. "Didn't know what they were doing" or the "true meaning of hate."

This guy was a hard-core supremacist who'd been indoctrinated overseas. He saw our Mesa crowd as "neo-Nazi idiots who read a couple pages of *Mein Kampf* and think that's enough." This guy was more ideology driven, focused on a hatred for immigrants, an appreciation of those supremacists who came before, and the inner desire to protect the White Race.

He and I went back inside where he and his buddy "showed

me the deal"—how to spot the phonies. The big secret was having brass eyes on the Doc Marten boots—the Chinese-made knock-offs weren't brass. Being the biggest phony in the room, I glanced down carefully at my own boots and, thankfully, Tawni had grabbed me the brass-eyed Doc Martens. These guys grinned, and I was thrilled my backup detective wasn't in the club anymore.

———

Now, I gotta be completely honest here. Part Two.

At the time, I simply thought I wanted out of the van. Twenty-some years later, after too many restless nights, and unexplained anger, and some therapy, and enough tears and talks between Tawni and me, I now know there was another element at play. I just didn't understand it yet: *a skinhead had tried to kill me.*

This shit was personal. And still is.

———

I got back home from The Nile around 2 a.m.

I was covered in the reek of sweat and smoke and took a long shower before crawling into bed. My arms and sides were bruised and sore from the mosh pit. My new Doc Martens now lay in a pile in the corner with my stinky clothes.

Tawni had woken up and asked how it went.

"It's not good," I said. I may have used other language.

I knew everything we were doing as cops was wrong. We'd been slow to react to the Latino and Black gangs growing in our neighborhoods and were clearly making the same mistake again. White gangs weren't yet considered a serious threat, yet The Nile had just been packed with eighty-plus White people, all angry, indoctrinated in racism, and coiled to strike.

Every person I met that night boasted about the "growing skinhead scene" in the Valley. Yes, it was alive and well and clearly not underground. It was standing out in the parking lot of The Nile theater.

The club was in a now-Latino neighborhood. Did the police have enough patrols to prevent "hunting trips" when the concert was over? The unmistakable potential for violence and illegal activity was huge, and yet no one was monitoring it. I couldn't yet understand...*why weren't we?*

By all definitions, these organizations were actually gangs. Dangerous, White-boy gangs. In our city. And growing in number every day.

"Try to get some sleep," Tawni said, but we both knew otherwise.

Here's a story… A kid named James, who everyone says is bright, is drawing swastikas on his middle-school notebooks and is fascinated with Hitler and WWII. His father died before James was born and the boy fights with his mother a lot; sometimes, police are even called to the house. As a teen, he's prescribed an antipsychotic for anger management and diagnosed with schizophrenia. He writes a high school essay about the values of White Pride, and his teacher notifies the school and his mother. On a senior trip to Europe, he keeps calling Germany the "Fatherland" and talks about other nations as inferior. He sometimes shouts out racial slurs or about Hitler to get reactions. James enlists in the Army after high school and is discharged four months later. He's now twenty, lives alone, and plays video games all night when not working at a grocery store. He hears about a rally in Charleston, a gathering of various alt-right and White Pride organizations, and drives down from Ohio alone in his first car. In the morning, he marches carrying a shield displaying the logo of Vanguard America, a national neo-Nazi group; he's never met them beyond being handed the shield for the morning protests. Two hours later, James turns down a street in his car, hits the gas, and plows into a large group of counterprotesters. Twenty-eight people are injured and a young woman is killed. The shield rests in the backseat of his car. James is arrested a mile away, keeps apologizing to the officer, and asks if anyone was hurt. He's told a woman has died, appears genuinely shocked, and starts to cry.

*James: Joe Ruiz, "Ohio Man Charged with Murder in Fatal Car Attack on Anti-White Nationalist March," NPR, August 17, 2017, https://www.npr.org/sections/thetwo-way/2017/08/13/543176250 /charlottesville-attack-james-alex-fields-jr

2

GOING UNDERCOVER

Challenge Accepted

At work on Monday, I shared all my intel about The Nile. All about the packed room of neo-Nazis bragging about organizing the rebirth of the White master race while joyfully singing about stomping someone to death.

No one was interested. No one.

For me, the night had provided a trove of intel; by night's end there were more than a hundred self-professed haters from all over the Valley in one location, at one time. But my fellow detectives and supervisor kind of laughed it all off, mainly interested in hearing more about my backup showing up dressed like a clown. No one had gotten killed, or even hurt. I hadn't seen any drug deals going on. There hadn't even been any reported vandalism outside the club that night. What was there to get worried about? Bad music? Bad tattoos?

Law enforcement is reactionary. Frustratingly so. I didn't think we should need an aggravated assault or murder before it got the department's attention.

Fine. Weeks later, I came across a report where a group of skinheads—as far as I could tell from their names and mugshots—had harassed some young Black women outside a downtown taco stand. These guys had baited the women with the usual slurs and name calling, and when one of the young women came forward to defend herself and her friends, they'd knocked her out cold. A couple of weeks later, the windows were smashed out of a local synagogue.

Neither case, however, was enough to get my colleagues interested in the boot-wearing Saturday-night clientele of The Nile. And I couldn't really blame them.

How could either of these cases possibly compete with the narcotics and new Latino gangs coming into town, the weekly drive-by shootings, the steroid market now sweeping the Valley, the underage sex trafficking? There were only so many detectives and cops, hours in a day, only so much budget.

Still, I cut a deal with my sergeant; if—and it was a big if—I was somehow up-to-date on all my other cases and everything else was covered, I could keep gathering names and intel at The Nile. There'd be no backup offered and no overtime paid. If I couldn't work it into my regular hours and do so safely without backup, I was to forfeit the entire project. Otherwise, he and I had an understanding: I'd become the White-boy gang expert in a department and world that had zero interest in White-boy gangs. I took the deal.

———

Long before I realized I wanted to be a cop, I was training to be one.

Raised in suburban Phoenix with three sisters (which means I never had *any* say in what was on the family TV) and small as a kid (the six foot four didn't come until late in high school), I mostly hid in my bedroom and watched the world go by outside my window. I even had a pair of binoculars to watch all the cars driving up and down our street, making mental notes of license-plate numbers and the exact times people were coming and going. Alfred Hitchcock could have made a movie about me, and I had no idea how many hours and years I'd spend in a van doing the same as a pro.

Another factor influencing my desire to be a cop was that there were a lot of bullies in our neighborhood. And not yet full size by half, I was an easy target. My walks to and from school were always filled with dread. Our neighborhood supposedly had "Emergency homes" you could go to if ever in trouble; they had a big "E" in the front window to let you know there was a haven there. They probably weren't meant for schoolyard bullying, but one day when the guys came at me, I made a beeline for an "E house" and banged on the door for several minutes. No one ever answered, and I got my ass kicked more than usual that afternoon for my efforts.

So, when a police officer spoke to my teen church group on career night, I perked up. Here was a chance to protect myself and maybe even be an "E" for someone else. It'd be another six years before it came to pass.

After Tawni gave the official, and quite reluctant, OK, I took the written test in Phoenix (already breaking her first if-you-want-to-be-a-cop rule) with fifteen hundred other guys looking to fill four hundred slots. While taking the test, I heard there was a better chance of making the cut in Mesa, headed east, and got into the academy. In the last weeks of training, however, I failed out. They told me I was "too nice" during the arrest simulations. Seriously. I'd try to toughen up my approach and was met with "Sometimes you gotta be a dick, Browning." They said I could reapply in six months.

Setting aside my upbringing, the recent two-year mission as a Christian, and a whole lifetime of amiable, reserved behavior, this peaceable giant now had six months to become "a dick." Challenge accepted and met, I guess.

I was sworn in as a Mesa police officer six months later.

I was a cop.

———

Admittedly, The Nile and the guys with shaved heads were not at the forefront of my mind for a while. I was working a huge steroid ring in town and had also been pulled into a "sex club" scene that reportedly involved minors. We thankfully found nothing regarding kids at this club, but it was a harrowing couple of months.

I made it out to The Nile when I could, about once a month for a while. I learned more names, was greeted warmly by those who'd met me before, and was still a big hit in the mosh pit.

I'd even learned to tell the "skins" from the "SHARPs"—again, same look but different ideologies on how the world should work. The truly extreme Right and Left, if you will, brought together by similar clothing and musical tastes. (How the SHARPs, who often commit violence in *defense* of open borders, put up with some of the anti-immigrant lyrics is still a mystery to me, but they did.)

I got folks talking, easier than you'd think, and over time built up quite a laundry list of organizations they belonged to, or had crossed paths with, including the local branch of the KKK, something called the "National Alliance," the Aryan Nations, the World Church of the Creator, the Unit 88 skins, and the Hammerskins. Other than the KKK, I'd never heard of any of them until now. But this crowd spoke about them like they were talking about the NFL or AARP.

While I was learning the ins and outs of American racism,

Tawni was busy at home with spelling tests and flash cards, raising our kids. There could not have been two more wide-ranging worlds. I'd be with a bunch of skinheads and get a call from an excited six-year-old reciting the newest vowel sounds he'd learned. I have to laugh now, but during that process, jumping from one extreme to another was disconcerting. Tawni didn't care. As far as she was concerned, our kids didn't have to suffer just because I was pretending to be a bad guy—I continued to take the calls.

Otherwise, from the start, I always tried to keep the work out of our house. There were no folders at home for my hate materials. I didn't want our kids to ever see that junk. Our home was my literal sanctuary, and unless I specifically wanted Tawni to see something, I kept it all in my car or at my work office.

———

I'd sometimes leave The Nile and go back into full cop mode, pulling over folk who'd just left the club. One night, for instance, five skins were kicked out because they were being too violent on the dance floor. A few blocks away, I pulled them over. They turned out to be a bunch of kids out of Phoenix. They didn't recognize me from the club, as they were too scattered from being pulled over. There were twin brothers, one mouthy kid who looked like he'd just gotten beaten up, and two quiet guys who looked more afraid than anything. All five of them looked like posers to me. I got their information, took their photos, and sent them off with my usual "I don't ever want to see you in Mesa again." The line usually worked and seemed the best way to avoid running into these guys at the club while undercover.

Then, I didn't think much of these five guys. They were just a bunch of punks looking to play tough on a Saturday night, right?

Yet, out of this group, one would eventually do prison time for a murder in Texas, another was involved in a Phoenix murder, one did time for tampering with a witness, and the fourth would be in and out of jail the rest of his life for a dozen different crimes.

One out of five ain't bad, huh?

Yes, our paths *would* cross again years later in terrible ways. But I did not yet understand the gateway effect, the small yet consequential steps these young people were taking by coming to such events and hearing such hate-filled rhetoric.

Speaking of the rhetoric, it was time I got some more myself. I had my new list of groups many of these neo-Nazis belonged to and figured I'd join some. It was time to come out of The Nile and into the bigger world.

To do so, I needed an undercover identity.

I needed Packy Von Fleckenger.

"PACKY"

These days, creating a new identity is full of complications with a lot of bureaucratic red tape. Because of social media, you have to create a whole digital footprint that goes back years. No one would ever believe some thirty-year-old just appeared online for the first time a week ago. Twenty years ago, thankfully, you only needed a driver's license and, if you were really going for it, a PO box.

One of the rites of passage in Special Investigations was picking an undercover name and getting a driver's license made. I wanted something "masculine" and easy to remember, but I didn't want to use a family name to maintain a distinct line between my real life and my undercover life. I'd also spent months growing out my mullet and even got my ear pierced.

I handed in my paper to the woman down at the Department of Motor Vehicles. "Are you sure?" she asked.

I studied the paper again. "Hold on a minute," I said. "You're right." I decided to add a middle name for a "German" flair. The picture taken; my new identity alive.

It was the birth of...Packy Von Fleckenger. (Didn't even put Patrick on the driver's license.) Yeah, I know. It sounds like a pseudonym the character Fletch might give and was actually a joke alias I used when I needed a fake name for whatever random reason. It's ridiculous. Tawni hated it from Day One.

Yet no one in the White supremacy movement ever questioned it. I simply became "Packy," and if the last name came up at all, it was to be congratulated for my "strong German name." One supremacist leader was particularly impressed with the "Von" part. He thought it was great. They were just glad to have a body with a pulse *and* a German-sounding name as White-pride icing. No further inquiry needed. That's how desperate these people were for fresh recruits.

And they *must* have been desperate. Or just had excellent customer-service skills. Within a couple of weeks, my new "Packy" PO box was full of pamphlets, and I was a card-carrying member of the KKK, Ayran Nation, and the National Alliance.

No matter the group, the literature all boiled down to the same old lines: Jewish people secretly ruled the world, Mexicans were invading the country, Black people were criminals, and the White race was at a precipice with two choices—either fight back or vanish from the earth. The specific talking points would change some with statistical or historical "proof" given, some "expert" quoted (they often quoted each other)—but there was no real discernible difference between these groups in terms of their philosophies. The

national branches focused more on Jewish and Black people. The
local Arizona groups were fixated on the Mexicans.

I'd started a small folder of all my White supremacy pamphlets
and membership information. Within a matter of weeks, I needed
another folder.

In lieu of actual action, rhetoric seemed to be the main goal of
each organization. I returned from nearly every trip to the PO box
with new pictures of the "Jewish rat" or caricatures of offensively
drawn Black men (exaggerated lips and broad noses) standing over
a beautiful White woman. The variety and magnitude of flyers,
posters, or stickers these guys could make that basically said the
same thing were shocking.

Membership dues were requested with every mailing. One of
the first things I realized was to never pay my dues on time and, even
then, never the full amount. Nothing would have screamed "undercover cop" louder. Few members *ever* paid their dues. Splurging on
a case of beer was considered a magnanimous sacrifice.

The real money in these operations came from older men,
often retired from surprisingly well paying jobs. Men who could
never quite leave the scene. In the Arizona chapter of the National
Alliance, for instance, there were four or five guys who really kept
the whole chapter afloat—lawyers' fees and armaments, hotel conference rooms, printing costs, postage, flags, and patches, paying
bands, the beer and food for parties. Within the Alliance, these
older retired men fronted the money for all of that.

For the most part, I discovered, skinheads are broke.

Jobs come and go. Apartments are usually shared by five or six
skins flopping on the couch and floor, one bedroom reserved for
the guy, usually the biggest wannabe in the group, whose name is
on the actual lease. Beer is bought by the very few who actually

have a full-time job. I'd quickly gathered that candid hate does not pay, as face and neck tattoos with racial slogans are rarely seen by prospective employers as a good thing. The only other way to make money is a life of crime, from small robberies and narcotics sales to home invasions.

For those White supremacists already in jail, supporters were encouraged to provide "outreach" by putting some money into their prison accounts; securing a job for when they got out; even helping out a "brother's" family when they could afford it. Few could. And so, few in prison rarely received any outreach.

Especially not from Packy.

My only goal was to send them more brothers.

TOO CLOSE TO HOME (PART I)

In 1999, Tawni and I decided to sell our first home and build another on an acre of land. Weeks behind schedule, of course, we were still under the fanciful belief that if you bought food and drinks for the construction crews, they'd work better and faster. Tawni and I made the Costco run and arrived at 6:00 a.m. with Gatorade, muffins, and doughnuts. No one showed up for another hour.

Finally, two framers arrived and walked up to the house pad. As they got closer, I saw one wore a shirt with the logo "Support your local hammers" with two crossed hammers. The other had a hat that read "AZ Hammers."

I thought to myself, "Nice, I have me some union workers."

We shared pleasantries and hooked them up with breakfast.

Then, as the pair turned to the pad, I saw the mark. On the left side of one of their necks was a tattoo of two crossed hammers surrounded by a circle of fire.

It finally clicked. I should have known but I didn't. I didn't want to know. It was safe at home. Until it wasn't.

Come on, Matt, I cursed myself. These guys weren't union workers; they were members of the Arizona Hammerskins, a neo-Nazi group I'd run into a few up at The Nile. The leader at the time was in prison serving a sentence on the attempted arson of a Jewish synagogue.

I couldn't believe it. I had all this intel on skin groups, all the hands-on research, but since I was at home on my own real turf, I'd completely dropped my guard. I didn't expect to see neo-Nazis at my house, so I hadn't noticed what was right in front of my face. I was so disappointed in myself.

Thankfully, I didn't recognize these two. And clearly, they didn't recognize me. The rest of the crew showed up, and I took that as a great time to pull Tawni aside and let her know what was going on.

As the two guys worked, we took their pictures. Everyone thought we were taking pics of the building process, but we were capturing the two skinheads' features and tattoos to help with future or past cases. We'd also picked up lunch for the framers. Amazingly, the neo-Nazis were the only two on the work crew who actually thanked us for the food. Eventually, as we were talking, I finally realized one of the two skins *was* the subject of an investigation my department was in the middle of. I wrote up a report later that same day, forwarded it to the detective in charge, and, a short time later, off to prison he went.

He probably still has no idea how they found him.

———

My real life officially intersected with my undercover life that day.

It's something I still worry about. In prison, time stops. Those convicted have all day to piece together how they screwed up their crimes—what and who got them caught, how to get ahold of those they feel have wronged them. I've wondered for years if the framer skin ever put the story together in his mind. The young married couple with the doughnuts and lunch. Has he figured out I was the one who sold him out?

I made a decision that day. No more lackadaisical Matt. I had to get serious 24/7 if I was to properly protect myself and my family and do this job right.

Tattoos became the key to spotting skinheads, and I became a self-taught expert in their symbolism. I recognized now, from The Nile, that tattoos told stories. I could now read who'd been to prison, who was Brotherhood (meaning Aryan Brotherhood, an organized White prison gang), Peckerwood (the minor league prison White boy crew who, if worthy, eventually fed into the Aryan Brotherhood), and Nations or skins—as they all had different styles of tattoos.

I was looking at *everyone's* tats. To this day, I still do. Judging who they are and what they are about without even speaking to them. In no time, it wasn't unusual for me to duck into an aisle at the grocery store and pretend to study the new packaging of Kraft Macaroni & Cheese just to get a closer look at a tattoo. As our children entered high school, I'd scan their friends'—and their parents'—tattoos also.

Visiting family in Germany years ago, we toured an enchanting little town somewhere between Koblenz and Trier, but I was mostly trying to get a closer look at the tattoo on some other tourist dad's right calf —an oversized, steroided-out bulldog carrying a UK flag in one hand and a bat in the other. The bulldog was even wearing a Skrewdriver T-shirt and Doc Marten steel-toed boots with red laces. *Who is this guy?* I wondered. *What crew is he with?* I moved in to get some photos and thought I was doing a pretty good job with the detective routine until I realized the little girl on his shoulders had followed me at each angle and with each picture. The guy's daughter caught me! Later, I sent the pics to law enforcement friends in the UK and Germany; turned out the guy *was* an old-school hooligan from England who'd decided family was more important than hate.

Another time, I was at home one night working on the truck with my sixteen-year-old and sent him on a run to the local auto parts store. He was gone a long time. When he got back, he showed me what'd taken so long: photos of a White guy with a shaved head and tattoos. He'd taken pictures of this skin's tattoos as "trophies" to show his dad and asked me to explain what every single tat was. On the back of this guy's neck was a big 88 just under what would be his hairline. My teen son said, "I knew you'd like this one, Dad." I agreed it was a good one and promised I'd use them when I taught. But I also recognized the tattoo and well knew the guy who wore it. I tried to shake it off. I mean, it was one thing for me to run into these guys, but it was an entirely different thing for my kids to be anywhere close to the ugliness. It was one of those times when I seriously questioned what I had done for so long and what I once again had exposed my family to.

Was all this tattoo observing hypervigilance, paranoia, fear, or merely due diligence? If I'd merely been looking for the right signs, I'd have noticed the "hammer" hat and T-shirt as the two framers stepped from their cars that day. And I'd know the young couple in front of me at the grocery store line were devout neo-Nazis.

It's not paranoia, I tell myself, if it's real.

TOO CLOSE TO HOME (PART II)

A couple months after our new house was finished, the entire family had Sunday dinner at Tawni's mom's place. After church, we loaded up the Suburban with our three boys to make the forty-minute trip to Glendale, where we were first greeted with the homey smell of roast beef and homemade bread.

Tawni is one of six kids, and it's always an adventure when her family gets together. Her sister was still living at home, and she was really excited when we arrived. She told Tawni she wanted us to meet her new friend. I knew the drill well enough; I was to be cordial to the new guy but mostly just wanted to get to important matters—eating.

"Matt," Tawni's sister said, "this is Chris."

Chris was wearing a wifebeater (this was Sunday dinner, remember) and had a goatee and a shaved head. *Here we go…* He looked me up and down as I surely did the same. His white socks were pulled up to his knees. Then, I realized this guy's shorts fell over his socks so you couldn't see any leg at all. Interesting. Still, the tattoo hunt continued.

Leery, I went to shake his hand when I saw a tattoo with the numbers 88 around his forearm (*remember*: 88 = HH = Heil Hitler).

"Nice tattoo," I said.

He bent down, nonchalantly, and pulled his sock down. "Here's another," he said. This tat depicted a man with a shaved head in a prison cell, trying to pull the bars apart to push his head through. It was surreal. I looked around and found that I was the only one in the room concerned.

Even Tawni was clueless. She was focused on situating the family around the table so we could eat. The kids were complaining they were hungry while my mother-in-law put the food on the table. *How could everyone act so normal? Did they not get it?* I was stunned. Here we had, no doubt, an ex-con with an 88 tattooed on his arm joining us for Sunday dinner.

I prepared myself for the worst. A safe place, a family home, had potentially become an explosive and dangerous environment.

———

A quick break for a peek behind the curtain. When Tawni and I first submitted our outline for this book, our new literary agent advised, "You can't have all these skinheads appearing in your life at the same time. It's like your world in Mesa was somehow filled with skinheads overnight. No one will believe it."

It was good advice. The truth was somehow hurting our true story.

But, to us, the whole Phoenix Valley *was* filled with skinheads overnight. And there was nothing paranormal or fictional or chronologically challenged about it.

They had been there all along. We just didn't know what to look for.

Not the boots or the tattoos. Not the extreme haircuts. Not the music.

It was if our eyes had been opened to a whole new reality, which now included neo-Nazis shopping at the mall or catching a smoke outside a local restaurant. Once you saw it, you could never again unsee it. Or perhaps a better metaphor would be that it was as if a light had flipped on in my head and there were roaches scurrying everywhere.

This is why it's so important for more of us—all of us—to recognize the signs and symbols, the "uniform" of the modern White supremacist.

Yes, our world was "suddenly" crawling with skinheads.

And I too quickly found myself eating dinner beside one.

———

With the food on the table and the kids sitting down, I went to take my seat at the only chair left. Tawni was on my right side and Chris, the 88 skinhead, was on my left. We all sat and blessed the food. I wasn't sure what to anticipate, but my whole body was poised on high alert.

"I understand you're an officer of the law," Chris said as he turned to me. His voice was very clear, no smile, just pure arrogance.

Looking straight ahead, I answered, "Yup" and tried to keep eating. At work, I knew how to handle situations like this; it was easy when you were on the street with five other detectives standing beside you. But this was different. I was at my in-laws' home with an invited and likely dangerous guest.

I waited for Chris's response, ready to hear anything from "Thank you for your service, sir" to fighting words. Tawni leaned closer and put her hand on my knee as she always does when she wants me to remain calm. Bizarrely, or maybe not, the rest of the family remained completely oblivious to anything going on.

"Well, you're not big enough to take me," the new boyfriend said.

I was younger then and gladly took the bait. "Reeeaaally?" I partially stood up. "Why don't we go outside for a little bit?"

This guy—ex-con, White supremacist—was clearly bad news, and I had no plans for letting anyone in my family become a part of it. Tawni quickly changed the topic and passed the mashed potatoes to him. Then we dined.

Sometimes the measures it takes for normal "civilians" to see what's going on around them are baffling. Here I was getting called out, readying to beat the living tar out of a cocky ex-con during a lazy Sunday dinner, and nobody saw or understood. *Did everybody think we were joking?*

After dinner, I took Tawni aside and explained Chris's tattoo and my feelings on the subject. "I don't want this guy around our family," I said. "I know what I'm talking about… This guy is no good."

After that, Tawni explained how, for some people, prison can be rehabilitating and that we didn't *really* know what his story was or what put him in jail. She continued that we shouldn't judge him without getting to know him, that repentance was real and that people can change, blah blah blah…

"Nowhere near *our* family, ever." There was little discussion after that.

I went to work the next day and told a few of the guys what had happened at Sunday dinner. After throwing his name around, I found out Chris had a violent prison record. His original charges were for drug smuggling in and out of Mexico, and he'd gotten into serious trouble in prison for things like fights and drugs; the prison guards, I learned later, hated him. I was both cop and protective brother now as Tawni and I actively tried to steer her sister away from him. But her sister just couldn't see it.

Thankfully, he and Tawni's sister broke it off a few months later. Before they split, however, he'd gotten criminally violent with her and verbally abused my mother-in-law.

Tawni swore to trust me on such things going forward.

And I swore to better trust myself.

THE NATIONAL ALLIANCE

My alter ego, Patrick Von Fleckenger, soon received *daily* voice-mails, literature, and email from different hate groups and organizations across the country hoping to connect. I knew, however, I could do the best close to home, so I continued to keep most of my outreach with local groups.

One day, Jerry Harbin contacted me.

Jerry was the leader of Arizona's National Alliance, a sizable White supremacy group based in West Virginia that had been making inroads into the American West. On a national level, especially back east, they were extensive, manifesting a strong history of violence, and ties with The Order, another major hate group.

In Arizona, they were now the hot new thing.

From our first call, I could tell Jerry Harbin was a different sort of fellow from your run-of-the-mill skinhead. He was very personal and motivated, even working at a local hospital. Jerry always proved overly excited to talk about "the cause" and spoke with obvious enthusiasm.

"We're starting a chapter in Phoenix," he said. "We'd like to meet you."

Sure, I said, and we picked a date. We would meet for lunch at a local Tempe hot spot—Denny's.

Prior to the meeting, I researched the National Alliance. Their national leader was Dr. William Pierce, a legendary supremacist and one apparently with failing health and quickly heading toward his death bed. For three decades, however, he'd been America's most renowned neo-Nazi. He'd been co-leader of the National Youth Alliance, a right-wing political organization in the late '60s, and founded the National Alliance in 1974. He was author of two supremacy "classics"—*The Turner Diaries* (1978) and *Hunter*

(1989), which both tell of White loners saving their race by attacking Jewish people, gay people, interracial couples, the liberal media, and a corrupt government. (*The Turner Diaries* has been directly linked to the Oklahoma City bombing, which killed 168 people, and multiple real-life hate groups, including the Order.[i])

I studied the group's positioning on race, religion, and culture. It seemed to me that every group wanted the same thing—in the name of protecting Whites, the submission or annihilation of any person, group, or race who wasn't White.

"*Here's much to do with hate, but more with love,*" Romeo says in the play when discussing the feud between the families. It is the same in White supremacy. Recruiters don't come at young minds promoting hatred of the other races—that comes later. What they *always* start with is love for the White race. *Do you see what they're doing to us? We're being replaced. Schools now teach that Whites are bad. White families are no longer safe. Whites are being silenced. Being denied jobs. Denied religious freedoms. Being raped and murdered.*

This group wasn't just loud rock music and beer and tattoos and girls. It was an actual ideology. It was grown men with jobs and money and political and social agendas.

I'd researched the violence the group was associated with: armored-car robberies to fund a racial war, shootouts with the police, political murders, ties to Timothy McVeigh and the Oklahoma City Bombing, and even a plot to bomb Disney World.

These guys were legit, and I was in. The most well-known hate organization in the United States since the '60s had asked for a sit-down meeting with me. I was beyond pumped. With thoughts of grandeur running through my head, including ideas for a RICO case (Racketeer Influenced and Corrupt Organizations; "big fish" federal charges) and *many* arrests, I went in to tell Sergeant Meza the great news. "You won't believe this," I said. "The mother-fricken National Alliance wants to sit down and talk with me."

Only knowing a little about the whole scene, but sensing my enthusiasm, John looked at me. "Let me get this straight... You're going to have brunch, at Denny's, on a Thursday morning with a bunch of middle-aged skinheads?"

"When you put it that way..." It suddenly *did* sound lame. "But, yeah."

John laughed, but not for long. He put on his game face and the planning session began. "Listen," he said. "I'll give you Gary and Todd for cover. Have them in a booth thirty minutes prior to your arrival, and have them get some pictures. Take as long as you need, but understand, you *have* to get something on the group so we can justify the time."

I know John and consider him a friend; we did a lot working gangs and the streets together. I also knew what little support we had from the department and that he was taking a big chance on me and my abilities to get the info. So, when he said "Get something," there was no doubt he meant it.

———

The day of the meeting, we briefed on the location, going over layout and overly long discussions of exit strategies, if my cover was blown and things got violent. For me, it was only going to be a quick lunch meeting. Gary and Todd, two intel detectives whom I trusted, happily took the cover position inside the restaurant—free lunch on the city.

I arrived promptly at 11:00 a.m. with the cover team already in place and directed my attention to a booth in the middle where four gentlemen sat. What caught my eye first was a man in his early twenties wearing a black, long-sleeved, button-up shirt and a black hat. On his collar was a red pin the size of a dime and, on the pin in large, bold, black print—as if he *weren't* sitting in the 21st century in a Denny's—was a swastika.

I approached the table. "Hey, is one of you Jerry?"

An older gentleman with gray hair in his mid-fifties stood. "I am," he said. "You must be Patrick."

After the typical greetings and platitudes, I sat down and ordered a classic Moons over my Hammy. While studying White supremacy, watching movies, and reading articles, I'd quickly learned a very important piece to this weird skinhead extremist puzzle: honor and respect are essential.

By showing respect you gain respect. Letters are written courteously and often with formal language befitting the 18th century: "*I hope this letter finds you in best regards*" or "*submitted in respect with my blood and honor.*"

Deference to crew leaders and recognized names in the White Pride movement shows you honor your heritage and the White race, special attention given to all those "who have fallen" before you.

Using this knowledge became a basis for my future success.

I told Jerry that it was a pleasure, and an honor, to meet him. "I've been looking a long time to find someone with the dedication that I can see you have," I said. Instantly, I'd gained respect from him, and even though I was the new guy, it already pushed me to a different level than the others sitting at the table.

Other than Jerry and the kid with the swastika pin, there was Elton Hall, an older man in his sixties who proved to be an actual Nazi. Neither German nor from the 1940s, he was still a full believer of the Third Reich's eugenicist agenda and ideology;

he genuinely believed in a White master race. The final guy at the table was a man in his late fifties, a local business owner focused on immigration issues he freely vented about.

The five of us then discussed who I was and what I wanted.

"Tell us about yourself," Jerry Harbin said. "And why you wish to become involved in the movement."

A thought finally struck me. In all the studying I'd done to pre- pare myself to be able to talk hate and their history, I'd forgotten a very important aspect: my own history. Patrick Von Fleckenger was only a driver's license. I hadn't crafted his back story yet. A major undercover failure.

We'd just bought that new property, and I was doing a ton of landscaping. So, Patrick suddenly became the new owner of a landscaping company. "I own a landscaping company," I started. There wasn't much after.

"A landscape company?" Elton asked, puzzled.

I'd already messed up. In the Valley, Latino workers predominantly man landscaping companies. *Now what, Matt?* I thought. Luckily, the server arrived to drop off coffee and food, providing me a quick minute to think. Right there, Patrick Von Fleckenger's hatred toward minorities and his strong anti- immigration views were born.

"I had three crews working for me," I explained. "Each crew was in charge of a truck and a trailer and equipment. A few months ago, I went on vacation to Idaho and left one of my Mexican workers in charge."

The guys all smiled and shook their heads like they knew the punchline.

"When I got back," I lied, "my yard was cleaned out. No trucks, no trailers, no equipment, no business."

Arizona's location, right along the border, made a dislike of Latinos a whole lot easier to pull off than any manufactured hatred toward Black or Jewish people. With this story, I was in—with no work or equipment, I had plenty of time to grow more hatred toward the Latinos. Jerry and his pals saw this and "totally understood."

For the next ten years, any time I couldn't take a phone call or was tied up with another case, I just told my supremacy "pals" I was in Idaho with my best friend's family because he'd "been killed by an illegal immigrant." These guys hated immigrants so much that they never questioned me on it.

The rest of the lunch was spent in weird, very quiet conversations between individuals, instead of the whole group. Jerry and I talked about how to grow the numbers in the East Valley, what my plans were for my business, and how nice it would be to have a business owner in the group who could give jobs to the White man (basically asking in a roundabout way if I'd employ the local skinheads).

During the meeting, the guy in the black shirt with a swastika pin sat quietly. Perhaps he was embarrassed about his clothing choice for the day. He'd adjusted his shirt and hat multiple times, almost as if to cover his pin as people walked by. WWII-fan Elton, meanwhile, was more concerned about the syrup that'd dripped on his button-down JC Penney shirt.

Almost two hours into the meeting, Jerry asked me a direct question that totally caught me off guard: "Would you be interested in running the East Valley chapter of the National Alliance?"

They wanted a Mesa branch, and they wanted me to run it. After two hours. Either I was a great liar, or they were just desperate. Based on the other guys sitting around the table, I assumed it was the latter.

Later, Jerry always seemed genuinely happy to see me. I often wondered what he saw in me, but I speculated he knew I could take care of business if called upon. Otherwise, I didn't carry any of that White boy bravado. I was in their world now but certainly wasn't one of them. Maybe he could somehow see that distinction and appreciated the difference.

I assured Jerry I was humbled and honored by his faith in me. However, it was a big step I couldn't take lightly, so I would need some time to mull it over. I shook everyone's hands and left the table.

After leaving Denny's, I drove around for a bit checking my mirrors and made a few stops along the way to make sure I wasn't being followed. I arrived back at my office and briefed Sergant Meza on what had just happened. I recounted the whole conversation and even shared the story of my fake landscaping company. John, being Mexican American, just shook his head.

"They want me to be the local president, John," I finally said.

He looked at me, amazed. "They want you to do *what?*"

I told him the rest.

"An undercover cop can't run a hate group in Mesa," he clarified.

Somewhere inside, I already knew what his answer would be, but I saw such a great opportunity at intel—names, addresses, planned attacks. With reluctance, I agreed with John. I'd never be able to instruct others to commit violence as a police officer. With John's support, I did, however, get approval from above to continue gathering intelligence on the organization.

—

As soon I had the chance, I called Tawni. "You won't believe it," I told her. "They want me to be president."

"Umm…how's that?"

For a variety of reasons, she wasn't as enthused as I was. It was too new to really understand it all. I explained in greater detail as much as I yet knew, anyway. In the end, she was simply proud of the work and just as shocked.

A few days later, I called Jerry Harbin and grudgingly told him that since I was trying to build my business again, I was presently unable to take him up on his offer. However, I assured him that I *did* want to stay an active member and do what I could to help the cause.

"That's good to hear, brother," the neo-Nazi said. "There's plenty of work still to be done."

A story... A suburban teen named Patrick notices his Dallas neighborhood has changed. Once 80% White, the population has doubled during his childhood, and now half of his neighbors are no longer of European descent. He is not the only one who has noticed the change. White supremacist groups target both his neighborhood and the local college with pamphlets arguing that "Muslims, Mexicans, Black people, and Jews" should return to "where they came from" or face "torture." The pamphlets also argue non-Whites are crime prone and a threat to White women. Patrick's suburban parents worry he is "a little lost, with few friends," but when he discusses current events in person, his ideas don't appear to be out of the mainstream. Patrick now spends roughly eight hours a day online, mostly on online message boards, and begins studying a theory known as the "Great Replacement," which argues Whites are systematically being replaced by the government, media, and liberals. He is now twenty-one and drives 650 miles to El Paso and enters a Walmart with a civilian version of the AK-47. That morning, on the online message board 8chan, he'd posted a "manifesto" citing other hate-crime shootings and the "Great Replacement" as inspirations for his mission. His thoughts focus on "the Hispanic invasion of Texas" and fear of a one-party state. Customers and employees hide under tables and in shipping containers behind the building. Patrick murders twenty-three people. Most all are Latino, and he later tells detectives he was "targeting Mexicans."

---

*Patrick: John Eligon, "The El Paso Screed, and the Racist Doctrine Behind It," *The New York Times*, August 7, 2019, www.nytimes.com/2019/08/07/us/el-paso-shooting-racism.html; Erin Ailworth, Georgia Wells, and Ian Lovett, "Lost in Life, El Paso Suspect Found a Dark World Online," *The Wall Street Journal*, August 8, 2019, https://www.wsj.com/articles/lost-in-life-el-paso-suspect-found-a-dark-world-online-11565308783.

HATE GROUPS

A Day at the Park

The park of my childhood had become Ground Zero for a small mob of neo-Nazis. Shaved heads, shiny boots, and actual banners with swastikas and iron crosses proudly waving side-by-side with the American flag.

There were also some hot dogs on the grill, plenty of beer in the coolers, and rock music blaring from an old portable boom box. Shirtless guys covered in tattoos joked and tossed up *sieg heils* while their skinbyrds pranced back and forth in some sort of impromptu fashion show to crude hoots and hollers. Several of their kids sat on the picnic tables and watched it all.

I also watched. Front-row seat, in fact. Wearing steel-toed Doc Martens, my arms crossed in tension. To my new Aryan "brothers," I was the tall, quiet guy with the scraggy mullet and the fixed subtle smile. The new guy who "hated Mexicans" as much as they did and would do *whatever* necessary to protect my White brothers and my race. I was also known—for whatever reason, probably just because I was tall and quiet—as the guy you didn't want to mess with. Perfect for a good guy hiding in plain sight.

Several groups had gathered together today. Mostly National Alliance members, Unit 88 skins, but also some Aryan Nations guys, a couple of Volksfront members, and one notoriously violent Hammerskin.

For a city that didn't have a White supremacy gang problem, there were sure a lot of White supremacy gangs represented in Phoenix today.

It'd been months since my first meeting at Denny's, and my entrance into the National Alliance had proven a bridge to a whole other world of White supremacy, a world I'd previously been completely unaware of.

By now, however, I'd met most of the supremacist groups in the Valley. Each one, ranging in membership from ten to a hundred people, had its own—I'm sure they'll love this perfect Yiddish word—*schtick*.

National Alliance—with whom I kept the most direct contact—were the older guys who loved rhetoric, had access to the most money, were interested in Hitler, wore polo shirts with a little NA on the chest, and were the fragile umbrella over the Valley's other groups. If you suggested this umbrella idea to any of the other groups, they'd laugh at you; according to them, the National Alliance was "all talk." That's exactly why Jerry Harbin, their leader, worked so hard to bring the other groups into his tent.

Unit 88 skins were the kind of guys and gals I'd met at The Nile. Shaved heads, tattoos, boots, and braces. Young, looking for an identity and a fight. The ones who showed up for events *outside* The Nile, the ones I was now hanging out with, were the hardcore adherents. They lived, in theory, by the "88 precepts"—which include in part[i]:

- It is our avowed duty and holy responsibility to assure and secure for all time the White race upon the face of this planet.
- Be fruitful and multiply. Do your part in helping to populate the world with your own kind. It is our immediate objective to relentlessly expand the White race and keep shrinking our enemies.
- The guiding principles of all your actions shall be "What is best for the White race?" Your first loyalty belongs to the White race.
- Show preferential treatment in your business dealings with members of your race. Phase out all dealings with Jews as soon as possible. Do not employ niggers or other coloreds. Remember the inferior-colored races are our deadly enemies.
- Decide in early youth that during your lifetime you will make at least one major lasting contribution to the White race.

Aryan Nations is a group formed in 1978 by Richard Butler (now deceased) and established upon militant antigovernment rhetoric of the *Posse Comita* (an 1878 act signed by President Rutherford B. Hayes, which limits the powers of the federal government and leans pro self-rule), which ultimately affixed racism to their cause to help swell numbers.[ii] Butler touted himself a military man and later told me, and anyone else within earshot, of his Army service in WWII. He believed Jewish people are the worst of all, the literal spawn of Satan and Eve. Butler's organization became most well known for its Aryan World Congress, a national meeting held each summer in Hayden Lake, Idaho, where hundreds of skins and White power leaders would gather to listen to speeches by "Pastor" Butler and have daily hate concerts.[iii] An avid Hitler-lover, Butler was taking Adolf's adage of "Who owns the youth gains the future" to heart and actively recruited skins by bringing top-rated White power hate bands to the compound.

It worked. The Aryan World Congress was soon internationally known as a "who's who of hate" extravaganza. It was a hate-filled finishing school where each organization shared the latest in White supremacy recruitment, promotion, legal advice, funding, violence, and criminal activity.

The Hammerskins (like the two guys who'd worked on our house) grew out of the punk rock scene in the '80s and officially organized in Dallas, Texas, in 1988. They grew quickly, becoming an international organization in 1990, opening chapters in Europe and adding their presence in Canada and Australia by 1991. Hammerskins had the reputation of being the true street warriors. Their membership was "by invitation only" and came with the responsibility to keep other races *and* other skinhead crews in check. (These guys made even the toughest Unit 88 guys look like wannabes.) Their hate crimes included assault, vandalism, arson, and murder. The Hammers were also a huge part in the production and promotion of White power hate rock.

Volksfront was a truly international organization. Their membership, in my experience, consisted of the most aggressive skinheads in the world. With chapters in Australia, the UK, Germany, Spain, Croatia, Netherlands, Canada, and the U.S., Volksfront was known as the premier White supremacist organization to be a member of. They'd started as a prison gang in 1994, but after the release of Randall Lee Krager, its founder and leader, from the Oregon Department of Corrections, it quickly grew in numbers *and* reputation.[iv] "VF" was also an invitation-only crew with a probation period for new prospects. They also had a notorious history of not playing well with the other crews and were in constant war both nationally and internationally with the Hammers. They had a violent reputation on the street, and within the ranks of law enforcement, it was well earned. Members were known to cross multiple states and even national borders to "take care" of individuals who'd talked trash about their organization. VF were methodical in their violence, and it worked; few ever talked about them, and this kept them off law enforcement radar and out of prison. (One VF member once planned to impale a rival supremacist crew member's face to his own hardwood floor with a dagger, leaving him for his brothers to find; he said he got his inspiration "from the Bible." He'd also claimed he wasn't truly violent but motivated to do it only "for the crew" and so his "reputation could go before him." Years later, he almost killed another rival crew's member with just his boots and a folding chair; his crew was probably very impressed.)

All of these groups had come together today.

The official reason for the gathering was to clean up a local park. Volunteerism at its finest, except with a major twist. The neighborhood, which was mostly White a decade before, was now mostly Latino, and these skins were going to tidy up to show "the Browns how to clean up their block" with the notion that "only Whites could keep America great." Mainly, they were looking to stir up some major shit.

To that end, the media had been invited and some reporters even showed up. I always made sure to turn away whenever I saw a camera revealed; I couldn't risk blowing my cover.

Our chosen spokesperson that day was a twenty-five-year-old skinhead named Josh Fiedler. This young man was impressive and said all the right things to the press: "giving back to the community" and all. I always believed Josh *could* have made something more of his life if he hadn't hooked up with this crew, such as becoming a great salesperson or maybe even been a teacher. Instead, he was out here laughing at Hitler jokes.

For two hours, we picked up trash and I hid my disgust as athletically challenged racists tried to play football and then argued over flag placement in the gazebo. I could hardly believe this was the same neighborhood where I'd grown up, the same gazebo I'd once played under. Tawni and her family had fed the ducks here when she was a girl, but the ducks had been replaced with half-naked skinbyrds covered in bad ink. It was pathetic. The real purpose of the day was only to intimidate or bait all the Mexican American families in the apartment complex directly across the street. The intimidation part wasn't working too well. The baiting, however...

By now, forty-plus counterprotestors had gathered along the edges of the park. They were all Latino men with their own wife-beater shirts and Nike Cortez shoes with a black Nike swoosh, long shorts, and socks pulled up to the knees. Most wore black-and-white checkered flannels with the top button done. Everyone was in uniform today.

The skins were counting on a confrontation and had purposely set up in the main gazebo to be seen by the whole neighborhood. They wanted a fight and wanted to be seen as victims. They were about to get their chance.

First came the yelling. "Fuck you, White boy!" "Dumb cracker." "White trash!"

My "brothers" fired back: "*Sieg heil!*", "Fuckin' wetback", "White power!" Several of the Latino men carried planks of wood and steel pipes. The skinheads were outnumbered and "outgunned."

Eventually, the guys from the neighborhood advanced, their enraged faces yelling for us to go home. (Not exactly the words they used.) As they approached, I held steady, trying to look like a loyal bouncer ready to bust some heads. I glanced over at Josh, his chest puffing out and his inked arms pumped in the air, urging the Latino guys on. I had my Glock .40 caliber tucked into my waistband, praying I wouldn't have to decide what to do if someone on either side pulled a knife or a gun. If I shot one of the Latino men, even if only in the leg to break up a fight, "my boys" would later give me red laces for my Doc Martens, having "shed blood for the cause." Or maybe it'd be a neo-Nazi I had to shoot or arrest; my undercover role would promptly end just as it was getting started.

I had a sudden thought of all the softball games I'd played in this same park. I wanted to puke. Someone shouted. The neighborhood guys charged the gazebo, and I braced myself in the "fight for America."

DAY BY DAY

Like most stories involving the National Alliance, and most true cop stories also, this one ends anticlimactically. The various gangs' members retreated. More slurs and threats were shouted by all, but then the police arrived, and everyone scattered in fifteen different directions. I was one of the ones who had vanished quickly back to my truck, as I couldn't have local patrol officers, people I'd recently trained in many cases, spotting me and potentially blowing my cover.

Even though the park scene had ended sans bloodshed, it *was* the closest we'd yet come to actual violence since I'd "joined" the National Alliance. Mostly, it was meetings, more talk, and tosssed-out bags of propaganda onto people's driveways. We'd stuff the literature, consisting of pamphlets about the dangers of Jewish people and the Mexican invasion and ways to join the National Alliance—into sandwich bags in the banquet room of a local Denny's.

These guys *loved* meeting at Denny's.

(It should be noted that Denny's—I didn't know this then— paid $54 million in a lawsuit in the 1990s netting the largest monetary damages ever for violations of the Civil Rights Act of 1964 for "ejecting Black customers, segregating Black from White customers, using racial epithets, failing to honor advertised specials for Black customers, and trying to limit the number of Black customers in a restaurant at any one time.")

I still wonder today what the staff ever thought about fifteen skinheads preparing racist materials in the back room on a Tuesday afternoon. We'd put pennies in the bags to weigh them down, but someone finally calculated that the group was spending more on the pennies than the Kinkos, printing costs. So, we switched to gravel, tossing these bags on driveways in predominantly White neighborhoods on Thursday nights. (On weekends, most of the guys were partying and too drunk to drive around.) As a cop, I couldn't help distribute this stuff, only prepare it. There were always strange rules about what was acceptable undercover work and what was crossing the line.

One day, while helping to wrap bags, I got grumpy and decided to call these guys out some: "We should pass these out in South Phoenix or Maryvale," I suggested. These were mostly Black and Latino neighborhoods. The others in the room laughed but then saw I was serious. "It'd really piss them off," I nudged, secretly mocking them.

"We'd get our asses kicked" came the honest response I'd expected.

This is precisely why the National Alliance needed the Unit 88s and Hammerskins around. Guys and gals who would use their fists and boots.

And they did.

In Mesa, one Hammerskin had been romantically propositioned in a bar by a man, and, after going back to this man's trailer, he and his Hammerskin buddy had beaten the guy to death. This did not go down as any kind of "hate crime"—just as a "normal" killing. The fact that both these guys were in a White supremacy group, which openly touted hatred of gay people, apparently had nothing to do with them beating a gay man to death. In another murder that same year, a young neo-Nazi shot and killed a Black man to earn *his* red laces. He went to jail on a simple murder charge, his gang leanings ignored.

Years later, I was brought in as an expert witness in another murder case. An eighteen-year-old named David had recently attended a party in his National Socialist Uniform, complete with steel-toed boots and a swastika armband. The party was a diverse mix of individuals, including a former friend who was part Latino. After, David picked a fight with his former friend and, during the dispute, called 911 and told the operator he was about to stab someone, which he did, plunging a knife into the teen's stomach. "You had it coming, you half spic," the 911 operator could hear David say as the man lay dying.

I gave testimony as an expert witness on the relevance of the boots and swastika and National Socialist gang and what one had to do to earn their red laces. Ultimately, after much back and forth between the defense and the judge, my testimony was tossed out and not included in the record or charges. It was "not deemed relevant in a racially motivated crime." The case proceeded as an everyday murder trial. Legally, race and David's new supremacy ties apparently had nothing to do with it.

Then, there were the definite hate crimes that lacked the testimony of any willing witnesses.

I once got a call from some Unit 88s I knew, on a violence "high" and desperate for me to meet them immediately; I did, and they told me their story. They'd been on a "hunting trip" in Sunnyslope, one organized to defend the honor of two "comrades" who'd been beaten up—one guy stabbed in the lung by a Latino drug dealer. In retaliation, a fellow "brother" had been challenged to earn his "reds" by beating *any* Mexican American he could find. He'd stabbed a random man multiple times; then the entire crew came in with a full-on "boot party," stomping, leaving the man for dead in a ditch. These guys were so excited telling their story, they even re-created the noises by stabbing a knife through a random piece of cardboard—SLASH, SLASH. "See! That's what it sounded like!" Over and over. I was sick. I thought of arresting them all on the spot, blowing my cover and dragging all four of them directly to jail.

Instead, I pulled myself together, excused myself, and quickly called my own real police "brothers" to help search for the victim. Nothing. I scoured police reports, called hospitals, walked, and re-walked the supposed crime scene with other officers. Nothing. No victim, no record, no hate crime—nothing. I have little doubt it happened; I even got the same story from two *more* sources. This man, an undocumented immigrant likely, had no doubt crawled to some house where he died or was stitched up quietly, fearing deportation.

Thus, crimes by White supremacists often go unreported. Undocumented persons fear deportation if they involve the police in any matter, let alone a crime. Additionally, a lot of times beat cops don't investigate to see if a crime stemmed from hate or bias, so it's not logged as such. Because of these issues, it's harder to see an upward trend of White supremacist violence. This is why it's so important to educate our cops. They have to know what they're actually looking at so we can get properly documented reports and, thus, the arrests and convictions we desperately need.

Another time, I was called to interview a Latino man who'd been beaten and sodomized with a plunger. *Who earned laces this time?* I wondered. But the victim was gone by the time I arrived. Again, I suspected the victim had fled to protect himself from possible deportation. I told Tawni about this specific crime and she cried. Seeing her tears flow so easily let me feel my own pain.

Sometimes, it was only a matter of witnessing an interracial couple walking down the street and jumping them. The neo-Nazis always beat the White woman up first for being "a traitor to her race" and then focused on her Black or Latino date, friend, or husband. These attacks were either reported as a generic assault or more commonly never reported at all. I'd hear about them later at some neo-Nazi barbecue—*Hey, did you hear what Stevie and Derek did in Gilbert?* But, there was never an open investigation connected to such crimes. There were always bigger fish to fry. Statistically the Valley has one murder *every* night, usually connected to gangs, drugs, or domestic violence and every form of criminal behavior in between. Police are busy. Where did some couple getting beaten up for five minutes find any time against all of that?

Again, there are only so many cops, so many hours in the day.

Witnesses, suspects, surveillances, and arrests—all that took time. Meeting with prosecutors, writing and executing search warrants, and booking guys into jail, going to court—that took even more time. Or often being called off your own cases to assist *other* squads on long-term surveillances, wires, and investigations. Now, throw in teaching at the academy, going to various seminars, helping to write policy, meeting with other agencies and organizations like the Anti-Defamation League (ADL), and attending more meetings... I often wonder how we found time to do any law enforcement work at all.

Most days, you'd get home late to go to bed and just get called out again for some drive-by shooting or homicide. Days off became hectic as you tried to cram everything in, because you never knew what was in store for you the next day back at work. And when I *was* home, Tawni was always supportive. That's not to say she liked it, but she saw what I was trying to do, and even pushed me to keep going. With, eventually, some minor adjustments...

By this time, most of my weekends were filled with skinhead meet-and-greets and daily phone calls with the "boiz." (Curious how they'd almost all of them adopted African American street slang, without any awareness of the irony.) Intelligence *was* flowing, and I was now providing genuine information on investigation leads to surrounding agencies. Professionally, I was gold.

One night I'd come home, proud as heck of the progress I'd made and all that was happening, the connections I'd been making, but Tawni's enthusiasm didn't match my own. That was rare. Still, I barreled through, explaining all that'd happened that day and what else I'd planned for the weekend. Still nothing. Mostly silence. *Then I knew...*

"You know," she finally said, "I didn't get married so I could go to church alone. And our kids..." She stopped. Nothing else was said. The next morning, Tawni sat in the last pew, me beside her, with our kids on each side, not alone, but as a family. If every White supremacist leader in the country wanted to gather with printouts of all their emails to hand to me over Sunday breakfast, they were out of luck. Church was no longer optional but a rare moment to be a family, to be together. It was a moment I needed, quite frankly, and another time Tawni saw what was so vital even when I didn't.

ODIN AND HITLER

The National Alliance held their monthly meetings at a local La Quinta. (Ironic, yes?)

Sergeant Meza agreed I'd been collecting some good info and secured the resources to pay for overtime. He would ensure a proper backup team for the Saturday morning meeting.

The first gathering I attended, I couldn't believe the turnout.

There must have been eighty chairs set up in the conference room, and it was *still* standing room only. All ages attended. From shaved heads and tats to dress shirts and bifocals. Elderly men and women came into the room and hugged the younger members of the crowd. There were youngsters and babies in strollers everywhere. A small boy, maybe four years old, wore red suspenders and tiny black Doc Marten boots with red shoelaces.

Remember now, White supremacy gangs in the Valley were "not a thing."

In front of the room, they'd set up a podium with a black flag with the National Alliance symbol, the life rune, draped over it. I claimed my customary seat on the aisle in the back row, an ideal location to scan the whole room and decipher the various associations such as who was hanging out with whom and which women were linked with which guys.

Elton Hall, the older Hitler fanatic I'd met at that first Denny's meeting, greeted me warmly. Behind us stood a group of sleeved-out (tatted in offensive racial tattoos, political ink, from wrist to neck), prison-graduate-looking guys. Some of the most vicious-looking skinheads I'd yet come across, more dangerous than the guys I'd met at The Nile. These were Unit 88 guys. Though they were a variety of sizes and shapes, they all stood arms crossed, glaring about the room, in steel-toed boots and red laces. As I attempted to memorize every detail of this particular group, two people occupied the open seats in front of me—a younger young woman in her early twenties who introduced herself as Natasha and a guy with tattoos from the top of his shaved head down to who knows where. "Hey, I'm Chris," the guy said and then turned to face the front. Tattooed on the back of his head in three-inch-tall black, bold letters was the word *CRACKER*.

The meeting began with several typical "Welcome, brothers and sisters" and "those dirty Mexicans are ruining our lives" speeches.

Then, Jerry Harbin came out and—there's no better expression for it—stole the show. I knew he was the same guy I'd met at Denny's, and we'd spoken on the phone several times since that first meeting, but *this* version of Jerry, in public speaking in front of close to hundred people, was someone else. Jerry often talked about his military service, but I later discovered he hadn't been infantry at all; instead, he'd been in charge of the theater, and he put on plays and films for the troops. And his theater skills were on full display this day.

The whole room hung on *every* word, and I could see firsthand how he'd managed to build the National Alliance in Arizona from solely himself as the single member to more than a hundred comrades in two short years.

Jerry was an Odinist, believing in the ancient Norse religion, and often began his meetings *as* Odin. He'd put on a large, heavy black robe with a hood and used a deep booming voice, speaking with the magnitude and archaic tone of a narrator at the start of a *Lord of the Rings* or *Conan* film. This went on for fifteen minutes. All about the glory and history, and destiny, of the White race. It was all quite asinine, but the crowd hung on every word transfixed and even broke into boisterous applause at the end. And there was more to come.

Jerry then took his robe off and laid it on the ground. Next, he directed our attention to the group of tough-looking skins I'd previously been eyeing in the back of the room. He said that he was "pleased and proud to present the Unit 88 skins as the new skinhead arm of the National Alliance" and introduced their leader, Paul Skalniak.

Paul Skalniak was overweight with a belly *and* a creepy mustache but otherwise unremarkable *except* for his supremacy affinities. He became, for me, one of those pains in your side that just won't go away, a nagging discomfort. He was an old-school skin from somewhere in Europe—at least, that's what he claimed. He now lived in a rough part of Glendale, and his house had become the meeting place for the Unit 88 guys and friends from other organizations. This guy was one of the few who didn't like me from the very start. Maybe he saw right through the bogus tales I'd been telling. (Years later, he'd put a "green light," a contract, on my life for putting several of his "boys" in jail, and to this day, according to one source, Paul cannot have a conversation about skins without my name coming up.)

Tonight, he stood directly behind me as he waved to the crowd.

Then, as if Odin weren't enough, Jerry provided the whole room a genuine, live Adolf Hitler speech. The mannerisms, the dialect, and the passion were all the same, waving his arms about like he'd watched Hitler speak a thousand times (which he had).

All Jerry was missing was the tweed suit and the silly little mustache. Speaking of the genetic and historic dominance of the White Race and its imminent fight for survival, Jerry—still playing his Hitler routine—also spoke of the importance of combining the Skinhead Movement with the overall White nationalist movement. The skins, he explained, were the "street soldiers," the much-needed "enforcers" of the National Alliance. They were the "recruiters of the youth" and "the eyes and ears of the street." After building up the skins' egos, Jerry carefully approached the importance of covering up one's tattoos. He asserted, "We do not want to scare people with all the hatred but bring them toward us." He assured the skins there was always a time and place for tats, but when one was out doing official National Alliance business— "God's work"—it was the time to wear long sleeves.

The skins behind me clearly ruffled a bit at this, but Jerry got the needed nod from their leader. Jerry finished his talk and got a standing ovation from the whole room—the 88 skins, not so much. Still, Jerry was visibly enormously proud of himself, strutting about at the front of the room. The meeting ended with the passing of a hat for dues.

I scanned the room again. There were several elderly men sitting and openly talking about World War II, how Jewish people had somehow "destroyed their lives," and how "Mexicans were rapidly destroying" the United States of America. Scattered throughout the retreating crowd were young men freshly out of prison and some, I'm sure, soon on their way back, all bragging about the tattoos they already had or the ones they planned on getting.

One kid, a guy I would later know as Brian (a.k.a. Tic Toc), lifted his shirt to show a tattoo of a skull with an alarm clock in its eyes. Another, named Sammy, was *completely* covered in ink and, later, proved to be a genuine psychopath who'd fallen in with these guys only as an opportunity to cause pain.

I placed myself as close as possible to eavesdrop as Jerry spoke to a few of the skins. Jerry said he'd heard about how they'd stolen an Israeli flag from a local deli and *sieg heil*ed in front of the establishment until the police were called. Chris, the kid who'd been sitting in front of me, broke into laughter. He turned to another skin. "I still got that flag hanging in my bedroom," he said proudly. And, like a displeased parent, Jerry attempted to regain focus and said that as much as he thought the whole situation was humorous and maybe even fitting, that kind of hooliganism would not be tolerated under his watch.

I escaped to my truck, drove around some making certain I hadn't been followed, and headed home. I looked forward to comparing notes with my backup team when we all got to the office the next day.

The meeting had confirmed all my suspicions regarding the local White supremacy movement. It *was* here, and it was growing.

THE KKK VISITS PHOENIX

Beyond being a compelling speaker and organizer and inviting folk to hang out at his house on the weekends, Jerry Harbin was never much of a warrior for the White race. His most revolutionary aggressive act? Leaving Denny's one day, he laid one of his National Alliance business cards on the table for our Latino server. "That's the only tip she needs," he said.

As we left, I dropped a twenty-dollar bill on the table. It didn't matter if these guys saw me do it—they always seemed to misconstrue my actions for something they weren't, always assuming the worst—and somehow it always worked in my favor.

One time, we were at another Denny's, and I asked the server, another Latino woman, what pies they had. I was just being nice. The table of National Alliance guys had been ignoring her all night and weren't buying anything beyond free coffee refills and water.

"Peanut butter or Oreo," she replied.

"Which do you like?" I asked.

"I love the peanut butter."

"Great." I smiled. "I'll have the Oreo."

It was a silly joke. Playful. She knew I was joking and smiled back.

Meanwhile, all the guys at the table laughed like it was the funniest thing they'd ever heard. "You ain't eating what that wetback eats! Ain't that right, Packy?" I was a hero for ten minutes because I'd taken the opposite choice of a Mexican American woman.

It was getting harder for me to go along with all the White supremacist bullshit. I knew how people should be treated.

Another weekend, I attended a Klan meeting at a Holiday Inn in downtown Phoenix. This one was hosted by a group who'd arrived from Southern California, the Knights of the KKK, and who were ultimately heading to Kentucky, picking up funding and recruits along the way. A small westside Phoenix Klan group was sponsoring their local visit I hadn't yet had much contact with. Even though "Packy" was a member at the national level, there hadn't been much going on locally.

This gathering was a perfect opportunity to monitor the activities of the granddaddy of White pride, the KKK, was up to. Though hooded Klansmen no longer paraded the streets and had become a caricature over time, the Klan's name and long history alone still brought trepidation and attention within the "civilian" world. It's still what people think of first when they think of a White supremacist.

I entered the Holiday Inn and saw the woman at the front desk was of a Middle Eastern ethnicity. It broke my heart to see her face as dozens of shaved and tatted Klansmen and neo-Nazis filed past her into the conference room. This was someone's sister, friend, daughter, colleague. This was a human being. And she looked absolutely terrified. "You OK?" I asked.

She looked up at the six-foot-four White guy with a mullet and earring, the one who'd come in with all the others. Somehow, she nodded.

"You'll be OK," I assured her. I didn't know what else to say. I'd probably scared her even more but told myself we'd passed some look that said, "I'm an undercover cop and you're safe." I was comforting myself more than her, I guess.

In a small meeting room, there must have only been a dozen chairs, with one long table and six unrobed local Klansmen graciously giving their ridiculous "hello brother" pleasantries. (I was, admittedly, disappointed that they were not in cloaks and pointed hoods, satisfying my naïve notions of the Klan.) On flagpoles in front of the room were a swastika and an Imperial Klans of America flag. There was also a Bible on the table.

As with most organizations, there was one "money" guy— someone who could pay for gas, one hotel room for six guys, and the conference room. This was clearly the old guy of the bunch, early sixties, receding gray hairline, wearing a faded blue short-sleeved, button-up shirt and khakis.

The five visiting Californians were all young, nineteen-to twenty-year-olds, unremarkable fellows, small in stature with little going for them. Believe me, these were not the high school athletes or homecoming king types. There was nothing much else for these young men to look forward to *except* moving to Kentucky to live on a compound spewing hate all day. When they walked in, it was like watching a flock of ducks fly past, a perfect "V" formation with the old guy in front and three guys on one side and two on the other. Bizarre. They may have been "idiots," but they were, I now knew, also dangerous.

This group had been directly connected to church burnings and the murders of African American and Jewish people. One Black teen in Louisiana had been found dead in the lake with his organs missing; the local KKK was suspected by the entire community, but the kid's death was officially ruled an "accidental drowning."

The meeting began with a welcome, followed by a prayer as one member of the group read a "Bible passage" about "muds," "spics," and Jews. Then, the time was turned over for the introduction of visitors.

"Great," I thought. "I have to do *this* all again." Introductions were brief. You gave your name, where you lived, why you were there. As this was transpiring, one of the California members took down all our names and a "survey" was being handed out: "What can YOU do for the KKK?" and "How much time and money are you willing to dedicate to building God's warriors?"

I sat and listened to a handful of twentysomethings from Mesa explain why they were there and how they were "ready to reach their potential." My turn approached far too quickly, and I was uneasy. No matter how many times I've done this, I always worry about what I'm going to say. I introduced myself and explained my ever-faithful landscaping fairytale. "I'm ready for a White world and prepared to do what it takes to make it happen!" I proclaimed. A statement met with head nods and lots of "Thank you, brother."

Introduction completed, the older man stood and thanked everyone for being there. He explained that the Imperial Klans of America (IKA), at that time the second biggest Klan group in America, was based out of Kentucky but that the new Phoenix chapter would be run out of Orange County, California. They were looking for "dedicated warriors" to "fight for the cause" and attend all required meetings and training events. The Klan, he claimed, was obtaining 30 acres outside of San Bernardino where they were planning to conduct training in firearms, close-quarter combat, and intimidation techniques.

We were told that the IKA were "mature skinheads" tired of the drinking lifestyle and wanted to be dedicated to changing the future of the White race. He adamantly drove home that they were not just a bunch of guys trying to figure out who was going to buy the next twelve-pack. After finishing with all the required paperwork, shaking everyone's hand, and even exchanging a few more man hugs, several new guys—yes, including Packy—were welcomed into the klavern.

The meeting was adjourned with a prayer and then several members approached me. Within a single hour of meeting this future Kentucky crew, I was asked if I'd like to join them in Kentucky and become their new head of security...the "Knight Hawk."

I'm here to protect the woman at the counter, I wanted to say, but instead told them I was "honored by their support" and that I'd "think about it."

———

While I was officially "thinking about" that offer, Arizona was about to become Ground Zero of White supremacy.

Our state had been chosen for the 2005 Aryan Fest—fashioned to be the biggest White Pride festival the United States had ever seen. Two days of bands, speeches, and a rare gathering of diverse supremacy clubs from across the entire world. The event was being sponsored by Volksfront and aimed to show true unity between the various organizations.

Volksfront had selected Arizona because they were getting chased out of Washington State, where they'd previously had a huge following. Membership in Washington *had* been very strong with a big base in the military; there was a VF "club house" just outside of Tacoma where training was given by active soldiers on everything from hand-to-hand combat to assault rifles. But, after a few military discharges and the recent brutal murder of a homeless man, they were seeking new territories.

(A quick aside on the murder. Four VF skinheads got drunk, bought two baseball bats, and went hunting for a Black man, *any* Black man, in an area where the homeless often stayed in Tacoma. But the first Black man they approached pulled out a machete, so they moved on. They attacked, instead, the next homeless person they came across, a White man, and beat him to death with bats, boots, rocks, and fists. You have to wonder how much ideology is really part of this violence?)

Fortunately for me, I'd been speaking with a detective in Washington for months before the planned Aryan Fest rolled out; we'd been swapping notes on our "White boy" gangs. So, it was total luck. Now these same VF guys were in *my* town, and I had a head start on them. And, when Volksfront asked Jerry Harbin and the National Alliance to lend a hand to the event, I again had a front-row seat.

I shared all of this intel with anyone who would listen, disseminated pertinent info to various agencies, and was lucky enough to have developed a trusted and loyal contact with Michelle, an aggressive, experienced investigator at the Anti-Defamation League (ADL). She proved as passionate about this work as I was and distributed info to her own circle of intelligence sources. While few in the United States cared about the National Alliance yet, Volksfront was a name people paid attention to, and more agencies started getting interested in the event, including Phoenix PD, DPS (state police), ATF, and the FBI.

The only drawback is that no one, including me, yet knew where the event was being held. It was still a secret, even among the various neo-Nazi groups, for fear of the government sweeping in and shutting it down. Jerry Harbin still wouldn't tell me where it was. I wonder now if *he* even knew.

The FBI had a source who claimed the event would be held at a certain time and place, but all his other information was garbage. They'd paid this guy $3,500 for info gathered at a meeting I'd actually attended, and his information was completely different from what I'd heard and was willing to share for free.

The FBI agent was furious I'd contradicted his intel.

I then informed him—and the rest of the room—that, too often, as much as half of the money White supremacists make comes from federal agents paying for "information." Before *that* part of the conversation got any more heated, we decided to focus on the task at hand.

Crew members, even trusted ones like Packy, were still being told the event site would be given later. The only clue we were given was to let other trusted people know there was "an airport close by" to fly into if needed, and a "few hotels to choose from if you didn't want to camp."

Simple enough. I pulled out a map and looked at parks near smaller airports in Arizona. There must have been fifty of them. I narrowed it down to half a dozen and eventually visited McDowell Mountain Regional Park in Fountain Hills to see if I could confirm.

This park is a large desert preserve with bike trails and hiking paths, and in the very northern part of the park, there's a large ramada and camping area. Perfect. Sure enough, I asked about reserving their ramada for a wedding party and was told it was already booked.

The sign-out sheet was hanging right up on the wall, and I looked at the name. Wouldn't you know it, it was the name of a guy who just happened to be a known supporter of Volksfront. *Boom!*

It wasn't exactly the most brilliant detective work, but it got the job done. We now had the location, and I contacted all the other agencies with the update.

ARYAN FEST

The big day arrived. Entering the park, visitors had to stop at a small "guard shack" just big enough for one ranger to sit at a small chair to collect an entry fee. This proved a natural place for us to grab photos and license plates on every vehicle. And the cars and motorcycles kept coming, sometimes six to eight deep, often with hate music blaring through cheap stereo systems and steam rolling out of overheating engines. Most of the cars were old, foreign four-doors with faded paint, limping through the park to the back pavilion. It was easy to spot the out-of-town supremacists; not only were they driving rentals, but they were also more courteous to the fee-taking ranger, trying not to bring attention to themselves in case law enforcement was to arrive.

Of course, law enforcement was already there, nabbing photos of haters from Volksfront, Aryan Nations, White Revolution, Unit 88, National Alliance, WCOTC (World Church of the Creator), the Klan, and a lot of independents—including their leaders. For me, this was unprecedented intelligence.

All in all, it was an impressive turnout. Most of these groups struggle to organize a barbecue and here, already, were 150 people. With a
weekend of cold and rain, there were few other campers, sightseers, or
mountain bikers to bother the neo-Nazis. The park was theirs. Over
the weekend, more than 500 people would visit the event.

The supremacists mingled in the ramada for hours, swapping
handclaps, *sieg heils*, lies, and a few girlfriends. Just about everyone
was drunk, most sneaking drugs when they could. (Volksfront's
leader, Randy Krager, would've flipped had he seen narcotics, as
most White supremacy groups profess drugs were created and distributed by the Black race to bring down good White men and,
so, not acceptable for "true Aryans.") There were tables set up for
attendees to purchase their annual supply of hate T-shirts, "How
to Make a Bomb" books, and horrible White power music CDs
for the car ride home. All this was going on while various hate
bands played their tunes—*all* of which were VF-aligned bands,
the group's greatest source of funding.

Surrounding us, as much as a mile away, were vacationers—er,
I mean surveillance trailers and campers stuffed with the Phoenix
PD, Department of Public Safety, ATF, and the FBI. Heck, even
the Royal Canadians sent down a team.

The Aryan Fest proved a success on many levels.

For the attendees and organizers, the fact that the event wasn't
shut down by cops meant they had "pulled a fast one" on law
enforcement. Also, Volksfront had designed the event to give every
group their props…and I had to admit they'd done a good job.

And, from the law enforcement perspective, there were no fights,
shootings, or assaults; the community didn't suffer for the event
being held, little overtime was paid, *and* the good guys now had
thousands of new photos, license plates, and names to work with.

———

Months after the event, a package bomb was sent to a Scottsdale, Arizona, city office and exploded upon opening by an unfortunate city employee, who lost a couple of fingers. Because of the photos taken at the guard shack, we were able to link the bomb maker, Dennis Mahon, with various hate organizations. This information was used at Mahon's sentencing hearing and added years onto his prison sentence. Intelligence gathering works.

BANNERS AND BEER

A couple of months later, Jerry Harbin and Arizona's sprouting National Alliance had their own big news. In September, Arizona was going to be "blessed" again—this time, by having new National Alliance leader Erich Gliebe come speak. William Pierce, the celebrated former leader of the National Alliance, had died, and trying to make a name for itself on the national front, Jerry Harbin had invited Gliebe (his heir apparent) out for a barbecue meeting. Harbin was determined to make this event even more impressive than the Aryan Fest.

Discussions of bands, flag ceremonies, and security were all deliberated on for what seemed hours. The chatter abruptly stopped, however, when Jerry called for silence and solemnly advised the group: "If there are any law enforcement among the congregation tonight, Constitutionally, by law, they are to introduce themselves right now."

What was this? It'd been months and none of these guys had ever made such a proclamation before. *Had I been made?* Also, everything he was saying was legally untrue.

"Any such individuals will be asked to leave and politely escorted from our meeting."

Sure, I thought. *"Hey y'all, I'm Detective Matt Browning from the Mesa Police Department. Shucks, guys, you found me out. I guess I'll be leavin' now."*

Everyone, including me, looked around, fully expecting someone to stand up. I half expected some other agent who actually believed this line of crap to take Jerry's pathetic bait. And, then it happened. I swear it did. Two guys wearing fanny packs actually stood in the back of the room and walked out. I couldn't believe it. To this day, I have no idea who they were working for. I was both embarrassed for my profession *and* disappointed to have lost a little possible help.

Now that "all" the impostors were chased out, talk continued, and it was determined that Unit 88 would oversee the flag ceremony and security at the barbecue. The next twenty minutes were spent arguing over whether these skins should wear security shirts or not. After much ado about truly nothing, the final decision was announced by Jerry, as if Adolf himself had spoken: "We are *not* paying for your security shirts. If you want them, *you* pay for them." (So absurd. They were so proud of these ridiculous security shirts. But, really, what else did they have? What other trophy or identity to share with the world?)

I'd found myself on the set-up committee and the welcome committee—work I should have been doing at my kids' schools, not for a White supremacist rally.

There was much less law surveillance this round. The National Alliance wasn't yet a big enough deal. At least, I'd convinced my bosses to let me have a camera guy and cover team. As with all skinhead events, I'd hoped to make a good impression by showing up with the beer. Grabbing my ice chest from home, I stopped at the local grocery store and filled up with beer and ice.

After helping unload tables and a few bags of chips, I was asked to wrap a couple of black and red streamers around a column and a podium to help impress the "esteemed" new national leader.

The 88 skins then arrived in a four-car caravan, including a future infamous border-bound red Nissan Sentra. Out of all the cars jumped shirtless skinheads, soon handed their brand-new white polo shirts boldly displaying the word "SECURITY" on the back.

Josh Fiedler gave me one of those "dude hugs" I tolerated but had grown to hate. "How you doing, brother?" he said. I wanted to explain my real brothers were a quarter mile away, recording everything.

I then sat back and watched as Jerry Harbin tried to show the Unit 88 guys how to do a flag ceremony. As an Eagle Scout, I'd been a part of enough flag ceremonies to know the drill, and watching these guys trying to figure it out was painful. Jerry picked out two of the skins, Josh and Chris, to carry the U.S. and National Alliance flags. Two other guys, Allen and Sammy, were supposed to take position *behind* Josh and Chris and march with them.

Sammy threw an actual fit. I felt like I was watching my own toddler son pouting about being asked to go to bed. Sammy thought he was "too good" to be second in the line and demanded to carry one of the flags instead. Eventually, Sammy ripped off his security shirt and stormed back to sit alone in the ramada. He was actually crying with frustration. He was met by several skinbyrds who assured him what a great guy he was and how they agreed he was "too good" to be "second in line." He had the words "SOBER SOUL" tatted across his bare stomach.

I'd come to understand how truly desperate most of these guys and gals were for a pat on the back from someone, *anyone*. All

Sammy wanted in this world was some sign of respect, even if it was just carrying a flag for thirty seconds, and he hadn't even gotten that. If only someone had gotten a paintbrush into this kid's hands, or a lacrosse stick, or a job at the local garage. *Something…*

Chris and Josh completed the flag ceremony rehearsal with only a few minor goose-stepping mistakes and returned to the ramada next to Sammy. As they walked over to him, both Josh and Chris reached down and rubbed his freshly shaved head as if to say, "It's OK, little brother. Your time will come."

Sammy, taking offense to their gesture, tossed his security shirt to the ground and stormed farther away to the parking lot. I figured this was a perfect time to take advantage of a situation and be hailed as the peacemaker, so I pulled the ice chest of beer out of my truck and placed it on the picnic bench.

"Who wants a beer?" I shouted. And, just as I had predicted, Sammy ran back from the parking lot like someone had just rung the lunch bell. So much for the "Sober Soul." I opened the ice chest and Sammy was the first to reach in as everyone else came around to get theirs. He pulled out the bottle of ice-cold, frosty Corona and displayed it so everyone could see.

Good call, I thought, and stood ready to start jovial conversations as a true "brother." But there were no conversations. All I heard was the sound of ice settling in the ice chest and more dead quiet.

I don't care who you are. As an undercover officer, you're bound to make some mistakes.

Sammy looked at the bottle, put it back into the ice chest, and walked away.

What the heck is going on? I thought. *Skinheads love free beer.*

Then everyone followed suit, leaving me with a case of iced-down beer. Finally, it clicked. Corona. A Mexican beer. *How clueless could I be?* I feared I had just blown everything—my cover, my case, my credibility—by bringing the wrong beer to the most important meeting of the year. I had to fix the situation, *if* I could, and fast. I quickly lugged the whole ice chest to my truck and headed back down the hill for a quick trip to the local grocery store. I hid the Corona and filled the chest with Heineken, a good "German beer."

Returning to the barbecue now with solid "White boy" beer, I was quickly forgiven and back in the game. After sitting around drinking for a while, the anticipatory arrival of Erich Gliebe came.

He'd arrived in a car driven by an older member of the National Alliance and the member's wife. Gliebe just seemed like a lonely guy sitting in the back seat of a red car. Though I hadn't heard much about him before the barbecue planning, Gliebe was the new national chair of the National Alliance. At this time, the National Alliance was profiting $1 million a year, just on paper, and its membership was in the thousands. He was also, perhaps more importantly to those in the movement, the CEO of Resistance Records, the largest and most profitable hate-production company in the country.

To be honest, he wasn't much to look at. He was a tall, almost gangly, balding, middle-aged man. Gliebe, I later learned, was a frustrated boxer (dubbed the "Aryan Barbarian"), who'd decided to hook up with National Alliance founder William Pierce while recovering from an elbow injury. After Pierce's death, a power struggle began between Gliebe and the National membership coordinator, Billy Roper. Rumor had it that Billy finally got sick of the battle, took those brothers he wanted, and formed his own break-off group, White Revolution. With Roper's departure, Gliebe was now free to step into the role of president of the National Alliance.

As he walked from the parking lot to the ramada, everyone acted as if the president of the United States had arrived. The crowd of forty-plus rushed over, each wanting to be the first racist to shake his hand. This was their new prophet and perhaps their ticket to somewhere more prominent within the White power hierarchy.

The flag ceremony went as planned and Josh and Chris looked like awkward, adolescent boys, goose-stepping and *sieg-heil*ing as they came forward and posted the flags. Jerry got up to say a few words and he revived his usual Hitler routine. He then introduced Josh Fiedler from Unit 88 and asked him to speak on the skinhead movement.

Josh marched to the front like a proud rooster fluffing its tail feathers. Behind him was his buddy Chris (whom Josh had invited to speak after because he felt bad for him). As Josh spoke, Chris stood at attention, acting as support and security. Though Josh was noted for his silver tongue, his speech today was short and with little substance. He was nervous, I think, that Gliebe was there. Still, after, he received all the obligatory Heil Hitlers and White Power chants from the crowd. Then, it was Chris's turn. He managed maybe a dozen words before both of them marched back down receiving handshakes from their brothers and the "good job" hugs from the skinbyrds.

Jerry Harbin now introduced Gliebe.

Years later, Gliebe married a stripper, which made him lots of enemies in the movement because she was "muddying the White race" with *her* "impure" behavior—and, according to inside info, also got heavily into cocaine, a huge no-no in true White nationalism. Tonight, however, he was still the king.

I stood among a group of neo-Nazis and listened intently to Gliebe's speech. To my direct right stood Brandon Miller—one of the young guys I'd pulled over at the traffic stop behind The Nile years before. I couldn't believe it. And he somehow didn't recognize me at all.

Gliebe started with the characteristic "thank you for having me" small talk. Then, he broke into an incredible and completely unexpected tirade. Gliebe proclaimed skinheads were a "disgrace" to the movement and should not be associated in any way with the National Alliance. He added tattoos were an ill-advised liability and needed to be covered, saying: "How does a skin ever expect to recruit good people into the movement when they're out there acting like undisciplined hooligans?"

My jaw dropped. This was both astonishing and awesome. *This guy really is a moron*, I thought. I didn't even need to look around me; I could feel the tension fill the whole park. There were some seriously pissed-off skins, skins with violent anger issues. This was going to get good. I didn't need my cover team for *me*, but I wondered if I was going to have to call them in for the guest of honor. Some skinheads started yelling obscenities while others booed and began packing up their stuff to leave. After Gliebe finished his speech, he requested that all the skins meet him over in the corner to discuss some "business."

He proceeded to apologize privately to the group, claiming that he had to say what he said to pacify the "older" people in the crowd. He claimed that he *personally* believed in the skinheads, believed they were the "street soldiers" for the National Alliance. He was nervous, I could tell, but doing his best to appease the skins. Either Gliebe was a master manipulator or the skins were more desperate than I thought. They accepted his explanation and "praise," and Gliebe made it to his car safely and left quickly without a single beer or burger.

The bands who were supposed to play the event had all backed out; this was typical. Volksfront, who managed, funded, and promoted White power bands, could always pull a great show together, not so much the other organizations who had to depend more on less-dependable punk garage bands who dabbled in White Pride music. There wasn't even any music on a boom box, just more unplanned talk.

Still, the congregation had grown bigger by this time and the sun was going down. There were now about a hundred attendees at the event. New skins had shown up, and I was happy to get to know guys I'd never met.

I heard the usual talk of pointing shotguns at people, hunting trips, boot parties, and other nightly beatdowns. Breaking the "Mexican's" nose and arm while dozens of onlookers watched—police never involved. Luring a Black drug dealer into their vehicle on the pretense of buying narcotics and then beating him unconscious. A group of six beating a Black man unconscious because he'd spilled beer on one of them. Yeah, they had plenty of stories…

Jerry was in high heaven because of the "great turnout" and his performance in front of Gliebe. And as far as *my* investigation went, I, too, was very happy with the intelligence I had gathered, and the inroads made.

But eight hours with these people was enough. My brain hurt, and my heart hurt some too. I released my cover team and engaged in my typical covert driving skills. Well past midnight, I finally made it home and was met outside by my beautiful wife, who threw her arms around me. As I held her, I realized: *This is peace. This is my life. This is real.*

———

It was the weekend and I just wanted to regroup and spend what was left of it with my family. I spent Sunday at church and just hung out with our kids. On Monday, I did the typical routine:

taking kids to school and then some alone time with Tawni. Throughout, my phone was ringing nonstop with calls from the FBI, DPS, ATF, and Mesa police—all wanting information on the barbecue.

They hadn't thought it important enough to commit resources or staff but wouldn't say no to any intel gathered. I finally just let the phone go to voicemail. Still, I'd be a liar if I didn't admit that it was nice to be the wanted man.

When I finally went back to work, we sat down to brief the barbecue and review all the information that'd been gained. Hours later, however, a sergeant asked, "Hey, did you use department money to get that beer?" Yeah, I had. "What happened to the Corona?" he questioned.

I told him truthfully that I'd given it to my cover team as a thank you for a long day's work. I received a reprimand and was instructed to purchase a case of Corona—with my own money—and place it into evidence *for destruction*. All that work and all the legit intelligence gained, not to mention the long hours away from my family…and *this* is what my department was worried about? I went to the closest grocery store, picked up the cheapest case of Pabst Blue Ribbon, my way of rebelling, and put it all into Property to be tossed out an hour later.

LEADER OF THE PACK

One group that wasn't worried about my Corona blunder was the National Alliance. A week or so after the event, I got a phone call from Jerry. "What's the chance of meeting with you for lunch?" he asked, and we arranged to meet at the local Denny's. I wasn't sure yet what this was about, and so I put together a quick surveillance team and headed to Phoenix; my "team" actually consisted of just a single guy in the parking lot.

Jerry and I arrived at the same time. He'd brought John, a newer member of the NA in his forties. John was one of the only members who actually had a good professional job, and he was going to school to become a polygrapher.

They both seemed excited to be there with me as we sat at a booth. There wasn't any small talk. Jerry informed me Gliebe had stayed with John and his wife while he was in town, and Gliebe had apparently expressed contempt for the local skins and their leadership. Jerry told me that, personally, he saw a very real need for the skins—as both the muscle and "cool" recruiters who could reach younger kids—*if* they could just be channeled properly. However, he also understood that they needed to be controlled and "educated in adult ways," to provide them with solid leadership and some old-fashioned discipline. *Good luck with that*, I thought.

"Would *you*," Jerry asked, "consider being the liaison between Unit 88 and all the other skinhead members for the National Alliance?"

"Me?"

What an opportunity—a detective in the *middle* of two groups, keeping intimate tabs on the 88 skins and National Alliance.

Is this really happening? I thought. I didn't have to pretend like I was taken aback because I was. My reputation had clearly been bolstered with all the barbecues and bonfires and the inroads I'd made.

Jerry's goal was to make Unit 88 the enforcement, recruitment, and model skinhead organization—all under the National Alliance banner. He wanted to begin weeklong boot camp training to take place on some land John owned north of town. Here, National Alliance indoctrination and close-quarter combat would be instructed. Firearms training and wilderness survival. It sounded more like a traditional American antigovernment militia group to me and, in truth, the lines were already blurring.

I agreed to their proposal and thanked them profusely for believing in me. In the parking lot, Jerry cautioned me that, again, Unit 88 was kind of out of control. He'd also heard of all the fights and assaults they'd committed, and he knew about more than I did.

He was particularly worried about Paul Skalniak, their leader. The one who'd stood behind me while Jerry did his best Odin and Hitler impersonations. Paul was *not* a leader but a party buddy who spent more time trying to be pals with the skins than providing any sense of leadership or genuine White pride ideology.

As I stood there, Jerry made a phone call to Josh and Chris, Unit 88 guys. He left a message advising them what had transpired between us and told them that they were to speak with me directly from then on. He hung up the phone, visibly upset. "It's after noon," Jerry griped. "They should be up and doing something productive." Shaking my hand, he added, "Packy, just take care of them and don't let them do anything stupid. Please…"

I was apparently now Unit 88s "mommy." Or daddy. You choose.

I immediately called my supervisor to let him know how the meeting went.

"You can't say no." I stopped him before he even got the words out. "I'm not the 'leader' of either group; I'm just a middleman," I pleaded.

We both knew this was an incredible opportunity for some great intel and arrests and, amazingly, I got the approval with the agreement that the whole thing would need to be worked very cautiously.

My supervisor asked, "Are these guys really that clueless?"

I responded, "I guess so."

———

If any further proof of their cluelessness was needed, the next Saturday I was at home doing work on my house, just trying to get caught up, when my work phone rang.

"Hello, Patrick," I heard. "It's Jerry." He told me he was sending over an invitation to the next private planning meeting he was organizing. An hour later, the email arrived.

Not only had he sent the promised invite, but he'd somehow *also* sent me a full membership roster of the Arizona National Alliance Chapter, as well as a few sub-chapters in California and other states. There were close to two hundred email addresses on this list. I almost fell over. I had been laying low for months and hadn't even asked for anybody's full names, let alone all their personal information. Yet here it was now in front of me—gold.

Addresses in hand, I started the long grind of processing dozens of court orders to various email providers to get the true identities of all involved. Putting their real names to prison records and driver's licenses, I was able to get the complete background on almost every member. I was certainly feeling some kind of "Detective of the Year" award would be appropriate.

OK, joking about an award. But maybe, now, other people would finally open their eyes to this White Pride problem. Maybe we could even put some bullies in jail. Stop the hate and violence *before* it happened. Shut down an actual hate organization growing in our community. It was only a matter of time now before the National Alliance and those connected to it were out of commission.

Or, at least, that's what I thought.

THE KLAN MEETS MY FAMILY

Our whole family loaded into the ol' blue Suburban and drove to Walmart for some shopping. I'd been working more and more and Tawni had been waiting for me to shop, not only to help wrangle the kids but to find some much-needed time together as a family. In her typical fashion, what is considered "ordinary" to everyone else was intended to be a meaningful event. It was, just not in the way we'd hoped.

We'd managed to fill our cart with more kids (three young boys and a baby girl) than items as we finally headed for the checkout. Then, I heard someone yell, "Hey, Packy! What the hell?"

Packy?

I froze. I knew this could happen—running into someone who knew my undercover persona while in my private life—but at Walmart, standing beside my family? This was 100% completely in my private life. And it rattled me.

With no time to process all that this entailed, I ignored the shoutout and continued to walk nonchalantly while trying to covertly tell Tawni to leave and take the kids to the car. To be fair, when I'd first started working in the Special Investigations Division, I *had* told Tawni, "If I ever tell you to go to the car, don't ask questions, just do it; I will explain it to you later."

Now, years later, Tawni was giving me one of her famous "You're not the boss of me" looks, and I again said more urgently, "Get out of here."

She stared at me, confused, and a bit irritated at my tone. Afterward, I found out she thought I'd wanted privacy to buy her an upcoming birthday gift and she wanted to tease me about what I might buy her at Walmart.

I just walked away from my family and toward the approaching

Klansmen. I had no choice. Behind me, Tawni finally understood the urgency and took the cart and all the kids down another aisle. I could hear our children: "Where's Daddy going?" "I want to go with Dad."

There, in the middle of our local Walmart, I was confronted by four KKK members I'd been avoiding for weeks. These were the same young California Klansmen I'd met at the local Holiday Inn.

All these guys ever wanted to do was get together and drink. There wasn't much intel to be had in that. Spending my time around a makeshift fire pit with guys barely old enough to drink legally, listening to some pipedream about how the White race will soon flourish again at some nonexistent KKK compound in Kentucky was not my idea of concrete police work. The idea of forfeiting another night with my family in return for very little usable information seemed…wasteful. I'd grown weary of coming home at night just to find everyone asleep.

"What the hell, brother," one grinned, clasping hands. "You just dog us like that?"

"You're supposed to be a Klansman," the guy next to him said.

I made up a story about going into Mexico to recover some of my stolen stuff. *Had they seen me with my family?* I didn't think so, but…I didn't give any of them time to speak or ask questions; I just talked their ears off until *they* said that they had to go.

"Just answer your fucking phone next time, Hoss. We're heading to Kentucky in a few weeks and want to get together before we leave."

"Definitely," I lied, filing away this alleged moving-date info for a later report.

By this time, Tawni had checked out and I found my family outside the Suburban playing silly games and waiting; I'd had the keys. I walked slowly to my car looking through the parking lot and over my shoulder with every step. I was also trying to figure out what I'd do if the Klansmen were outside. Would I just walk past my family, strand them in the parking lot for another half hour, and hope Tawni understood? Should I just let it be known that "Packy" had a wife and family of four kids? The KKK guys were going to Kentucky soon, apparently. What could it matter?

We loaded the stuff quickly and started to leave. Pulling away, I glanced back and saw these Klansmen outside the store and looking around the parking lot. I literally watched in the rearview mirror as one of the guys pulled out his cell phone and my phone started ringing. *You gotta be kidding me.*

"Where you at, brother? We're gonna get some drinks."

Brother, again. I winced with revulsion every time they said it; and they all say it constantly. "Sorry, guys," I said, glancing at Tawni. "Already long gone. How 'bout another time?"

We never got that drink, and I got half a dozen "fuck you" voicemails before they left for Kentucky.

Turns out, there was no actual compound waiting there and, to my knowledge, they never got one built either. Still, for months after, I got phone calls about coming down and donating my time and fictitious construction know-how to help build said compound… and to "hang out with my brothers."

Turns out, if I'd really wanted to do that, all I had to do was go to church.

White supremacy wasn't only in the parks and clubs.

It was, I soon learned, also being preached to the choir.

A young man named Wade is first demoted and then finally discharged for excessive drinking after six years in the Army. He attends
Hammerfest, a White power music festival in Georgia and, excited by
the music, relocates to Orange, a city in Southern California that has a
booming White pride rock scene. He can play guitar and sing and spends
the next decade touring the country via the festival circuit in bands with
names like Blue Eyed Devils, Celtic Warrior, Max Resist, and Definite
Hate, who release an album, *Violent Victory*. He now has many tattoos:
838 ("Hail the Crossed Hammers"); a *W* and *P* on each hand for White
Pride; a huge Celtic cross; and the number 14 encircled in flames (for
David Lane's now-canonic fourteen-word motto). Wade forms his own
band, End Apathy and promotes their music on Stormfront, the largest
neo-Nazi web forum in the world. On the site, he also supports his belief
in "White genocide," blasts "race traitors" as well as the "dirt people,"
and buys White power merchandise. He earns his patch and full membership into the Northern Hammerskins. He moves to Milwaukee to stay
with a new girlfriend; they break up months later, and he stops going to
work and falls months behind in his rent. He drives to a Sikh gurdwara
(temple) down the street from a restaurant where he briefly worked. He
shoots nine people and kills six of them. Wade puts the pistol to his own
temple and kills himself in the gurdwara parking lot.

---

*Wade: "Sikh Temple Killer Wade Michael Page Radicalized in Army," *Intelligence Report*,
November 11, 2012, https://www.splcenter.org/fighting-hate/intelligence-report/2012/sikh
-temple-killer-wade-michael-page-radicalized-army; "Sikh temple shooting was suspect Wade
Michael Page was a white supremacist," CBS News, August 6, 2012; Dinesh Ramde, "Wisconsin
Temple Shooting: Oak Creek Incident Leaves At Least 7 Dead," *Huffington Post*, August 5, 2012.

A QUESTION OF FAITH

A Great Multitude

These were color photographs taken covertly by another detective.

The photos showed chairs, orange barrels, and sawhorses carefully arranged across an otherwise-empty parking lot. They showed more than a dozen people, mostly men but some women too, crouched behind makeshift barricades and cover. Suburbanites clutching firearms. Preparing for war.

"Are those...*paintball* rifles?" I asked, my face no doubt scrunched in confusion.

"Some." The other detective was smiling, shaking his head. He was a seasoned street crimes detective and part of SCAT (Special Crimes Apprehension Team), an undercover squad used for major cases and arrests. He was a short, husky Latino man who knew the streets of Mesa well and wasn't afraid of getting the tough work done. "BB guns, also," he said.

Several times a month, apparently, twelve to twenty people gathered in the same parking lot. Doing drills or playing some kind of grown-up "cops and robbers." Finally, several neighbors had called the police, concerned.

"What church is this again?" I asked.

"Mesa Bible," he repeated. "Just off Gilbert." He'd said it looked like genuine military training. Then, he said, "Crazy White people is *your* thing."

"Guess I'll head out there," I agreed, and he quickly dropped the folder that had held the photos onto my desk.

He'd not come to me as a concerned colleague who understood my mission but rather as someone who had "better things to do." He, and many others, often made comments like "When you're done looking into White people and want to play for real, let me know." (To be clear, this guy is a great cop and we got along well for years. But for him, unless someone was going directly to jail, an investigation was a waste of time.)

"Let me know if there's any *real* crime there," he smirked and walked out. I have a vague memory of him playfully flipping me off as he left.

I, meanwhile, was going to church.

———

Church wasn't ever a chore in my life. Tawni always says to make a better life, folk just "need a little more faith." Over the years, I've come to totally believe her. I'd grown up with both church and faith. My dad had us up every morning at 5:00 a.m. to read the Bible as a family and he held leadership roles in the church; I was a genuine preacher's (bishop's) son. At one point, he was responsible for four-thousand-some church members and I traveled with him throughout the Valley so he could make his visits and not have to drive alone. Because of that, I have a lot of good memories of just my dad and me. I'd met my friends at church; Sundays were spent in Sunday school and Wednesday nights were our "youth group"—playing softball, basketball, and, yes, sometimes skipping to go to a convenience store or McDonald's. I first saw Tawni at a church softball game, then a church dance. A lot of good things happened for me because I was at church functions. And when I experimented with alcohol as a teenager, it was a church member who caught me and promptly told my dad, ending my "research."

I certainly appreciated the way I was raised and the faith my parents instilled. It provided the foundation I needed to get through some of the more difficult times in my life. When I graduated from high school, like most young men in my church, I prepared to go on a two-year mission. However, it wasn't a sure thing with me. It really wasn't until I'd started dating Tawni that I grasped a mission would be in my future. Tawni knew from an early age that she would only marry a return missionary, just as our church taught she should. No question, then; I was going.

One Sunday afternoon, I spoke with my bishop and got the paperwork to start the mission process. Sitting in the chapel in the back row was my dad, talking to another leader of the church when I walked up and said, "Hey, can you hold this for me, so I don't lose it?" I handed him the mission papers and walked away to be with my friends. I looked back and saw the biggest smile I'd ever seen on my dad's face. Two months later, I was on a plane to Provo, Utah, to spend a week at the mission training center before I went to the Tulsa mission, which covered all of Oklahoma and parts of Texas, Arkansas, Missouri, and Kansas.

Two years came and went, some weeks faster than others. I met some good people, and one in particular was the Police Chief of Joplin, Missouri, Mike Wightman. Mike allowed me to visit the police station, sit in his office, and just talk about police work. I realize (as I write this now) it was through the church that I'd met the two people who influenced me to become a police officer: Steve Checketts, one of my youth leaders, and Chief Wightman.

I returned home wanting to be a police officer, and the mission also set the groundwork for a lot of my adult life. I now understood how to talk to people I had absolutely nothing in common with; I could knock on any door without anxiety about who would answer or fear of rejection, and I learned that Tawni was right when she said, "Everyone needs a little more faith in their lives." Especially me.

I would not be finding him at Mesa Bible.

———

Prior to the Bible study I was planning to attend, I did a drive-by of the church. At first, it looked like ten thousand other small churches spread across the United States. One story, mostly brick, a big cross on the side that faced 8th Avenue, the main street. There was a display out front promoting counseling, Bible study, and "Mert Pekrul, Pastor."

From the side street, however, the church looked more like a rundown motel, a row of seven red doors running along all that brick. No windows. The whole building had maybe six windows total, none bigger than a typical flatscreen TV. Someone had built a small fortress in the middle of Mesa.

There were also four cars in the parking lot, and I rolled through for a closer look. One plate read "Washitaw Nation." It was not a plate I'd ever seen before, and my first assumption was that it was for some western Indigenous tribe I'd never heard of. I filed the name away, and the answers I needed came later that week from my department's SCAT team—these weren't just some Bible-thumping retirees.

This residential church was also an active militia group. A

real-deal antigovernment sovereign citizen organization. My first, but certainly not my last.

While modern militia groups exist in fifty-plus flavors and have a genuine resemblance to those militias that existed before Ben Franklin was a child, the main ingredient in these modern groups has almost always been the same: mistrust of the government combined with a sense of vigilante justice and preparation. They believe that the government is either (a) not doing its job or (b) corrupt and tyrannical. And, in either case, citizens must organize and act themselves.

The Washitaw Nation, I learned, *was* originally a group of Native Americans involved with the Louisiana Purchase.[i] The tribe believed the purchase was a fraud in which the U.S. government bought a few hundred acres from Napoleon and used that as false pretext to grab another *500 million* acres of Native land. Sometime within the last hundred years, the "Washitaw Nation" had become a mishmash of mostly *White* people spread across the whole USA.

In any case, because of the original "bogus deal" in 1803, the updated Washitaw Indians now alleged they were sovereign citizens with no obligations to the government—no taxes, no laws, and no governmental authority, including any law enforcement except for the elected sheriff.

To become a member of Arizona's version of the Washitaw Nation (varied groups across the country use this same name), you first needed to talk with Mesa Bible Church pastor Merton Pekrul. After, you'd be pressed to transfer nearly all your money, vehicle registrations, property deeds, and business associations into Washitaw Nation bank accounts. In exchange, you'd receive new, *albeit bogus*, birth certificates, state ID cards, and passports—all for "official" Washitaw Nation documents. When that was done, Pekrul would have new members send notarized letters to the county recorder and all state offices stating they were no longer affiliated with the United States of America.

It was a meaningless gesture, legally, but I still collected copies of these inane letters from different government agencies and sources to keep up on what was happening. I did some other digging, also.

There were, I found, already fifty-plus local known members.

I'd never heard of this Washitaw Nation group, and I had lived in the valley for twenty-plus years. *How was that even possible?*

Easy. Even though the SCAT team worked down the hall, they'd never once mentioned them to the other investigation squads. But we were all guilty of that. Each team, even mine, was territorial. Even in a post-9/11 world, no one was talking to each other. Every department, even teams within the same building, had its own concerns, budgets, and—most importantly—egos and turf. We were all too busy, haughty, or foolish to help the other crews.

And, on top of that, members of the church were your typical "neighbors next door," people you wouldn't ever consider being a threat. They were bank tellers and car salespeople and hairdressers. Not one I later looked up had a criminal record. Not one. At neo-Nazi gatherings, 70% of the crowd had been arrested at some point.

This group had, I soon learned, first appeared on authorities' radar in 1996 when supporting a Montana militia known as the Montana Freemen—one of the largest and most famous in the country—during its infamous eighty-one-day stand-off with federal agents.[ii] During the standoff, supporters of the Montana group had come to Phoenix to purchase large SUVs using counterfeit money orders and driving them back to Montana to aid in the militia's cause. The SUVs were to be used as escape vehicles for when the government decided to raid. Further, these guys genuinely believed the government was soon to collapse, putting the militias in charge, and the SUVs would prove crucial for the new militia-run America. Arizona-supplied money orders would also cover guns and ammo as needed. I couldn't believe this type of activity was going on in Mesa.

I knew enough about militias and antigovernment groups then to know they often *also* attracted White supremacists. Oklahoma City Bombing's Timothy McVeigh, Ruby Ridge's Randy Weaver, and Robert Mathews, leader of the Order, were "militia members" who'd also dabbled within the National Alliance and Aryan Nations. There was good cause to at least check this Washitaw group out.

My cover story this time was simple enough. I called a few days prior just to make sure the Bible-study class was still happening and spoke directly to the church pastor, Pekrul. He confirmed the day and time of the class and then asked who I was. I told him I was Patrick and had just moved my family into the neighborhood because I was looking for a better place for my kids to grow up. I claimed I was from Aravaca, an extremely small southern Arizona town that undocumented immigrants and cartels use as a "watering hole" on their way up north from the border. I suspected just mentioning the town would catapult me right where I needed to be with this guy, and anyone else who was remotely antigovernment or anti-immigration would understand why I'd want to get my family out. I'd suspected right.

Once again, I was welcomed right into their little hate club.

"Brother Patrick," the pastor said, "I look forward to meeting you."

———

After dinner, Tawni had good-humoredly prepared me by singing some old gospel tunes before I readied to "go to church." Then she got more serious. "Don't let them get in your head," she said.

The concern, I thought then, was absurd.

"It's often a slow and steady road to Hell," she clarified. "And these people are most likely on it."

Pulling into the church parking lot, I thought about her parting words. A lot.

Thanks to the photographs, I could perfectly visualize the barricades and orange barrels the church members had recently used to practice urban warfare. I wondered where they kept them. There were six portable trailers behind the church, and I was later told they were used as extra classrooms for Bible school on Sundays. (Another one, next to the church, was—I found out later—full of guns, ammo, and explosives.)

The parking lot was scattered with a dozen more vehicles, half with Washitaw Nation license plates.

On most undercover operations, we would normally "four point" the building, having a full team set up early to grab plates and pictures and a rescue team set in a van in full entry gear waiting for the call if something went wrong. For me, I had John in a car across the street from the church in a school parking lot, updating workstation files and reading reports. At least he was there.

I parked my red Chevy pickup and headed for church.

Taped on the front doors of the church were papers stating the church was "on sovereign land" and "no law enforcement" would be allowed on the property; "only the local sheriff" had legal jurisdiction over them.

Then, another sign: "THIS CHURCH IS PROTECTED BY GOD AND HIS .357." My thoughts ran to feeling the weight of the Glock on my ankle and the blue Ford Taurus with John, my backup, across the street.

Inside, I'd hoped to get a chance to look around by myself. Instead, at least ten men and women were already there for the Bible study. It almost felt like I was in my own church-except half these guys had guns on their hips in full exposure.

"Hello, Patrick?"

I turned to my right to be greeted by a gentleman in his fifties wearing brown slacks and a yellow shirt. He stretched out his hand. "It's good to have you here," he said. "Let me show you where Bible Study is." It was Pekrul, of course, and he clearly knew I was the guy he'd spoken to on the phone.

I simply said, "Thank you, sir... I feel like I'm home," and then we walked to the left down a short hall to a classroom. There, about fifteen people, more men than women, were already seated in metal chairs and making small talk until Mert walked back in with a cup of coffee from the hallway table and said, "We ready to start?"

He first introduced a younger man who stood to offer a short prayer. In the prayer, this guy gave thanks to God for "being who we are," and I tried not to read too much into it but soon understood fully.

After the prayer, Mert Pekrul presided over the study. We started with readings from the book of John, and Pekrul was on his soapbox, the sermon well on its way. I grabbed a loaner Bible and soon found myself confused. Overly confused. Typical Bible talk had quickly shifted to other topics, which were being presented as if Pekrul were reading them *directly* from the New Testament.

I double-checked the pages for the words "mud peoples" and "serpent seeds" and "lazy Jews" knowing I wouldn't find them in the text. Meanwhile, the others in attendance merely nodded and agreed with the sermon, shouting out their own views and hatred toward, mostly, Jewish people. Comments also flew of how the government was destroying the Constitution with no care for its true citizens and that Black people were the lowest form of society.

There wasn't a shaved head or showing tattoo in the room. Yet, for the next hour, I might as well have been at a Klan rally, or a Skin show in The Nile Theater.

As if my first militia meeting weren't enough, I was now also formally meeting an offshoot of the Christian Identity movement.

———

While there are a hundred blends of Christianity with White supremacy, corrupting organized religion to reinforce and endorse discrimination, Christian Identity is a good keystone to start from. To understand them is to understand the other ninety-nine.

Some things to know:

They believe the Bible, when connected to other apocryphal texts, "proves" White Europeans ("*Adam*ites") are God's chosen people, direct descendants from Abel. This idea has its origins in British Israelism, a centuries-old pseudo-archaeological belief that Brits are "genetically, racially, and linguistically the direct descendants" of the Ten Lost Tribes of ancient Israel. Some devotees even claim the Virgin Mary was raised in the British Isles and returned again with Jesus after giving birth in Bethlehem.

They believe, in turn, that Jewish people are the cursed offspring of Cain (an idea with roots going back to the Middle Ages), who was conceived when Eve lay with the snake/Satan; thus, Jewish people are often called the "serpent seed" or "two-seedline" theory. They believe there was also an inferior race on

Earth *before* Adam and Eve, "beasts" of the field—which the religion teaches is the Black race—which God eventually put Adam and Eve in charge of.

Christian Identitarians also believe, as most Christians do, that Jesus will one day return to reign over a new Heavenly Kingdom on Earth. A "Golden Age" or "World to Come"—a special time (promised in Revelation) in which Heaven on Earth occurs for a thousand years *before* the Final Judgment. In the Christian Identitarian version of Heaven on Earth, however, adherents add the belief that Whites will again "assume their rightful place" and all non-Whites will be exterminated or enslaved to serve Whites, who are the only ones who may ultimately enter paradise.

Some other beliefs include that God finds interracial marriages a sin and the Bible shows dozens of injunctions against it; European nations were founded by the Ten Lost Tribes of ancient Israel; a state of racial purity must be achieved in the U.S.; the government is controlled by Jewish people and seeks to thwart this plan via systemic White replacement; political change can only be achieved through force, but an armed insurrection against the current government would fail; creation of a "White Aryan bastion" or ethno-state of pure Whites somewhere in the U.S. is the first step.[iii]

Americans developed most of these beliefs starting in the 1940s via the KKK and throughout the 1970s and '80s via the Aryan Nations, The Order, and various militia and isolationist groups.

There is no one "leader" connected to these beliefs, nor are they attached to any one organization or Christian denomination. They are simply touted, shared, and legitimized by individuals, White supremacist sects, and fringe Protestant congregations spread across the whole country.

And, principally, in *prisons*—where Whites are outnumbered two to one and often looking for some lifeline of hope and "impending command."[iv]

Adherents could also assert the Catholic Church itself as "supporting" their beliefs. In 1493, Pope Alexander VI issued *Inter Caetera*, an edict that included the Doctrine of Discovery, which gave European explorers the right to confiscate any non-Christian lands they "discovered" on behalf of their Christian Monarchs.[v] Those non-Christians already living in such lands could be converted, enslaved, or killed. Thus, God's voice on Earth had given official permission to subjugate non-Europeans (non-Whites) in lands throughout Africa, The Americas, and the Pacific—permission exercised with abundance for the next four hundred years.

What was White supremacy, argued Christian Identitarians, if not a continuation of such doctrine?

The most dangerous adherents to these ideas call themselves the Phineas Priesthood.

Phineas appears in the Old Testament in Exodus, an Israelite who murders an Israelite man and his Midianite wife for intermingling two tribes and is, in certain interpretations of the scriptures, rewarded by God for adopting an early stand against interracial couples. (How a Jewish guy became the namesake for antisemitic White racists is an ironic mystery.)

Their symbol is the letter *P* with a horizontal line through it, representing the spear Phineas drove through the offending spouses.

In the early and mid-1990s, this group was connected to multiple bank robberies and bombings from the Pacific Northwest and Oklahoma. But part of what makes them dangerous is that there *is* no collective group. No meetings. No leader. No dues.

They scheme and act alone, chosen "by God" to protect God-sanctioned racial purity. Over time, I learned to identify these individuals and quickly reevaluate their position with an investigation knowing they are no joke. They believe wholeheartedly they are doing the will of God and can make head-shaved Hammerskins look like Cub Scouts. They are zealots completely willing to kill, and die, for the cause of God-sanctioned White supremacy.

———

Mert Pekrul was now telling the story of Jesus and the Syrophoenician (says Mark) or Canaanite (says Matthew) woman who asks Jesus to help her daughter who is possessed by a demon. Jesus refuses, telling the woman his mission is for the children of Israel and that he will not give his "children's" food to "dogs." Dogs.

Those in the pews around me nodded in agreement.

I couldn't believe what I was hearing. I didn't remember this Bible passage at all and opened the Bible to the section Pekrul was working from. In the very next lines, the Gentile woman persists, and Jesus tells her to go home where her daughter is already healed. These passages were not read tonight. Later, I'd learn that the "dog/children" wording is more like "puppy/children" and a metaphor for who will be saved *first*—the implications being that all will be saved in time, but Christians first. (Still not a flawless message, but I guess Matthew and Mark were writing for a specific audience.) Pekrul had simply skipped this part entirely.

Instead, we'd moved on to some more generic praising of the Lord, singing a song and saying a traditional prayer. I couldn't help but think of the million-plus paintings of blue-eyed, fair-skinned Jesus—an image that'd hung in my own house growing up. The

casual propagation of a "White Jesus" and a "White God" that I
hadn't really considered, or admittedly questioned, until just now.

The meeting ended. I stuck around and spent time bouncing back and forth from the hall to the classroom trying to hear
everything being said. I'd worked my way into a conversation
with the man who gave the opening prayer who was now talking
about the ham radio at his home and the doomsday-type "podcast" he put out on it, which revolved around preparing for the
government's collapse and the impending religious End Days. He
was also spouting his beliefs that the influx of immigrants was
planned and funded by the "Jew government" with plans to take
over neighborhoods and cities.

It was the same language I heard around bonfires with skinheads. But this guy looked more like a geometry teacher. *He's nuts*,
I thought, foolishly dismissing him. But no one else thought so
and, rather, all nodded in agreement at every sentence.

My time was quickly running out, and my main objective became
to find Pekrul to talk with him again. I thought that if I could schedule a "counseling" session with him (as advertised on the sign out
front), I'd be able to develop a relationship and get more information.
But he was gone. Snuck out right after the prayer. I focused back on
the "Ham radio man" and, testing the waters, told them I'd heard
about some kind of training they were doing out back.

My knowledge of their training didn't make them nervous at
all. In fact, they were excited to tell me all about it. It *was* training for the End-of-Days Rapture or the government's impending
collapse, or both. America, they assured me, had quickly become
"a lawless welfare state" and it was only a matter of time before
Western Civilization buckled under the mobs of "godless, unedu-
cated, and lazy Blacks, Mexicans, and Jews."

What really piqued my interest was when they proudly told me that several of the trainings had been conducted by Bo Gritz.

Gritz was a nationally known veteran and antigovernment activist who'd run for president of the United States several times and now offered training across the country in paramilitary and survivalist skills. This Green Beret was also famous for his negotiations at Ruby Ridge (where a White separatist, someone who believes the races should live apart, and members of his family were killed in a standoff with federal agents), and his rumored White nationalist ties were hard for anyone working this stuff to ignore. To hear his name connected with *this* crew was beyond interesting.

I'd seen and heard enough, called my one-man cover team, and we both went home. I was exhausted. I tried to explain what had happened to Tawni, but it was still hard at first to process, let alone talk about.

The old gospel standards Tawni sang earlier were now replaced with questions of faith and doctrine. She always asked the hard questions, the ones I would rather escape. I knew I'd be back to the grind at my own church, a *real* church, on Sunday. A church with no open-carry guns and no teaching that Jewish people are the spawn of Satan. We got into bed and opened our King James Bibles together and read from John. We ended the night together in prayer. Something we probably should have done a whole lot more often.

———

According to a study conducted by the Public Religion Research Institute in 2020, 72% of evangelical White Protestants believe police shootings of Black people are isolated incidents instead of a pattern, where only 30% of religiously unaffiliated Whites say the same.[vi] And, close to 80% of Catholics see Confederate monuments as "symbols of Southern heritage." Non-religiously affiliated Whites were recorded at 45%.[vii]

In 2001, 87% of Christian churches in the United States were completely segregated between only White or Black parishioners.[viii] According to the Equal Justice Initiative, 86% of churches in the nation still have no significant racial diversity.

———

I'd like to claim my visit to Mesa Bible began a serious investigation into their activities as a militia with supremacist ties. But I can't.

In real life, there are budgets and managers and limited resources. And a major piece of the story of the rise of White supremacy in America is the fact that we simply didn't, and don't, commit the resources to this issue that we should. And no matter how much I screamed or begged, other matters were deemed more grievous and took precedence.

Instead, I got busy with other investigations—murder for hire, gangs, long-term surveillances on child and drug trafficking cases, and more gangs—and *tried* to keep up my contacts with Pekrul. But I never had the chance to attend any more Bible meetings. (I try and tell myself it would have only been more of the same. But I wonder, and it bothers me still today.)

Sources, I found later, claimed actual guns, not only the paintball or BB kind, were stored at the church for the "Final Days" and a standoff with government entities. Later, I learned of vehicles with bogus registrations and license plates driving all around Mesa, all associated with Pekrul and the church. I eventually found myself crossing paths with many of the Washitaw Nation members in other places and organizations.

What I discovered that night was important—a quick "baptism," if you will, in understanding religious zealots in the White nationalist world. These people had the same hatred for other races that the Skins and other neo-Nazis did, but they also trusted they had God on their side. The Bible and prophecy, they truly believe, said as much.

They are mixing religious ideology with a potentially violent ideology, a historic recipe for destruction. Richard Butler, the founder of the Aryan Nations, maybe said it best: "The cornerstone for any society is faith. Once a man believes his fight is for God and country, he becomes invincible."[ix]

While I would have to let the Mesa Bible Church go, I'd still confirmed my instincts were accurate: the line between religion and hate was extremely thin, and the militias and White supremacy movement were closer than I had ever realized.

THE WORLD CHURCH OF THE CREATOR

By this time, I was fronting as a Klansman and a member of the Aryan Nations and National Alliance. After my visit to Mesa Bible Church, "Packy" made sure to also join the World Church of the Creator (WCOTC, COTC).

WCOTC is a movement started by Ukrainian-born Ben Klassen, who eventually became a Florida Republican state legislator. He was famous for popularizing the whole "Racial Holy War" (RAHOWA) phrase within the White national movement and claiming "Jews created Christianity to make the White man weaker." Ben ultimately ended up committing suicide, but his "church's" influence over the entire Christian Identity movement continues today.

Unlike other Identity groups who allow anyone in regardless of age or other group affiliations, WCOTC is reserved only for those who identify as skinheads. The Creators I met were all members and associates of Unit 88 skins or attended National Alliance meetings. Creator "reverends" had been arrested for murder, armed robbery, firebombing a NAACP office, plotting to blow up landmarks on the East Coast and Black churches, witness intimidation, and conspiring to assassinate Rodney King for "his part" in the LA. riots of 1992.

But have you ever heard of them until now? Shouldn't you have?

When I joined undercover, their leader was Matt Hale, a cop's son who'd earned a law degree but was refused a license because of his ongoing racial activities.ˣ He'd appeared on NBC's the *Today* show multiple times as a "leader of the White Pride movement" and garnered national attention when he built a website to recruit *children* to the movement. (Hale, at the writing of this book, is serving a forty-year sentence for threatening a federal judge and her family.)

WCOTC was, and is, extremely significant in the prison system because it is one of the rare cliques prisons still allowed to meet as a "true religious group." Thus, the prison systems allow imprisoned neo-Nazis to gather for "church" where they mostly discuss hate, recruiting goals, the future paradise of a White heaven, and other supremacy-related business.

Until 2001, the group had tax-exempt status as a nonprofit charity.

SACRIFICIAL LAMB

It was the morning after Christmas.

The screams of our children woke us. Not with screams of play or a silly argument, but instead, screams of terror.

I sprang from my bed, almost exactly like the guy in that *Night Before Christmas* story. Almost.

Our house is on an acre of land in a citrus grove. It was a dream come true. Both Tawni and I were suburban kids and knew nothing of the farming way of life. However, our nine-year-old son was excited to embrace this new lifestyle and begged us to let him join the local 4-H club. This was a new adventure, and we'd been excited to buy him a baby lamb to raise, one he'd cared for diligently for months and sold for $650. Now he was ten and on to lamb number two. The sheen of newness had worn off a bit, and he was a little less excited about feeding the newcomer and had brought on his little brother as a partner. They'd named the lamb Glory.

"I thought she was...sleeping," my younger son now sobbed. He'd been the one up early that morning to feed the lamb. When he'd found that Glory had gotten out of her pen but wouldn't stir from the back porch, he'd gotten his big brother.

Our ten-year-old better realized what they were looking at on the porch. That's when the screams began.

The lamb was dead. She'd been killed. Someone had clearly rested a shotgun against her rump and pulled the trigger. The hole was enormous. But there was no blood on the porch.

The lamb pen sat no more than twenty yards from the house, and its gate was always secured with a wire acting as a lock. The gate was closed, but the wire was now gone, and through the backyard, I could see drag marks. Someone had stolen Glory from the pen, shot her somewhere farther away from the house, and dragged her back again for us to find on the porch. They'd clearly done all this Christmas night.

"Who did this?" our ten-year-old asked, dismayed.

Tawni and I looked at each other. This wasn't some random act of violence. Someone had wanted to send me a message. Probably someone with a shaved head or lightning bolts tattoo. A skinhead or neo-Nazi. Soldiers of Odin, maybe. The American Vanguard. An anti-government extremist. One of the KKK guys from Kentucky? At this point, it could even be a fellow cop who'd grown tired of me trying to root out all the active racists in our town.

By this point, there were so many suspects.

I called the sheriff's department (who took nearly ten hours to get out to the house). Still attempting to keep my undercover life separate from my real life, I tried to explain the situation and was met with a blank stare. The cop wasn't even going to file a report until I made him.

The whole thing was a mind screw, for sure. Someone was showing me they knew I was a cop and where I lived...and there wasn't much I could do about it. My supervisors would feign concern, but nothing would be done. As careful as I'd been for all these years with who I was and what I did, in that moment I thought it was completely up to me to keep my family safe. No one else was going to do it for me.

Boy was I wrong.

After the kids were somewhat settled, the cop gone again, and my brother-in-law helped me put Glory to rest, Tawni tracked me down.

"Who did this?" she asked.

I shrugged. "Could be a hundred people," I said.

And the sad thing was…it really could have been. Maybe more.

"I want their names," she said. It wasn't a request. "All of them."

Now I finally understood, and I recognized the look. "Tawni, we——"

"They came to our house…" she said. "Our *home*. On Christmas. And murdered our sons' pet. They're sending you, sending our family, a message."

"Yes," I admitted.

"I want to know who these people are," Tawni said again. "And the next time you go undercover…" I already knew what would follow. "I'm coming with you."

My wife, the deputy.

Now, there were two of us.

A young man named Ben grows up in a wealthy Chicago suburb. His father is a physician, and his mother is a lawyer. He attends one of the best public schools in the country, has many Jewish friends, and leans "left" politically. He withdraws from the University of Chicago after beating and choking his college girlfriend with a belt. Once a student of the Bible and Koran, he now instead reads *The Turner Diaries*, *Mein Kampf*, and materials from the National Alliance. He enrolls at Indiana University, changes his major from English to Criminal Justice, and meets Matt Hale, the new leader of the World Church of the Creator, who is openly recruiting on Indiana's campus. Ben soon distributes WCOTC materials on campus and throughout Bloomington neighborhoods and wins the "Creator of the Year" award from Hale for his "enthusiasm." A year later, he loads up his Ford Taurus with guns, ammo, and thousands in cash and returns to Chicago. There, he first targets a known Orthodox Jewish neighborhood and shoots six people. Then he murders an insurance executive, a Black man, standing by his two children outside their home. He fires at an Asian couple in a passing car. Then two more Black men. Then six Asian students. He finally returns to Bloomington, where he murders a Korean grad student who was on his way to church. In a high-speed chase with police, Bens shoots himself twice in the head, crashes his car, then shoots himself in the heart, ending his life at twenty-one years old.

*Ben: "The Logic of Extremism," *Intelligence Report*, September 15, 1999, www.splcenter.org /fighting-hate/intelligence-report/1999/logic-extremism; www.washingtonpost.com/archive /politics/1999/07/05/midwest-gun-spree-suspect-is-dead/f503592b-34b7–4958-b7fd -47e1928b73f3/; Kirsten Scharnberg and Ray Long, "KILLER'S PARENTS: WE DIDN'T TEACH HATE," *Chicago Tribune*, August 27, 1999, https://www.chicagotribune.com /news/ct-xpm-1999-08-27-9908270162-story.html.

5

SKINBYRDS & DRAGONS

Skinbyrd "Charly"

The club in Tempe was filled with neo-Nazis again. All the tattoos and shaved heads. The deafening music and screaming lead singer. The stink of sweat. The miniskirts and Doc Martens. The mosh pit of raging testosterone.

And my wife.

Tawni had claimed a spot back by one of the few standup tables, nursing her concoction of Red Bull and cranberry juice. She was not alone.

Three skinheads had gathered around the table. They looked like electrons around a nucleus or moths gathered around a flame, or maybe wolves around prey. But looks can be deceiving. A closer examination revealed moths caught in a spider's web. Wolves in the crosshairs.

Dressing for our first undercover night, Tawni joked, "I'm just going to wear my hoops and heels and be me. I hope that's OK because I don't know how else to do this."

For whatever reason, her sincerity made me laugh. "Exactly what you need to be," I said. "You." I just let her do her thing.

She'd found her tightest jeans and a black T-shirt. She's five seven and blond. I'm not bragging—and Tawni will deny it—but these guys never had a chance.

I understood. As a teen, playing church softball one summer, my attention was drawn to a tall blond walking up to the field. She wore blue silk running shorts and a Mickey Mouse shirt. I was done—head over heels. But she looked like she was in her twenties and light-years out of my league. Turns out she was fifteen and still light-years out of my league. I did everything in my power that night to impress her, and nothing I did worked. Months later, while attempting to get some other guy's attention, she approached me (she says because I was the tallest guy she saw) and asked me to dance.

Twenty-some years later, we were undercover together at some neo-Nazi dive bar in Tempe. *Ain't life curious?*

We'd entered the club, presenting ourselves as a couple. Packy, who half the room already knew well, and his girlfriend Charlotte, Charly for short.

Tawni and I also understood, however, that we'd do better separate, so "Packy" spent most of his time near the stage, talking to regulars and pretending to watch the band. I mostly kept away and let her do her thing; I wasn't foolish.

Guys looking to impress—in *any* environment—never shut up. (That first night when she'd donned a Mickey Mouse tee, I'd literally tripped over the baseball equipment in an effort to talk to her.) Neo-Nazis were, ultimately, still just *men*.

The "moths" and "wolves" changed every now and again, but they were always there. Talking. She never paid for a drink, and I never had to buy her one. These guys could barely scrape up enough for a six-pack and the bar's cover charge, but they somehow found a way to keep bringing drinks to whatever tabletop where she'd set up shop.

Fresh meat, they assumed. A new face to astonish with stories

of how tough they were, how connected they were. *Good, boys…
Just keep talking…*

She hated the constant gay sex jokes and "f-bombs" every third
word. She eventually asked if they could just have a five-minute
conversation *without* it. The neo-Nazis thought this was hilarious.
She was just being herself and it was working. In undercover work,
it almost always does.

Talking about the evening afterward, Tawni just thought the
whole thing was…sad.

In the skinheads, she saw a train wreck of the worst kind of
the "male species" with their fragile egos, toxic masculinity, and
hypocrisy. "None of these guys are loyal to their brothers." She
understood that after only one night. "They'd fall all over themselves to betray each other if it meant getting the girl." She was
also saddened by a lot of them, as she was empathetic to their
stories, including the various paths that'd brought them to this
point such as addiction, poverty, broken homes, and physical and
sexual abuse.

Of course, any intel she got was completely unusable in any
court of law. There was nothing sanctioned or legal about bringing my wife on the job. My supervisors had zero idea I'd started
bringing Tawni with me. They never would have approved it. Ever.
If they'd known, I would have been taken out of special investigations and maybe even fired.

And we had no backup. Just each other.

She'd had no training in undercover work, but then…neither
had I. There are no special classes you take in detective school
to go undercover. You can either do it—bullshit your way into a
group of dangerous strangers—or you can't.

Tawni could.

———

She proved to get amazing stuff. It was impressive. Tawni is a nat-ural listener and people have always tended to confide in her, and the neo-Nazis at this club in Tempe—and other circles we'd even-tually infiltrate together—were no different. (Years later, Tawni would turn this gift into a lead role on the *Escaping Polygamy* TV program, working with women trapped within that subculture.)

So, I wasn't surprised that her first night was a success and she was already "in" with some of these guys. She, however, couldn't believe how easily they were played and how simple it was for her to get real information.

I'd also reluctantly helped Tawni—but at *her* insistence—set up profiles for "Charly" on various neo-Nazi-type websites and chatrooms and then gave her the basics: *Only talk about what you know; Don't try to be something you're not; Let them teach you and when they want to talk; Just shut up and listen.*

When not at the clubs, Tawni studied mugshots, online chat boards, names, and tattoos, and we began sharing more intel. She was a natural, and she worked quickly. We could go to a White power concert or bar, split up to talk to the patrons, and still have time for a late dinner or movie that same night.

As "Packy and Charly Date Nights" went on, men told her things they wouldn't tell another man. Mostly in the first two weeks of getting to know her, but then they'd always want to take it to the next level. "Charly" would make up some excuse and stealthily, but politely, withdraw from the "relationship." Poor guys, I think there were a lot of broken hearts in our local Skinhead circles.

Tawni was conflicted about it. For the greater good, she'd tricked these guys and, being who she is, she couldn't help but feel bad about that. She realized she was trivializing and manipulating them in a manner men often did with women. Exploiting them, and her own sexuality...for the cause.

It was also a love/hate thing for *me*. Having her there.

I'd agreed to make it happen—as if I had a choice—and yet I still didn't really want Tawni anywhere near this world. She was reality and light *outside* of this dark environment. Having her surrounded by these guys—guys I hated, most who'd done jail time—was difficult. I was constantly caught between wanting to rescue her and yet letting her do her thing.

We worked great together but...it was also tough. (Still can be.)

But, oh, the info she gathered.

Our goal was never necessarily to find "criminal activity" but, rather, to better link the individuals, draw out connections, and build organizational charts to understand who the players were to find out who connected to whom. And with that intel in hand, I was able to both get *more* information out of these crews and verify what I already knew.

Tawni's information was the foundation. It became the concrete floor I needed to build the rest of the house on certain individuals and organizations. *Who were the shot callers? The leaders? Who needed to be watched? Who was the weak link caught in a tough situation with no ready way out? Who'd had the bad childhood? Who was running from what? What were their weaknesses? Who seemed hard core but was actually soft and might be easily flipped into an informant? Who was a killer?*

She somehow found the soft side of these guys. As she put it, she wanted to get into their hearts and minds—all so that she could protect our family.

Maybe, I realized soon, there were other motives...

On the way to one club, she'd asked: "If I get something important that you need, some worthwhile intel… Can we just go out after and…be us?"

I realized I'd been so preoccupied with so many things that, even while spending literal time at home, I'd been neglecting her. Tawni's grandma once admitted she'd started fishing to be with her grandpa, taking up his favorite hobby as her own just so they could spend time together. I cringed knowing, perhaps, that was happening here as well. It also made me love her more.

We both found it'd become easier to talk about work while at home. She and I were on the same page now, shared the same language and details when it came to my undercover work.

I also found that I came down from my Packy persona more readily when I worked with Tawni. Coming home solo, I'd often sit in the driveway for an hour, decompressing, before coming back into the house. With Tawni beside me however, we'd simply come home together or even go out on a normal date following a couple hours in places like The Nile.

It made it easier to know what was real and what wasn't.

———

Then, one night, coming home from a neo-Nazi bar, she asked, "You ever hear the name 'Ready' before? 'JT Ready'?"

Affirmative. Big time…

I'd first heard of JT Ready at a local law enforcement meeting as a "somebody" who was far too zealous on the anti-immigration front.

An easy enough name to file away for later, and I had.

I did some digging and found he'd been arrested in high school for assault, ending up on parole. He had joined the Marines, but was quickly dismissed from the elite Reconnaissance Company, court-martialed twice, and soon discharged. There was also a story he'd shot a Mexican American man "in self-defense."

This was exactly the kind of guy I wanted on our radar.

I had no idea yet how long he'd stay there.

"What have *you* heard about JT Ready?" I asked.

"His name just keeps coming up," she said. "New hot shot in town or something, I guess. An organizer."

That he was.

JT READY

Speak the devil's name...

JT Ready soon started attending National Alliance meetings. Standing beside Jerry Harbin, working the crowd like he'd been there for years.

He was a big guy. Not in a muscular kind of way, but 6-foot, always pushing three hundred-plus pounds; just a big dude. When he came into the room, you would know it immediately. But not, I admit, in a bad way.

Of most of the supremacist guys I'd been working, you could almost *feel* their presence—the hair-on-your-neck-standing-up-type thing or the sense that something foul had just entered the room.

But not JT.

He, and the next tier of supremacists I was soon to meet, were different.

JT was more like a "congenial uncle" type. "Hi, how are you?", "Nice to see you." He was not at all "scary" or coarse or off-putting like the others at all. He had no offensive tattoos on display, no entourage of skins behind him, no muttering an "f-bomb" every third word. No shaved head. Just a big guy, working the crowd.

And he was always working his way to the front. He *needed* to be seen and *needed* to be respected for who he thought and believed he was. "I'm JT Ready, not some dumb skinhead, but JT Ready the founder and organizer of numerous ant-immigration groups, private border patrol units." Those who knew JT always approached him first. And those who didn't know him yet, *he* approached. Plainly put, he acted like a quintessential politician. And I would soon find out that there was a reason for that: people in the movement liked JT. *Still do.*

Jerry Harbin—who I thought might get jealous or concerned about this new prince in the kingdom—was apparently thrilled to have JT around. He was pleased with *any* growth of membership, and Jerry believed JT Ready would soon bring a lot of people with him. Jerry loved the numbers.

The First Defenders Corp was JT's first real footprint into the White supremacy scene. This was the group he'd organized and run out of Mesa with cofounder John "Jack" Foote, an ex-military guy from Texas who'd first managed Ranch Rescue, another huge border militia group in Arizona. (When you go down the rabbit hole of border-activism militias, the names eventually all blur together; they tend to all be involved and intertwined.)

The First Defenders Corp was touted to be the "premier border militia" in the nation with special training, weapons, and even a military surplus transport vehicle purchased to haul people and supplies through the rugged terrain of Arizona.

Later, I had reliable source information that JT and Jack were doing "dope rips" on the border—capturing drug mules crossing into the U.S. as "concerned citizens" but only giving *half* of the confiscated drugs to Border Patrol, keeping the other half for personal use and to fund their own lives and border operations.

But I wasn't ever allowed to work this case or prove it beyond my sources, my supervisors deeming the border too far out of my jurisdiction in Mesa. And when I passed the info farther south, law enforcement didn't really know what to do with it: *How important was JT Ready's selling some stolen weed and coke in an area of the world where the drug cartels were selling children to pedophiles and cutting off people's heads and hands?*

In any case, the First Defenders Corp was just the first of *many* organizations for JT. He was also a member of National Vanguard (an offshoot of National Alliance), United for a Sovereign America (USA), America First (which JT founded), Civil Defense Corp, the Minuteman Project, the National Socialist Movement (JT became head of the Southwest region), the Ready Rangers and, later, the U.S. Border Guard—whose name and uniforms were chosen specifically to confuse immigrants with the actual U.S. Border Patrol.

Eventually, JT belonged to as many groups as "Packy" did and had a role in almost every border and racist political organization in the state.

Over the next year or so, JT eventually became the local poster boy for the anti-immigrant cause—a *nativist*. ("Nativists" is a catch-all term for those who supporting policies that protect the interests of native-born or established inhabitants against those of immigrants; you'll find them in every century and country.) He was even getting political backing via association from major politicians in Arizona, including the infamous Joe Arpaio in Maricopa County (who'd notoriously put thousands of immigrants in tents in the desert) and Russell Pearce, an influential nativist Arizona

state legislator who referred to JT as his "son." He'd also garnered
the support of local businessmen, including the most successful car
dealership magnate in town (Kia, a Korean company, dealership in
not unfamiliar hypocrisy).[i]

Many saw him as a motivator, a visionary, a concerned citizen
who was making changes and exposing the evils in our government; a man who was "saving the U.S." and had the charisma to
get people behind him.

He soon also worked with Mothers Against Illegal Aliens (a
self-styled MADD for border activism), manning booths across
the valley with moms and kids and further legitimizing himself
in the community. He was constantly at various border rallies and
political events, and I had to admit he and his supporters were
getting people to listen. He was always doing...*something*.

JT was like many of the skinhead thugs I'd come across, a guy
with real potential, an ability to create something great, but somewhere along the way, something had caused a wrong turn in his
life. JT could have really made a difference—been a good guy. He
had a lot of gifts and was often truly likable.

But he also organized Hitler "birthday parties." And what he was
doing along the border was unforgivable. He and his various crews
were hunting and hurting immigrants, and it needed to be stopped.

On a personal level, I found him to be psychotic. He was full of
fear and hate, and all the rhetoric about cartel "narco terrorists" and
human smuggling and illegal-immigration concerns was merely a
front for his own paramilitary fantasies.

I wanted him off the streets, off our border. I knew he was
dangerous.

At first, JT liked me. But it didn't take too many more inter-
actions before it became clear that he and Packy weren't going to

get along very well. First, he always seemed a little worried about me taking any of his leadership potential and grandeur. Packy was respected in the National Alliance, and I was always the *other* big guy in the room, so I made sure to stand down.

But he probably also sensed I understood him on a deeper level than he wanted anyone to. That I had his number. And I did.

But was there anything I could actually do about it?

There were always other matters to take care of first.

Including solving a skinhead murder.

SKINBYRD JESSICA

One of Mesa's homicide detectives called and asked if I was interested in taking a supplemental report from a woman who thought "some skinheads had committed a crime." I said sure.

Five minutes later, my desk phone rang, and the caller identified herself. I didn't recognize the name, but she started a long rant about some friends and her ex-boyfriend. Honestly, I was losing interest fast. Then she threw out a name. "Do you know who Sean Gaines is?" she asked.

I sat straight up. "I sure do," I said. My interest turned from getting off the phone to finding out everything I possibly could.

Gaines was one of the rougher supremacists in town. A husky guy, 230 pounds, five feet ten. He was described as an "animal" but had been raised by one from the age of fifteen, when his mother dropped him off at his father's—a meth cook/dealer who'd soon taught his son how to fight, weigh, cook, and sell drugs, as well as hotwire and steal cars for cash. His dad, and associates, even taught Sean how to murder and did so right in front of him. Shooting men in the head, slitting throats, and Sean once described to me, in detail, what it was like to put a body through a wood chipper—because his dad made him do it. Sean never had a chance. He'd become a racist skinhead in prison. Before this, he was just another teen who genuinely loved hip-hop and rap, one who idolized Black rap stars.

The woman on the phone told me that, ten months earlier, her boyfriend, Jeremy Johnson—a skin and a "fresh cut" who was just getting into the scene, and who I had been seeing around—had come home late, sat on their bed and cried. Not knowing what had happened, she'd tried to console him, but he wouldn't say anything more. After some prodding, Jeremy eventually told her he'd been out with Sean Gaines, and they'd used the trunk of her car to "dump a guy in the desert."

That was all she could ever pry out of him. It was enough. But she'd never done anything with the story—never told anyone. As time went on, however, Jeremy had apparently grown more violent and began abusing her. she eventually moved to California to get away from him. There, She kept thinking back to how Jeremy had borrowed her car the evening he had been so upset and decided to finally go to her local police.

Finding her credible, they'd pulled her trunk's carpet and jack out of her car. There was blood residue on both. *Ladies and gentlemen, we have ourselves a homicide*...There was a victim somewhere, "dumped in the desert," but we had no body or any other information to corroborate any of it.

I began looking into Jeremy's local skin friends and found that Jessica Nelson, a Unit 88 skinbyrd and acquaintance of Sean Gaines, had been staying at a home in Phoenix with a man named Bruce Mathis along with Bruce's wife and brother, Mark Mathes.

Wouldn't you know it, no one had seen Mark since last February. And his brother had filed a missing person's report a week *after* Jeremy had borrowed his girlfriend's car.

The two incidents were clearly connected but we couldn't yet link them.

We were obviously early in the investigation, so I decided the best thing to do was not pull anyone in for questioning until we had a body. The risk in scaring these guys off and not getting anything of value was greater than the reward. Thanks to Packy, I already knew where all the key players were or how to get a hold of them. We had the upper hand. Plus, none of them would even expect the police were after them for a murder that happened more than a year ago.

I'd been making a reputation for myself as the guy in the know when it came to the militias and the White Pride scene in the Valley. The FBI's Joint Terrorism Task Force asked me to come over to their squad and work this case with them.

Eventually, an agent got a call from a young girl who said a group was on their way up I-17 to Flagstaff when a friend of hers pointed to the Crown King/Table Mesa area and said, "*That's* where they dumped that guy."

Finally, we had a location to start looking.

I organized a search party full of Mesa Gang detectives and we all made the hour drive up to Table Mesa, a place our family had spent many a weekend four-wheeling and sleeping in the back of my truck. After a long, hot day with no luck, all the gang guys decided to head out and I sat on the side of a hill, looking down on the Agua Fria River, just hoping to find something. *Nothing.*

I called the Yavapai County Sheriff's office, the county just north of Maricopa County, to see if they'd possibly found something. *Anything.* It was a Saturday, so I left a message with the on-call detective.

Monday morning, as I was staring at one of the many wall charts I'd constructed with copies of pictures, strings, scotch tape, just like in all the movies, my cell phone started ringing with a number from northern Arizona. It was a detective from Yavapai County, and he wanted to know if I had a minute.

"Please tell me you have something."

A month or so before, some men target shooting had found bones in a little cave. The bones were now with the Yavapai County Office of the Medical Examiner.

"I'll be there in a couple hours," I said, but the medical examiner wouldn't be in Prescott for another few days. I would have to wait. Not wanting to jinx myself, I told no one, except Tawni, of course. We were both stoked. Wednesday couldn't come fast enough.

Finally, I was on my way to Prescott. The Prescott deputy sheriff there first offered to take me to the place where the bones had been found. South of Prescott, heading toward Phoenix, are some great old mining communities, "ghost towns." "Where *are* we going?" I finally asked.

"A place called Swastika Hill," he replied.

"Are you kidding me?"

"Nope, an old Indigenous site that has had that name for a hundred years or more. Don't ask me why or how it got its name, but if you look on the maps, they all say 'Swastika Hill' or 'Swastika Mine.'"

We climbed up into one of the mountains a bit more and then he pulled over to a spot beside a guardrail. Over the rail was a twenty-foot drop. "That's where the bones were found," he said. "Not much to look at, but this is it."

We headed to the office of the medical examiner, an unremarkable building in downtown Prescott. The examiner played his part well and was mid-chew in a sandwich as he walked over to the freezer and pulled out a brown grocery sack. Again, with the sandwich in one hand, he reached in and pulled out a jawbone with some teeth, and a large leg bone.

"How much you need?" he asked. He'd pulled free a battery-operated angle saw and proceeded to cut an inch-long section of bone. Despite all my years in police work, I'd never seen this before, and it was intriguing. Bone dust went everywhere, and the smell of bone being cut nearly choked me. I went back to my truck, pulled out the cup holder from the dash, and gently placed the newly labeled jar and sample into my cup holder. I think I stared at that bone the entire way back to Mesa.

There, I marched straight into the crime lab and asked how long it would take to compare this bone fragment to the blood recovered from the inside of the girlfriend's car. I was told it could take weeks. I guess they could tell I was a little disappointed and they promised to expedite it for me.

Two days later, I got the call.

"Hey Matt, it's a match. The blood from the car trunk and the bone came from the same person."

———

We flew in the Phoenix Police helicopter to Lake Havasu City to interview Jeremy, the sobbing boyfriend of our original source, at the local police station there. Traveling by helicopter, it was almost peaceful fifty feet above the ground, almost like we were chasing the javalina and coyotes rather than going to interview a neo-Nazi killer. I knew Jeremy was going straight to jail but as soon as he got locked up, he'd never talk. He'd have other things to worry about. If we couldn't get him to flip now, we never would.

Jeremy quickly broke down again, as I knew he would. We'd interviewed him first because he was our weakest link. I wasn't at all worried about interviewing him myself or blowing my cover. He and Packy hadn't officially ever met.

Jeremy confessed the bones and blood *were* those of Mark Mathes. He expressed relief at finally coming clean, stating he'd been having nightmares for months. He also admitted to murdering Mark with three other people: Sean Gaines, Patrick Bearup, and Jessica Nelson.

Through further interrogation of the four of them, we were finally able to piece together what had happened.

Mark Mathes had apparently stolen $200 out of Jessica's purse. The popular skinbyrd was furious and told Sean Gaines about it. Gaines decided it was the perfect opportunity for Jeremy to "shed blood for the cause." (Keep in mind, Mark Mathes was as White as anybody could be; the "cause" was only to avenge a wronged skinbyrd.)

Accompanied by a knife, a shotgun, and a baseball bat, the trio of skins had surrounded Mark in his backyard and extacted their revenge. They then dragged his body out to the alley and threw him—still alive—into the trunk of the Honda. Reaching the remote mine, whose unusual name was not lost on the group, they'd popped the trunk and yanked Mark out, stripped him of all his clothes, and threw him back on the ground. They rendered more kicks and punches, but they wanted to obtain a ruby ring Mark always wore; his fingers, however, were as swollen as his face. When Jessica's metal nail file couldn't saw through his finger, Patrick "found" some wire cutters and snapped it off. Mark's naked body was tossed over the side of the road. To ensure a close, Sean pulled out his shotgun and shot Mark one time in the head.

The four then took Mark's clothes to a dumpster, burned them, and headed back to Phoenix. Once home, Jeremy promptly broke down in front of his girlfriend. Still, the evening seemed successful to the trio of killers. A duty well done for a vindicated skinbyrd... and Jeremy had earned his red laces.

With the mounting evidence and testimony, we had them all.

Meanwhile, my supervisors were not interested.

The crime didn't happen in Mesa, so why would Mesa foot the bill for further investigation? The *only* reason Mesa had done the DNA test for me was because I'd asked the lab and, to CYA (cover my ass), I'd convinced the powers that be that "some of the crimes" *had* taken place in Mesa.

It was the story of my career.

Law enforcement is a money-making operation. Tax dollars are not enough to fund police departments. The focus in law enforcement is, "How are we going to recoup the money we spend on cases, and even *make* money on top of it?" One way is seizing assets. Drug dealers have a lot of assets.

White supremacy groups rarely hold assets. No money in the crimes you're investigating translates into little support from the department heads.

The most damning reason, however...

If we pursued these crimes for what they were, the city would have to admit *there was a problem*. A new problem. One most citizens had zero idea about. And what mayor, police chief, or township committee would ever want that?

I was furious. *What was I even working this horrific stuff for?* Crime does *not* follow jurisdictional boundaries—especially White-boy crime. But what could I do? I quickly changed my focus to writing the search warrants and preparing for the next days' events. No one was going to stop me from arresting three more supremacists for murder.

These three neo-Nazis now had the taste of blood, new and fresh in their mouths. They were, so far, getting away with it, and unless we did *something*, they would 100% strike again.

DUNGEONS & DRAGONS

Richard Butler—one of the godfathers of White supremacy and the founder of Aryan Nations—was in town to give a speech, and "Packy" was part of the group invited to hang out with him and his entourage afterward.

Butler brought years of experience, lists of well-known violent movement associates and, when he was younger, a very charismatic way of leading. He was smart, a chemical engineer who claimed to have the patent on Fix-A-Flat. Seeing the skins meeting Butler was like watching little kids meeting their sports heroes; trembling and nervous, they would ask for a picture and permission to even shake his hand. (There would, later, be an unfillable void after he died and things moved toward the lone-wolf mentality. The movement is most dangerous when there is good leadership and definitely a top-down mentality.)

It proved an extremely long two-day event for the aging Butler. His physical weakness combined with the dry Arizona heat took it all out of him. Packy hung close by throughout, listening to side conversations and trying to remember every tattoo he saw. I think it was my lack of desire to be noticed or braggadocio that eventually drew Butler toward me. He called me over.

Butler told me how he was once a leader in the movement, "full of the power of God with the ability and motivation to wipe out the Jews and Blacks." He then told me about how he hated his time in WWII because he'd been fighting against something he believed in—Hitler's hatred of the Jews. He claimed he'd used all his money and talents to build the Aryan Nations and convert as many as he could to Christian Identity. You could tell it was a speech he'd given a thousand times. In turn, I explained my make-believe dilemmas with undocumented immigrants and my struggling lawncare business, that I spent a lot of time in Idaho taking care of a close friend's family after he was killed by a drunk Mexican.

Like so many before, the supremacy leader bit. "Patrick," he said. "I'd like you to join my organization and help manage my security."

What?

"You are strong and calm, and moral. We, *I*, need more of that." He patted my arm. "It will be a big commitment full of travel and long hours. Patrick, take your time. And then let me know."

The Aryan Nations saw the passing of Richard Butler as imminent, and skinhead crews across the country were breaking away into new groups. The jockeying for position and struggles over leadership had already begun, and it would be a *perfect* time to get in and be a part of the impending infighting and power struggles, a perfect time to gather information. I really *wanted* this gig and was going to figure out how to get it. Screw jurisdictions. But I also knew better.

After the day's events, I was invited to join Butler and a very select few at a local bar. One guy there was someone I recognized immediately from the Aryan Fest, "Dungeons & Dragons."

James was a six-foot, 260-pound, long-haired thirtysomething who donned black military-style pants and a long black duster-style trench coat. He also always wore a black leather belt with half a dozen multipurpose tools in leather holders, two buck knives, and one fixed four-inch blade in a scabbard, all topped off with a small, black leather fanny pack for his "special" tools, I'd supposed. I'd dubbed James "Dungeons & Dragons" years before because he always looked outfitted for some medieval quest.

This guy's arrogance and ego were palpable. James was, you just knew, pure evil. He'd also already put away five eight-ounce glasses of Yeager. And his New Jersey accent and brash East-Coast way of speaking nearly got us all kicked out of this empty hotel bar. Mercifully, while I carefully talked my way *out* of a job with Richard Butler, "Dungeons & Dragons" vanished for a long while, then rejoined us only later for a quick goodbye.

It was late and I had a forty-minute drive home. I spoke to Tawni on the phone and checked for a tail the whole way. After numerous side roads and U-turns, I made it home, tacking on an extra fifteen minutes to keep my cover, and family, safe.

———

Days later, I learned that when James, "Dungeons & Dragons," snuck off, he'd sexually assaulted a fourteen-year-old girl in the same hotel where the bar was located. A few floors above me.

I was wrecked.

All I could do was go over again and again and again what I might have said or done differently that night that could have prevented this crime. And, as if beating myself up enough wasn't enough, my supervisors asked, "Why couldn't you stop him?"

As if I could now somehow personally follow every monster I came across 24/7. It was maddening. Because (a) there was no way I could have stopped him and (b) I had the same damning questions. It didn't matter how much I had already stopped. The ones that get away haunt you.

I often wonder about law enforcement stories where they are *always* able to stop the bad guy. Like they did everything right at the right time and "just had this feeling." I guess I'm guilty of that, also. Not here, though.

I failed. I missed something. I wasn't in the right place, only close to it.

I can only hope it helps other cops somewhere hear the truth. Because I know fails like this one really take their toll.

These are the days I'd started sitting in the driveway for too long to compose myself before I went back into the house. I was routinely sharing drinks and jokes and talk of "kicking niggers to death" with racists, rapist, and killers. It was mentally and emotionally exhausting. I *needed* the driveway time, some kind of makeshift decompression chamber between the world of White supremacy and the world of the Browning family.

But each month, each decompression seemed to be taking longer and longer.

I'd begun to sneak home for an hour during the day just to visit Tawni, sit on the couch, even take a nap. Or she'd come out to my truck in the driveway and just sit with me, sometimes for hours, before we both went back inside. It always helped, but how much?

THE ACCIDENT

We'd borrowed a small bobcat tractor from a friend to do some landscaping in the backyard. Tawni was six months pregnant with our fifth and final baby, and her doctors had put her on bed rest. The kids loved to see the tractor work and enjoyed it even more when I'd let them sit on my lap and drive around the yard. And I loved spending time with them, which I never got to do as much as I wanted to.

I'd started with my almost-four-year-old son and two-year-old daughter on my lap, but it made operating the tractor a bit hard. I had my son get out of the cab and stand along the fence while I moved some dirt. I told him to stay back and promised I'd put him back on my lap *after* I got the load. Confirming he was out of the way, I pulled forward and scooped up a load of dirt. With my daughter in my lap, I began to back up. When I looked back, my son was gone. My heart stopped; my stomach dropped. I jumped from the tractor. *Where had my head really been?*

I later found out that I was about to back over his stick "sword" and he ran to get it. As he'd bent down to pick it up, the tractor hit him in the head and knocked him down, and the back tire ran halfway across his body.

He was transported by helicopter to the county trauma hospital, then transferred to Phoenix Children's Hospital. Tawni and I were in complete turmoil; the needles, shots, crying, worrying, praying. Hospital staff ran around trying to prep our son for an emergency surgery, and we were signing release papers as quickly as they handed them to us. He had emergency surgery for his kidney and his spleen among other internal issues. The artery to his kidney was twisted, and but for a trickle of blood keeping it alive, we would have lost it.

Then, I remembered something…

Jerry Harbin, the leader of the National Alliance, had been bragging for months how he'd been spreading the "word of Odin" to all the children he came in contact with…at Phoenix Children's Hospital.

Jerry was a respiratory technician at *this* hospital.

This was where he'd go into his patients' rooms and pass out footballs and stuffed animals along with necklaces with Thor's hammer on them while he'd enlighten the children about Thor, Valhalla, and the Norse gods.

Odinism—also often called Ásatrú or Wotanism—is an ancient Nordic religion dating as far back as 500 BC that thrived throughout Scandinavia, Germany, and other areas of northwestern Europe.[ii] It's perhaps most famous for being the "Viking religion," which ended pretty much *with* the Vikings—during the Christianization of Scandinavia—and which took place between the 8th and the 12th centuries as the powerful Holy Roman Empire spread north and west. It became, like all previous European religions, a "pagan" faith.

Yet, to White supremacists, it is considered to be the purest and "Whitest" religion, symbolic, for them, of the Germanic and Scandinavian Vikings and kingdoms that thrived a thousand years ago—the Aryan ideal.

A 1999 FBI report labeled Odinism, unjustly or not, a "White supremacist ideology that lends itself to violence."[iii] White supremacist pamphlets, posters, websites, and song lyrics typically feature Norse gods and goddesses, Norse runes and symbols, and imagery connected to magic. Odinism entered the American prison system in the late 1980s, spread by adherents such as Else Christensen, a Danish ex-Nazi who founded and led Odinist prison groups across the country. By the early 2000s, the Anti-Defamation League had labeled Ásatrú "one of the faiths that incarcerated White supremacists found most often."[iv] David Lane, a member of The Order, promoted Ásatrú during his lifetime incarceration.

In 2005, the Supreme Court sided with an Ásatrú inmate by upholding a federal law requiring state prisons to accommodate prisoners' religious affiliations.[v] An estimated twenty thousand people in the United States consider themselves Asatruars or Odinists.[vi] Many simply believe in an earlier religion. Many believe in an earlier religion because of its ties to White supremacy.

White warlike gods. White warlike heroes.

And a clearly White afterlife.

Meanwhile, everyone at the hospital, from colleagues to patients and their families—just assumed Jerry was a nice guy.

My heart had stopped for the second time that day. *Was Jerry working today? Was I really going to have to worry about him, about blowing my cover, at a time like this?*

I explained the situation to Tawni, and we rushed to the nurses' station. To her credit, the charge nurse understood, was mortified, and without question placed all kinds of restrictions on our son's room and computer information. We were on some kind of high-security clearance list, and the hospital took it all very seriously. I just wanted to take care of my kid.

All these people I'd worked with and developed intelligence on were now coming full circle into my life. *Was all the worrying worth it? Was I really making a difference?*

Our son was in the hospital for two weeks, mostly in intensive care. He ultimately recovered nicely, by the way. Eventually, he became the football captain and homecoming king, went overseas on service missions, and is currently playing college football. We are proud and blessed parents. It *was* a miracle.

But when we should have been focused entirely on our son, we were, instead, now focused on helping our son heal *and* keeping off Jerry Harbin's radar. The two worlds had crossed again and the whole ordeal had proven horrific in every way.

But it was only a hint of things to come. We were soon to face a new group in the White supremacy movement.

My coworkers. Cops.

My ideas of horrific were about to change.

Nathan is twenty-eight years old. He was an honor roll student in high school, award-winning member of the jazz band, and in the honors program at Dartmouth as a biology major. He is recently married, has a PhD, a good job, and no criminal record of any kind. On a notebook beside his bed are pages and pages which read things like "White people are the world's apex predators"; "Whites in the USA are waking up. FACT"; "Blacks are fucking losers. All of them"; "Whites will play the knockout game with niggers. All its gonna take is a lil nudge, then Whites in the US will snap and kill all the shittskins"; "Racism is good. Natural. Killing shittskins is in our blood. We need to do it"; "1,000,000 yrs. of evolution molded me to hate these subhumans"; "I'm done. They fuckking suck." The final page of his diary reads, "Jesus Christ I hate niggers." He buys a gun and four days later steals a plumbing company's truck and smashes it into a residential building near his condo. People come outside to see what happened. Nathan, gun drawn, walks past the White bystanders and targets the only two African Americans who've come out to help: Ramona Cooper, sixty, a veteran staff sergeant in the U.S. Air Force, and David Green, fifty-eight, a retired state police trooper. Police arrive, and Nathan is killed in a shootout. There are no known ties to any particular hate group.

---

*Nathan: Michael Yoshida, WHDH TV 7News "Suspect Wrote that Whites are 'Apex Predators': Killings of Black Woman and Man in Winthrop Being Investigated as a Hate Crime," June 28, 2021, https://whdh.com/news/da-suspect-wrote-that-whites-are-apex-predators-killings-of -black-woman-and-man-in-winthrop-being-investigated-as-hate-crime/; https://whdh.com /news/white-race-is-superior-da-releases-excerpts-from-journals-kept-by-man-who-killed-2 -in-apparent-hate-crime-in-winthrop-2/.

QUIS CUSTODIET IPSOS CUSTODES

The Cadet

This guy already knew all of it. The specific gang tattoos and White pride symbology. The bands. Terms like "boot party" and "feather-wood" (another name for skinbyrd) and "RAHOWA." How the gangs worked together in prison. He even recognized many of the specific local neo-Nazis I was mentioning, shaking his head with a half smile.

I'd taken two-plus years and countless hours to learn as much, and this student where I was teaching a seminar on White supremacy to a room of about twenty-five could have easily stepped in as a co-teacher. He had clearly been close to the White pride scene for years, and this group *loves* proving how much they're part of the club, so he'd been easy to draw out.

"Now...," I'd bait, "anyone know what '88' means?" He raised his hand and gave the correct answer: Heil Hitler. *Hmm...* "OK, does anyone know what the 'fourteen words' are?" He again raised his hand. "What about the 88 precepts?" Yeah, he knew his stuff well, all right.

The biggest problem, however, was that I was doing this training at the local police academy.

This man was a cadet and less than a month away from becoming a sworn-in Mesa police officer.

The last few weeks of the academy were spent teaching

advanced modules to the recruits. My module was on the local White pride gangs. Because I talked about cases, people, identifiers, and mostly because I was undercover, my class was saved for the tail end of the academy.

After class, I walked up to my star student. "Are you a skinhead?" I asked as if joking. I wasn't. "Or do you just hang out with them?"

"I've known a few," he answered.

I spent the rest of the afternoon asking around about this trainee. We even gave his application a closer look and discovered he'd lied about some previous work experience. I went to the recruit-training officers and told them they needed to drop this guy. He was a White supremacist, or had been one, or hung out with them. Not the kind of person we wanted protecting the Phoenix Valley. Thankfully, I'd spent enough time working at the academy and knew the training staff, and there was a mutual respect. With the falsified application in hand, the staff did not question me whatsoever. The cadet was immediately terminated.

I'd been tossed out of the academy the first time for being "too nice." This wasn't that. There would be no second chances for this cadet. And I felt surprisingly good about it, honestly. My experience had enabled me to spot this man and prevent the Mesa Police Department from making a terrible, and potentially deadly, hire.

Now, I just needed to do it another ten thousand times.

———

There *are* police in the White supremacy movement. And soldiers.

And, yes, there are also dentists and mechanics and geometry teachers who speak of Jewish or Black or Latino or gay people as inferior, as dangerous.

But these other professions aren't hired and sworn to protect the rest of us from the bad guys, from violence, from injustice.

It *is* different.

Still, I *am* one of them. I find myself wanting to shout: *What about the cop who saved the Black guy from the burning car? Or the Black and White cop I know who've worked together for years to help Latino gang members rehabilitate? Or the cop who—*

Some more recognition for all those doing their jobs well. For thirty years, nearly all of the men and women I've worked with genuinely wanted to help take care of their communities. And they do so without prejudice or racial bias; rather, more often appreciating, and *mending*, racial inequities on a daily basis—often years ahead of and far beyond today's most vocal armchair activist. Talking to law enforcement across the world, I've found and heard the same—overwhelmingly good cops, and a small number of bad cops who give law enforcement a bad name.

And so, I'm not oblivious. I understand, truly, when some colleagues get up and leave the room when I get to this part of my presentation on White supremacy. Not because they're supremacists themselves. It's interpreted instead as an attack of our brothers and sisters in blue. To accuse one is to accuse all.

(I know. This chapter is the one I've avoided writing the longest. But I've also never condoned any sacrosanct "thin blue line." Right is right, and you can't very well look yourself in the mirror knowing you've backed up what you know to be wrong.)

Law enforcement is a representation of society. If a city hires two hundred cops, statistically someone in that group is going to harbor extremist views.

There are eight hundred thousand police officers in the United States. If "only" 1% are supremacists, that's eight thousand dangerous racists on our streets. And that's just police officers. Imagine the additional millions in ancillary positions within law enforcement. Now imagine a number *higher* than 1%.

The scary part is that it takes far less than that to become a real problem.

———

White nationalists actively recruit police and military personnel into their ranks. When approaching militia groups, when I actually told them I was a veteran cop, they were *more* pleased to have me onboard. Detective Matt Browning had far more value to them than struggling lawncare manager Packy Von Fleckenger.

During several meetings with the National Alliance, Jerry begged members, the few who might be eligible, to apply and infiltrate their local police departments. Not to necessarily enforce the law but to learn the tactics of "urban warfare" and to be used as sources of intelligence for the cause.

For decades, biker gangs and the drug cartels have successfully gotten girlfriends and siblings and even their children to become clerks, janitors, dispatchers, and secretaries inside state and local justice system departments—becoming their eyes and ears, gathering intelligence via various databases on ongoing investigations, undercover operations, and the private addresses of witnesses, cops, and judges.

The White supremacy movement has been trying to catch up.

Jerry eventually asked me, of course, as everyone already thought of me as the "security guy" by now. He suggested it might be a good replacement for Packy's struggling lawncare service.

I told him I couldn't imagine ever being a damn cop. Funny stuff.

Months later, however, he asserted there was a "bright candidate" already forging his way through the academy process. And it *wasn't* the guy I'd gotten tossed out.

No longer funny.

I left that meeting early and went straight to my office to start doing checks on recent candidates. I must have rifled through fifty applications and then BINGO—I'd found one of the biggest, non-felonious (at the time), White-boy names in the valley. This guy, who'd been drummed out of the military, was a prominent White Pride influencer (who is still active as of this writing). Active with the Vinlanders *and* Tea Party but never arrested—a rare neo-Nazi candidate.

We quickly pulled his application, issuing a "Thanks, but no thanks" letter.

Two down, ten thousand to go...

Who watches the watchmen?

THE GHOST SKIN

An FBI memo in 2006 finally, specifically, warned law enforcementand the military that they were the targets of an active campaign by White supremacists to infiltrate their ranks[i]. The FBI dubbed such infiltrators "ghost skins"—or people maintaining normal exteriors to blend in and hide their true aims.

But it's not just an "American" thing.

During an investigation Tawni and I did years ago—one involving Volksfront, once the biggest supremacy group in the world—it became blatantly clear the military was involved in this movement in countries all over the world. Sources told us members of the

Spanish military, for instance, were ardent members of Volksfront; and some of their most important, and violent, members.

The UK calls them "insider threats." National Action is a banned terrorist group within the UK whose ultimate goal is to secure a "free, White Britain" and whose members, including military veterans and active police, have been arrested for a variety of charges ranging from illegal recruitment to possession of illegal weapons, including guns stockpiled for their "upcoming race war."

North of the United States, in Canada, the RCMP (Royal Canadian Mounted Police) and military police found colleagues actively pursuing plots to harm and "execute" law enforcement and others in authority.[ii] In 2018, the Canadian Military Criminal Intelligence Section identified at least *six* different hate groups within Canadian Armed Forces, from Hammerskins to Soldiers of Odin, a group with violent European White supremacist roots.[iii]

The Canadian report confirmed what I'd been seeing in the U.S. for years: "Drawing on their training and deployment experience, current and former military members find that their skills are valued by these groups" affording "them the ability to gain positions of leadership."[iv]

Soldiers and cops have specialized weapons training and other paramilitary expertise. They *are* the most highly sought-after recruits.

Racists trained in combat and weapons with authority and intel over their communities. *What could possibly go wrong?*

———

The "Lynwood Vikings" was a secret clique of Los Angeles officers who had matching tattoos and targeted Black and Latino people. Their shared tattoos included 988 (the code for when an officer shoots someone) and a skeleton carrying an AK and wearing a *stahlhelm*, those distinctive steel helmets Nazi soldiers wore in WWII. Supervisors later described the tattoos as "a mark of pride," and the police station openly displayed a map of East LA redrawn in the shape of Africa.[v]

A federal judge ultimately renamed the group a "neo-Nazi, White supremacist gang" and the city paid millions in settlements. Similar White police clubs in town included the "Jump Out Boys," "Red Devils," "Grim Reapers," and "Regulators."

But it's not just an LA thing.

Across the country, police speak about the officer with a Confederate-flag tattoo on his back, or the one who plays bass in the town's White pride band, or the one caught distributing KKK literature at a local mall during his off hours.

Or the firebombing of a Black family's home in Kentucky, which ultimately led to the arrest of a Jefferson County police officer.[vi] The officer proved to be the local Klan leader of a *forty*-member Klan subgroup called the Confederate Officers Patriot Squad (COPS), half of whom were active police officers. His involvement in the KKK, it was revealed, had been known by his own local department for years and was tolerated as long as he didn't publicize it.

Or the Border Patrol officer who intentionally ran over a Guatemalan migrant with his car shortly after texting that Guatemalans were "disgusting subhuman shit unworthy of being kindling for a fire" and "mindless murdering savages."[vii] He received three years' probation and 150 hours of community service.

Or the Virginia officer assigned to a local high school who recruited at the school on behalf of the Identify Evropa White nationalist group.[viii] Or the Ohioan thirty-year military veteran, now police chief, who tells off-color jokes and puts a Ku Klux Klan sign on a Black officer's desk. Or the Florida police deputy chief and fire chief posting pictures of themselves in KKK robes.

Or the Portland cop who erected a memorial shrine to Nazi-era German "war heroes" in a public park, who wears swastikas and gets married in Hitler's mountain town retreat, and claims he's just a "history geek."[ix] Or the veteran Michigan cop, who'd shot and killed a Black man a few years before, with KKK materials and racist flags in plain view in the online pics of his home for sale.[x]

Or the FBI and ATF agents outed by Alabama militia (who were angry with ATF over the handling of the Waco siege) who'd routinely attended the "Good Ole Boy Roundup" in Tennessee—a xenophobic conference that promoted products like mugs and T-shirts with MLK in a crossfire site and "hunting for niggers" licenses.[xi]

Or the lieutenant in the U.S. Coast Guard, who'd also been a Marine for six years, a self-identified White nationalist who promoted the idea of a "White homeland" and claimed online that "Much blood will have to be spilled" he'd then stockpiled weapons with the aim to "kill Democrats" because their "liberalist/globalist ideology is destroying traditional peoples, especially White."[xii]

Or...

You get the idea.

———

Closer to home, it was no secret the Phoenix police employed one of the most notable problematic police officers in the nation, Jack McLamb.

Looking at Jack and his organization, Police Against the New World Order, will help to contextualize more national groups like Oath Keepers and Three Percenter. What *begins* as "antigovernment" or "anti-immigration" or "pro-Constitution"—all common world views—often quickly morphs and escalates into something else as it attracts more-aggressive and dangerous followers.

Jack was antigovernment and a nativist who believed the borders should be completely locked down. He'd picketed the Phoenix Police Department—*where he worked*—about "The New World Order" (an emerging totalitarian world government) and law enforcement violating their oaths by enforcing "unlawful commands" (concerns involving freedom of speech, search and seizures, the Second Amendment, etc.) He'd also helped with negotiations at the both the Montana Freemen standoff and at Ruby Ridge. He ran an antigovernment short-wave radio show and had penned *Operation Vampire Killer 2000: American Police Action Plan for Stopping World Government Rule*, a booklet that promoted the recruiting of law enforcement and military to fight against the "ongoing, elitist covert operation which has been installed in the American system with great stealth and cunning."

He believed the U.S. government was actually *fostering* narcotics trafficking with an underlying hope to start a race war and that it, Al Gore in particular, planned to reduce the world population by 90%.

Jack would travel to teach law enforcement tactics and New World Order concerns to anyone who'd listen, even arguing the unconstitutionality of a traffic stop, something he, himself, was tasked to perform. Later, he was a regular speaker at various Patriot events—still donning his police uniform and running Police Against the New World Order. He'd also teamed up with Bo Gritz and Jerry Gillespie, a former state Senator who'd led

Arizona's charge against Martin Luther King Jr.'s Birthday Day as a national holiday.

He was doing all of this in the open, zero secrecy needed. He never crossed lines enough to lose his job, and even continued the activities when he retired, still officially an active officer.

Now, we enter the gray area.

Is being in support of tighter border security necessarily racist? If three hundred thousand undocumented Canadians were entering the U.S. every month, would Jack and his supporters head North? Unknown. To say anything more would be only speculation. But the truth remains:

Anti*government* groups, events, and agendas—regardless of actual motivation—attract White supremacists. Their interests and concerns intersect.

Does the fact that Jack and his supporters had bought acres and acres of land in Idaho with plans to live separate from the rest of America and a by-invite only community constitute White supremacy? I can't say, but many of his followers certainly believed so, that he was preparing a "White homeland."

And so, whether or not Jack believed this almost no longer matters. Almost.

———

I'd recently started working undercover within a group called the U.S. Constitution Rangers, following the lead of a name I'd gathered while at the Mesa Bible Church. The Rangers were another staunchly antigovernment militia and less so a White supremacy group—although, several members *did* straddle both worlds.

The group identified as Sovereign Citizens, a movement

historically made up of right-wing antigovernment White Americans who believe the federal government has been corrupted since 1871, when the "real Constitution" was "taken and replaced by a fake."

One of the first things I learned about the United States Constitution Rangers in Arizona was that cops were training them— not retirees or guys who'd been kicked off the force, but active police officers teaching this militant antigovernment group everything from hand-to-hand combat and modifying assault rifles to the best ways to get out of a ticket. And their main target was *other cops.*

These guys were helping the Rangers target members of law enforcement for committing what *they* deemed "constitutional violations"—stopping and citing citizens without, they argued, Constitutional authority. The Rangers would record random traffic stops, then follow the person who'd just been pulled over and question them to gather "evidence" and "testimony" to use later if they "felt their rights had been violated." They often put out decoys to *trigger* a traffic stop—a staged driving-offense simply to confront, bait, and entrap an officer.

It starts with a simple traffic stop, speeding maybe. The Ranger-trained driver slides a piece of paper through a barely cracked window: *"I am a sovereign citizen and you have no legal rights to stop or detain me."* No driver's license, car insurance, or vehicle registration is ever given. Due to the fact that they are "traveling" in a "mode of conveyance" instead of a motor vehicle, traffic laws— *technically*—have no jurisdiction over them. (To explain this fully would take another twenty pages and would still take a week in court arguing about legalize and the letter of law to *maybe* sort out; it is this confusion the Sovereign Citizens depend on.)

The cop writes a ticket anyway and, to avoid further altercation with the driver, simply writes "refused" on the signature line of the citation. They then circle the court date and slide the citation back through the window. Done.

But this, for many, is only the start. What happens next, *very* quickly, is that the person you cited, or their Sovereign Citizens allies, takes the following steps: (1) checks the officer's personnel file (something any citizen can do), hoping for a home address and family names; (2) contacts a "sovereign PI" (a Sovereign Citizen specifically tasked with surveillance work) to track the cop down, follow them to and from work, and take pictures, including of family; (3) flies a false lien with the county against the cop for up to millions of dollars (a legal document submitted to satisfy debts and obligations, but one based entirely on fraudulent statements—a typical tool of harassment in "paper terrorism" often against government officials). Months or even years later, the officer goes to buy or sell their house or car, and the bogus lien pulls up: *bam...no luck for you.* The officer must now work for many months to get the fictitious liens removed.

All in retaliation for conducting a simple traffic stop, a retaliation built upon technicalities and methods *taught by other police officers.* And bogus filings and "paper terrorism," as bad as they are, are often just a start.

This group—and others like them—also holds "sovereign courts," or "constitutional court," assemblies with no *actual* validity often convoked in some garage or basement. Sovereign Citizens act as the prosecution, defense, witnesses, and jury for the offending officer. The pretend trail is held and *always* finds the cop "guilty of treason." False liens, of course, are ordered. Then false complaints are filed with the officer's employer. A fictitious "arrest warrant" may even be issued as the Sovereign Citizens take their make-believe justice one step further.

This is what happened to a Metro Police Officer in Las Vegas who was "arrested" by four men and handcuffed to a hook in some garage to "serve time" for violations of their rights and the breach of his oath to protect the Constitution. This officer waited hours to be executed but was eventually freed. (I got this story first-hand from an original SIN member who'd worked the case undercover as a Sovereign Citizen.) The officer, humiliated, never reported the incident.

In Mesa, Sovereign Citizens came to an officer's home and attempted an arrest, which led to drawn guns and a quick retreat. Other times, there was no retreat. Actual violence is *always* on the table. One group, the Wolverine Watchmen, recently plotted to kidnap Michigan governor Gretchen Whitmer and to "try her for treason" for her handling of the COVID-19 pandemic. In another publicized attack, two West Memphis police officers stopped a father and son on a routine traffic stop.[xiii] The sixteen-year-old exited the van with an AK-47-style rifle and killed both officers. Two hours later, another shootout ensued in a Walmart parking lot, where both father and son were killed. Jerry Kane, the father, was a self-identified Sovereign Citizen who'd traveled the country giving seminars on how to forestall foreclosures, maintained that money is fictious and insisted that nobody needs a driver's license.

Go to any gun show or far-right rally and you'll be able to identify Sovereign Citizens pretty easily: they hand out pocket-sized books that contain the U.S. Constitution; antitax books, Prepper pamphlets (a Prepper is a survivalist preparing for the end of the world or society), and materials; and pre-made "I am a Sovereign Citizen" flyers with explanations for law enforcement if they're stopped.

In 2011, the FBI labeled Sovereign Citizens as domestic

terrorists and a threat to law enforcement.[xiv] They left out who'd been training them—cops. They also left out that many of its members were linked directly to White supremacy.

———

I was outside, washing off our driveway with a hose in one hand and holding my baby daughter in the other. We live at the end of a somewhat long road, which makes it nice because if someone ever comes to the end of the street, I know they're coming to our house. And someone was.

A white Crown Victoria pulled by, turned around slowly, and then came to a stop directly in front of my driveway. I called out for Tawni.

The car looked exactly like an unmarked police car, complete with tinted windows and antennae on the trunk. I assumed it was either a Mesa County Sheriff's Office (MCSO) detective who knew me or there was some other type of surveillance in my neighborhood.

The driver's window was rolled down only enough for me to see the very top of the driver's head. Something just wasn't right. Laying down the hose and giving my daughter to Tawni, I started toward the car.

It was a nice day, and as I walked, I'd placed my right hand on my hip checking for my gun. I didn't have it. *I'm at home. I'm supposed to be safe. I shouldn't need to carry a gun when I'm at my home.* Our house sits just sixty feet off the street, but the walk felt like it took forever. As I approached, the driver pulled forward a couple of feet but then stopped again.

The driver just looked back at me staring me down. It was

the cadet from the training class who'd known too much. The one who'd been fired.

At our home.

"Something you want to talk about?" I asked, approaching faster.

The driver continued to glare at me as he crept his car in front of our house.

"Hey, jackass, I'm right here!" I yelled and slammed the back of the trunk.

He sped away and I watched as he ignored the stop sign at the far end of the street and vanished back toward the main roads.

"What was that?" Tawni asked, coming down the driveway.

I told her. She shook her head as she went back into the home with our daughter. It was disturbing. Tawni had already been through a lot with me and my career choice, which she'd never really wanted in the first place though fully supported. There's just something unnerving, toxic, when the "bad dudes" are blatantly seeking you out, at your house—especially in front of your children.

Standing alone on the driveway again, I allowed the adrenaline to work its way through my system as best I could. This guy could have shot me easily. It was likely that he had a gun in the seat beside him but had chickened out. My whole body had tensed for the worst. This time, in front of my own home.

The worst part about this guy showing up at my house was that after a number of phone calls to supervisors and my cop "brothers," there was no follow-up investigation. The guy wasn't arrested or even contacted.

I was on my own again. And for whatever reason, that was the hardest part to take. Not because of some skinhead or druggie—but because of some guy who'd been two weeks from becoming a Mesa police officer.

Ultimately, I learned this disgraced recruit had called one of his academy friends, a newly sworn cop, my new colleague—who gave him my home address. Nice way to start your career: giving your "brother's" personal information to a pissed off ex-employee. I was furious.

I thought about those active police officers who wore their government-bought "raid gear" while standing guard on the border as part of the Minuteman Project—a new border militia.

A classified FBI Counterterrorism Policy Guide in 2015 specified "militia extremists, White supremacist extremists, and sovereign citizen extremists often have identified active links to law-enforcement officers."

Though I appreciated this was finally being acknowledged in the open, it was frustrating. I'd known this for well over a decade-but had learned it the hard way. My greatest fear—I could now admit—wasn't being caught by the "bad guys" I was investigating; it was being outed by another cop.

The bad guys didn't know who I really was; my fellow cops did.

———

Recently, Tawni and I have been trying to work with a group along the border who helps new immigrants who've recently crossed— yes, primarily illegally. This activist group has been pressured— mailed threats of violence, damaged vehicles, harassment, destruction of water and first aid supplies left out for the refugees—by border militias *and* local law enforcement.

When Tawni and I offered to play some role in helping them avoid such intimidation, it has been—so far—spurned. I'm not yet trusted because I *was* a cop, and they have concern I'm some kind of spy working *for* the militias.

We'd driven down to meet with them in person to talk better and found two police cars parked in front of their location. The entire town only *has* two police cars. It makes it kind of difficult to assist "illegals" needing food, water, medical care, trauma counseling, and legal assistance with two police cars parked outside your door. But the cars, they're told, are there for "*their* protection."

Their fear of law enforcement *is* understood.

Mine had been there for years.

THE OATH KEEPERS

A journalist friend of mine called one day.

He had a list of Oath Keepers—a national antigovernment paramilitary organization made up largely of active and retired cops and soldiers. Scarcely formed in 2009, they were the new kids on the block whose stated goal is to protect the Constitution against forces foreign *and* domestic. I'd been invited to similar meetings with these types—as a cop named Matt, *not* as Packy—for years.

Oath Keepers started from the premise that any oath taken by law enforcement or military is not an oath you retire from, but rather, it's for life. That whenever government violates the rights of its citizens, it is the duty of those who've taken an oath to defend those rights to take corrective actions.

JT Ready often preached the same. "All enemies foreign and domestic," he'd tell the room. "That's what I swore into. When we took that oath, it was for life. It didn't say five years after you get out or ten years after you get out that now you burn the Constitution. No, that's a lifetime commitment…whether you're a civilian now or not."

Oath Keepers was founded by Elmer Stewart Rhodes, a Yale

Law School graduate and former U.S. Army paratrooper and, a onetime Arizona Supreme Court justice law clerk who'd taken inspiration from the notion that Adolf Hitler could have been stopped if German soldiers and police had refused to follow orders. He reasoned that a totalitarian police state cannot happen in the United States if the majority of police and soldiers simply obey their oaths to defend the Constitution against a potential dictatorial leader or faction.

While the group wasn't officially a White Pride group—in fact, Rhodes publicly bristles at any such accusations, arguing that his is a "civic nationalist" organization and not a "White nationalist" one—it had certainly attracted members and supporters from that world.[xv]

Did it help, perhaps, that Rhodes had Valhalla tattooed on one arm? That he and other Oath Keepers have marched beside Identity Evropa "identitarians" interested in "preserving Western culture" who've also been labeled neo-Nazis? Or the years of Rhodes's anti-Muslim rhetoric, providing security for ACT For America—the largest anti-Muslim organization in the country?

"I think it makes sense for a guy like you to have this list," my reporter friend said. "Someone who might actually use it. I'm just sitting on it here. You want a copy?"

Always happy to get more info and cross-reference the groups I was investigating, I was excited. "Sure," I said. "How many names we talking?"

"North of thirty thousand."

Good thing I was already sitting down. I'd expected a few thousand, tops.

"*Thirty* thousand?" I repeated.

Holy… Wow.

——

Two weeks later, finally, I got the full list on a thumb drive via snail mail. The thirty-two thousand names were mostly folk in the criminal justice business, cops, and U.S. military. I now had their names, agencies, military branch, rank, dues paid, whether they were active duty or retired—more information than I could have dreamed of.

But going through the list was mentally draining and logistically taxing. I found myself getting increasingly upset with each page.

The Oath Keepers group wasn't officially formed until March 2009, but the amalgamation of military and cops and extremism wasn't something new. I'd been tracking it since 1994. This was just the newest name and apparently far larger and more organized than even I'd realized.

Richard Mack, a former Arizona sheriff, for instance, had started a group called the Constitutional Sheriffs & Peace Officers Association (CSPOA).[xvi] Mack teaches that because the sheriff is the only elected law man in the county, it's *his* word, and *only* his word, that binds. It was the same old philosophy I'd heard at Mesa Bible Church and taught in "sovereign citizen" meetings across the country.

A similar group are the Three Percenters, also called 3%ers or III%ers. (The name is derived from the disputed claim that "only 3%" of the colonists fought against "the King's tyranny" during the American Revolution.) Its hot buttons are gun ownership rights and resistance to the ever-expanding authority of the U.S. federal government. Police and military types have also flocked to this group. And, as with the Oath Keepers, while not created as hate or White supremacy organizations, the antigovernment, survivalist, far-right leanings of these organizations is a breeding ground for those with more-racial agendas. That Confederate and Nazi imagery sporadically appear beside or on 3% patches, T-shirts, hats, and flyers is—irrespective of original aims—revealing. (One 3%ers crew was implicated in the firebombing of a mosque in Rochester, Minnesota.)

And, when talking about any of these groups during presentations—that these extreme groups are being trained by police officers and military personnel and many are within their ranks—I never witnessed alarm or outrage.

More telling, there was no *surprise* either.

There is no easy answer to why extremists are drawn to law enforcement.

Does the military "teach hate" through war? Does law enforcement appeal to some who want revenge or orderliness through extremism?

Those in law enforcement usually lean politically conservative. They're willing to risk their lives every day for existing laws, for keeping the world *as it is*—not as it "might be." The United States Constitution Rangers openly promote themselves as defenders of the Constitution. Why *wouldn't* someone in law enforcement, who took an oath to the same end, support that?

But, as some militias evolved from strictly antigovernment into antigovernment with varying degrees of White-pride agendas, many in law enforcement have *remained* allies with those fringe groups.

This is not entirely a right-wing issue. The NFAC (Not Fucking Around Coalition) is a left-wing Black armed militia of current and ex-military and law enforcement. And Antifa also recruits similar resources when it can find them.

Extremism on all sides exists in law enforcement, I would argue, because those of us in law enforcement are told daily that we are the only ones protecting our cities and streets. An "us against them" mentality is forced down our throats from day one as each one of us ultimately decides what, exactly, we're protecting our cities and streets from.

THE DEPUTY

The sheriff of Yavapai County, two hours away, invited me north to interview one of his deputies. The sheriff wanted to know whether his deputy of eight years still had any ties to the Aryan Nations.

Still???!

I couldn't understand why the guy hadn't already been dismissed but then began convincing the sheriff, and myself, that this officer could be a fount of information on the local—

"Just confirm if he's still associated with the group or not," the sheriff replied. "That's it."

Skeptical, I made the trip north and sat down with this guy, Justin. It may go down as the shortest and most concise interview I've ever done.

"Are you a member of the Aryan Nations?"

"I was."

"What did you do for them?"

"I was the youth recruiter."

He and I stared at each other quietly for a while. I'd already heard enough. A guy who'd once recruited for a neo-Nazi organization should find a vocation other than being a cop. "Do you still have affiliations with the Nations?" I asked simply.

"No comment."

"Are you still active?"

"I have no comment."

"Ever met Pastor Butler?" Butler, now deceased, was the founder of Aryan Nations and a "spiritual godfather" of the White supremacist movement.

"No comment?"

"Never met him?"

"What do you think?" the deputy replied, as if insulted by the question.

I honestly wasn't sure if that meant "yes" or "no."

"If you think I'm going to tell you what I know," he continued, "and *who* I know…you're wasting your time. I don't know why you were asked to interview me 'cause I'm telling you the same thing I told the sheriff: I just want to be a cop."

"So, it would be pointless for me to ask you any more questions?"

"I HAVE NO COMMENT."

I sat there contemplating my next move. I knew arguing with this guy wasn't going to accomplish much, so I turned off the recorder, leaned forward, and signaled for the deputy to come in closer.

In my best dramatic sotto voce I said, "You just wanna be a cop?"

"Yeah."

"You don't have the right, courage, or balls for it," I told him. "Real cops *protect* what you want to destroy. Know that I'll do everything I can think of to make sure you're not wearing that badge for long."

Justin leaned back, looked at me, and simply said, "Fuck you."

Fair enough.

I told the sheriff his guy was unquestionably bad news and that I was 99% sure he was still connected to White supremacy. The sheriff looked away, then asked if I could prove it.

"No," I admitted. "You'd have to make a real investigation out of it. Get Internal Affairs or the FBI to—"

He stopped me. I wasn't surprised. The sheriff admitted he knew about Justin's White-pride past. But if and until the deputy broke a law in an obvious way, nothing would be done.

Months later, we discovered Justin hadn't just been the youth recruiter but, rather, the entire Washington State leader for the Aryan Nations. He'd specialized in booking White power bands for festivals and had been a regular speaker at Richard Butler's Aryan Youth Action Conference, indoctrinating youth.

Perfect ideology for one who was hired to protect and serve, wouldn't you say?

Not long after our interview, Justin was arrested for drug charges and went to prison. He faced seven felony counts, including contributing to the delinquency of a minor (for sexual actions against the family babysitter), and involving a minor in a drug offense as he'd sent his sixteen-year-old son to buy cocaine from a local drug dealer.

One more down.

Could we chase out another hundred bad cops? A thousand?

Maybe, someday, all of them?

————

At an International Association of Chiefs of Police Conference that Tawni and I recently attended in Philadelphia, there was a large counter-protest in front of the convention center denouncing *all* police.

A woman in her early seventies held a sign that read "KOPS and KLAN WORK HAND IN HAND!!"

It proved visceral for Tawni. And, before I could advise otherwise, she'd already marched up to the protester.

"See that guy over there?" Tawni asked, pointing my way. "He *abhors* racism. He was an undercover cop for years in White supremacist groups and put these guys in jail. He got racist cops fired. At great sacrifice to him. And his kids, and our family."

"Well"—the woman looked directly at Tawni—"he obviously didn't do enough."

Tawni was stunned, angry, and sad.

And though I love Tawni for sticking up for me and the hundreds of thousands of cops like me, I also agreed with the lady. We haven't done enough.

But we're still trying, ma'am. We really are.

Patrik is a reservist in the Canadian Armed Forces and is a combat engineer with military-explosives training. He is also a chief neo-Nazi recruiter for The Base, an international paramilitary White supremacist group, tasked with forming and uniting cells across the globe. In 2019, Patrik enters the United States to meet racist comrades, including American military, and attends several military style training "hate" camps in Massachusetts. He posts videos outlining his radicalized views against Jewish and gay people and argues that violence is "the only way," promoting the derailment of trains, an upcoming civil war, and the poisoning of city water sources. "The time for talk has ended," he warns. "If you think politics is a solution, you are a damn fool. It is the system that is fomenting violent revolution, not us, and they shall now reap what they have sown." He transports firearms and ammunition across state lines with intent to commit a violent stand at a pro-gun rally in Virginia but is arrested. A month later, a Royal Canadian Artillery veteran and active Canadian Ranger drives more than two days to reach Ottawa from Manitoba. There are high-powered firearms in his pickup, and he carries his military ID with him to aid him in evading the police later. He rams his black Dodge into the gates of the estate where Canadian prime minister Justin Trudeau now lives, angry at Trudeau for being a "communist" and a "dictator" and for his stances on gun control and COVID. After an armed standoff with security, the soldier surrenders. It is the first known attempt to assassinate a sitting Canadian prime minister.

---

*Patrik: Karen Pauls and Angela Johnson, "Ex-reservist Patrik Mathews and others planned violent revolution, U.S. prosecutors say" CBC News, January 21, 2020, https://www.cbc.ca/news/canada/manitoba/patrick-mathews-base-violent-revolution-1.5435323; Mack Lamoureux and Ben Makuch, "Canadian Soldier Turned Neo-Nazi Terrorist Sentenced to 9 Years in US Prison" October 28, 2021, https://www.vice.com/en/article/5dgzpa/patrik-mathews-canadian-soldier-sentenced-nine-years.

HATE CRIMES

Cole

When someone is kicked to death, each kick strikes the head with the force of a frontal car crash at 30-plus miles per hour. In the last minutes of his life, Cole had been in up to twenty "car crashes." And more were coming.

He was twenty years old. He'd just interviewed for a bartender job at River City Pockets, a Phoenix pool hall, and was waiting for a taxi to take him to his girlfriend's apartment; she was sick with the flu, and he was coming to make her some soup. Then, half a dozen neo-Nazis were tossed from the pool hall and those plans ended—along with Cole's life.

"What are you looking at?" taunted Samuel Compton, a shaved-head brute of six feet and change.

Cole had tried to look away. He was five feet nine and weighed 130 pounds. He wore glasses and had a pacemaker. He'd been born with a heart defect, and for the first year of his life, he'd fought to live while his father stayed awake each night to watch him and make sure he didn't stop breathing.

When Cole didn't answer, Samuel Compton marched the short distance between them and punched Cole straight in the face. Compton was wearing brass knuckles. Cole's glasses snapped and flew off into the night, his nose and right eye socket fractured. Before he truly understood what had just happened, he was on the ground and blood was running down his face onto the pavement. But this kid had been fighting for life since the day he'd been born, and he wasn't done yet. He crawled back to his feet and ran.

All six skinheads chased after. One knocked him back to the ground and then several started kicking. A "boot party." For fun. The group, said witnesses after, cheered and laughed the whole time.

It didn't matter that their victim was White. To bridge that gap, they called him a "wigger" throughout. Kicking with bare feet can lead to fatal injuries. Cole's attackers wore boots. Steel-toed boots. "No... Please..." Cole got out, his attackers would later admit in court. "I was just waiting—"

The kicking continued.

There were fractures of his calvarium (skullcap) and facial bones. Brain contusions. Intra-cerebral hemorrhage. Deep gashes to his forehead and left eyebrow. Blood covered both his eyes, so the first police officers to arrive couldn't even tell if they were open anymore. Forensics labs typically find sole-imprint patterns in the adipose, a soft tissue between the head and skull. You can actually see the imprints, like an X-ray captured in the bruising. Cole had been kicked so hard, there were no such patterns; it all bled together into one shape.

Earlier that same day, Cole and his father, Cole Sr., had argued over some car payments Cole was behind on. It's why he was looking for a second job. These two always got along, but their last discussion had been heated. This fact would haunt the boy's father for the rest of his life. If Cole thought of it in his final moments, we would never know.

Earlier that same day, I'd been invited to go out drinking with these same killers. "Packy! Bro… We're going to the pool hall tonight… Let's hang out, bro!"

I'd declined.

How things would have changed had I agreed to join them…

I think about it every day.

Cole's upper thorax and diaphragm were crushed. There were fractures in his lower jaw and forearms, showing he'd tried to defend himself. Teeth were missing. His liver ruptured. There were lacerations to the back of the head and fractures of the parietal and temporal bone—all in the arched pattern of a wide steel-toed boot. His thoracic vertebrae and hyoid bone (spine and neck) were cracked. External and internal blood loss would kill him. The blood stain would remain on the sidewalk for too many weeks.

The last kick was described in court as if they'd kicked a football. Stepped back and eyed an imaginary goal and then came at Cole's head with those steel-toed Doc Martens. The group cheered. And then they ran.

———

It was mid-October and the weather was beautiful. Tawni and I were out for dinner with friends. We spoke of the things normal people speak of and had just ordered our food when my cell phone went off.

"Hey, Matt," a Phoenix homicide detective, Paul Dalton, said. "Need a favor."

He told me of Cole's murder and that, according to witnesses, the suspects were White men "with loads of tattoos." He'd been told I was the guy who would be able to help identify them. And, sure enough: one of the suspects had "CRACKER" tattooed on the back of his head.

"Chris Whitley," I said. The kid I'd sat behind and first met at a National Alliance meeting. A guy I'd shared beers with a dozen times since.

"They weren't kidding about you," the detective said. "How fast can you get here?"

I started making my phone calls to get all the approvals from the powers that be (it takes far more calls and authorizations than you'd ever think for a Mesa detective to help a Phoenix detective ten miles away). I kissed Tawni and left her as the third wheel at the restaurant. I was already in Phoenix when I was given—unenthusiastically by my superiors—the approval to assist.

I first drove to the apartment where Whitley and his friends had been living, hoping to catch them there. I sat outside in my truck and waited until, eventually, Phoenix PD showed up and cleared the house, but nobody was inside.

Entering the apartment, I wasn't surprised by what I found. On the wall hung a swastika flag. Beneath it, a pair of the shiniest spit-shined Docs I'd ever seen. Hate music blared on the stereo in the empty apartment.

I was fully debriefed on what had happened.

The group—Chris Whitley, Sammy Compton, Justin Larue, Brandon Miller, Cassandra Wood, and Kelly Coffman—had all been inside the bar, River City Pockets, playing pool. At some point, Cassandra got into a fight with another random barfly and ended up breaking *her* orbital socket. An enormous Black security guard, a collegiate offensive lineman no less, proceeded to throw all six out. Sammy, humiliated, was the first out the door and he'd spotted Cole Bailey.

After attacking Cole, of course, like most "White nationalists" and "street soldiers," they all ran like cowards. Brandon, I was told, had already been caught, driving away from the scene, blood still on his boots, and had been arrested for murder.

The other five were still on the run.

I sorted through all the names of all the members of Unit 88 whom I'd met or knew from the National Alliance meetings, and one who kept coming to mind was Jason Keith, a.k.a. Slick. Slick had just been released from prison and had moved to Apache Junction, an area at the far east end of Phoenix. Having been raised in Phoenix, I said to myself, "If I wanted to get out of town but didn't have the means to do so, the furthest place I would go would be Apache Junction." This area was full of White boys, tweakers hooked on crystal meth, and actual meth labs—a perfect place for this particular crew to easily hide.

I called the Phoenix detective and shared my suspicions. Due to the late hour and lack of manpower, he said he wasn't able to follow up on it that night. So, I started making calls to my own guys in Mesa to see if *they* could help. Of course, I got the whole "It's not a Mesa homicide, Matt. Who will pay for the overtime?" routine and was unable to get my squad together.

The following morning, sans approval, I went to Apache Junction myself and checked Jason's house. As I suspected, my five skins *had* been there the night before but had left earlier in the morning as news of the murder spread across town. I'd missed them by hours.

My phone burst with calls from both law enforcement *and* the White supremacist underworld. Jerry Harbin was calling anxiously to know if I'd (as Packy) heard anything as I pumped him for information of my own. I was consumed. I reminded my supervisors: "This is *murder*. An innocent kid was murdered. If we can help, does it really matter whose case it is?"

I needed some quick backup and called new friends: the FBI.

———

All FBI field offices have task forces that partner with local law enforcement. The cops selected are paid by their PD, but the FBI pays any overtime and provides a nice car, fancier guns, and the opportunity to work special cases. It's a sought-after gig, and when the FBI came calling with their Desert Hawk Fugitive Task Force, I applied and was selected. I was now putting in between sixty and eighty hours a week.

It was grueling but rewarding. It had also given me new friends.

Some of my partners from the FBI's Fugitive Task Force joined in on the pursuit of Cole's killers and pulled over Josh Fiedler and his girlfriend to have a little chat; they questioned him on what he was doing and if he'd seen Chris or Sammy. Of course, Josh had "no idea" what they were talking about, and he was released with a citation for driving on a suspended license.

The hunt continued.

Phoenix PD stayed aggressive on this one and it felt good, but we knew the suspects were on the run and time was not our friend. Phoenix PD decided to get creative and contacted *America's Most Wanted*.

This popular program was credited with capturing more than a thousand criminals, including seventeen on the FBI's "Ten Most Wanted" list. It was a great break to get their attention on this one. The program just needed to know more about the case, so the producers asked the Phoenix team if I would participate.

I had grave and immediate concerns about being a part of any media, especially TV. But I didn't even ask for approval from my Mesa supervisors. If it was good enough for the Phoenix guys, it was good enough for me.

The production crew flew out to Phoenix, popped up a studio in a hotel room, and everything was set.

Before filming started, however, I had to know a few things. "You guys realize I am still undercover in this group, right?" I voiced. "I really don't want to be burned now." They hadn't known. *This is not going well,* I thought.

The producer—Mary, a wonderful person who soon became a family friend—made a quick phone call and then promised they'd hide my identity by covering my face and altering my voice.

I had so much to lose and still wasn't keen on any of it but agreed to proceed. It was unnerving: the lights, cameras, the crew, and mics—trying to strategically answer the questions, but not entirely blow my cover. I know I wasted far more tape than they'd planned to use because I was either looking down or at the wrong spot during the interview. But we got through it.

We recorded in December, but the episode wouldn't air until February. Two months to wait. Now, I truly felt like it had been a waste of my time and a threat for no return.

Meanwhile, just before the new year, I got a call from Phoenix detective Dalton. Chris Whitley, a main suspect, was back in town and being set up by a "friend" of his, Patrick Bearup. (Bearup was a skinhead and the son of a longtime local officer then running for sheriff.) Bearup had reached out to Cole Bailey Sr., the victim's father, and arranged to set Chris up for $500.

Cole Bailey Sr. had called Phoenix PD and set up the meeting at—no surprise—a local Denny's restaurant. There, Patrick collected his $500, and Mr. Bailey, along with two friends of his own, walked into the Denny's to speak with Chris. We never found out what Cole's father said. I can only imagine.

Shortly after they met, members of the Fugitive Task Force, who were already seated inside the restaurant, arrested Chris. I watched as he came out of the restaurant handcuffed and carrying a "doggy bag" with his half-eaten hamburger and fries. He was taken to the Phoenix PD to be interviewed. I followed and set myself up in the interview monitoring room.

There were no secret mics or earpieces where I could speak to Detective Dalton during the interview. Instead, I'd watch and listen, take notes, get frustrated, and then Dalton would come out on "breaks" to debrief with me and pace how we were doing. Even though Chris wouldn't confess, he was still booked on charges of second-degree murder.

Meanwhile, a warrant had been issued for Cassandra Wood's arrest in connection to the original bar fight that led to the death of Cole. Perfect, I thought; I'll find and arrest her and interview *her* about the murder.

I'd heard a rumor that after Cole was killed, Cassandra had resolved to put her life straight and, apparently, being a mechanic was part of her new dream. I'd done some low-level mechanic work back as a teen and knew Arizona Automotive Institute was the first place to check. The AAI was a school with a history of taking every high school dropout, tweaker, and broken person trying to "get their lives together"—and some did, but the clientele could be… rough. Cassandra Wood-type rough.

I drove through the student parking lot looking for her older blue Ford Bronco. I parked and waited. Half an hour went by and sure enough, Cassandra and her blue Bronco pulled up.

I called Detective Dalton and told him I had her, and he asked if I could get her to Phoenix PD to be interviewed. Following procedure, I needed backup for the arrest and called my new friends with the FBI Fugitive Task Force again. Shortly after, Danny got there. Danny always had some wild idea to get the job done and he didn't disappoint this time either: he came up with the plan that I'd pose as Cassandra's "beneficiary" to see how much she still owed in tuition. Knowing the school would need to get Cassandra's permission to talk with me, Danny was going to wait by the receptionist door and arrest her before she even made her way into the bursar's office. No cover blown for Packy; she'd never even see me.

It worked like a charm. I did my thing, Danny did his, and Cassandra Wood was off to the Phoenix PD to be booked on her warrant and interviewed by Detective Dalton.

But, she had nothing to say either.

Meanwhile, the *America's Most Wanted* show finally aired. Sammy Compton and Justin Larue were the last two people connected with the murder we hadn't pulled in. Sammy had been seen bouncing around all over Arizona and California for months and was picked up in Bakersville, California, only days after the episode aired. Larue was still MIA, but the show *had* found one more.

A month later, I got the call from Paul telling me that Brandon—the first skin they'd arrested the night of the murder—had been released from jail. All his charges were dropped.

"You have *got* to be kidding me." I couldn't believe it.

Paul explained that the only witness who actually made a statement had moved to Texas and was refusing to return for trial. Not only was he refusing to return, but the witness had also recanted his statement and was now saying he had no idea what'd happened that night, that he did not see anything.

Someone had gotten to him.

———

I couldn't let Brandon go and couldn't get this case off my mind. One night, I'd started looking through some old pictures and happened upon one I'd forgotten I had: Brandon and his small little crew of thugs. I'd taken it years before when they were thrown out of The Nile Theater in Mesa. Yup, Brandon was one of the first skins I'd ever talked to. I stared at the old photo in amazement. I couldn't get him in jail that night long ago, but now I was determined to get him rearrested on these murder charges.

Fine. If the only witness had taken off to Texas and wouldn't come back, I would go to him. I reached out again to the FBI and briefed my FBI supervisor. My boss was a great guy, incredibly involved in his work, and I was confident I could quickly get this approved. I quickly learned otherwise.

First, they told me, the FBI budget was to be spent only on official "FBI cases," not local charges. Second, if there was an FBI office close to the witness, *they* were to handle the interview. Third, of course, I got the dreaded "It's not that big of deal, Matt." It was *"only one"* local murder.

I continued to argue. "Even if we brief the local agents, they'll have no clue how to interview someone about a skinhead murder."

My supervisor looked at me blankly. "They're FBI agents for a reason, Matt. They can interview just as good as you. Write up the lead and send it."

I did as I was told. The lead written and sent to Texas. Protocol says the interview should have been completed in thirty days. It took three months, a lot of phone calls, and a few threats to even get the interview done. I never received a copy of that report; I doubt there was ever one written.

I did finally get ahold of the FBI agent, who explained simply: "The witness didn't want to talk…. So, we left."

"Nice," I said. "You should be real proud of your work." I hung up.

———

The more Tawni learned as she worked beside me, the more the ineffectiveness of local law enforcement and the FBI perplexed her. Much more than even I was…which was saying something. "There's so much good that *could* be done," she'd say.

I tried reassuring her that she just didn't understand. She agreed and was happy about it. "Why would I *want* to understand? Then, I might condone it also." Tawni was an outsider realizing "business as usual" often stood directly in the way of getting the job done. It made no sense to send an agent from another state, one who wasn't going to take the time to truly understand the case, to interview important murder witnesses. This one was a real blow for us both.

Disheartening to her. For me, it was crushing.

———

Justin Larue, the final suspect, was finally picked up in Washington in July on a DUI warrant, headed to work on a crab boat. He was held on Cole's murder warrant and extradited back to Phoenix.

Ultimately, Sammy and Chris both got more than twenty years for Cole's murder. Larue got sixteen. Cassandra Wood got probation for the original bar fight. The other skinbyrd got nothing. And Brandon, caught fleeing the scene, also didn't serve a day for the crime.

JT

JT Ready, I learned, was now running for the Arizona House of Representatives. His chief platform, of course, was cracking down on undocumented immigration, which posed a threat, he advocated, to the entire U.S. health care system. He also wanted to improve the education system by addressing "this mass illegal influx of foreign students who do not even embrace the same language and culture as Americans and who spread tuberculosis, whooping cough, lice, and other third-world biological diseases to our children."

His language let everyone in Phoenix know who and what he was about: "We need some can-do, kick-butt American Patriots to get back in office. Now, I might be the first one to advocate this, but I firmly believe in having a mine field across the border… It is 100% effective." He'd also attempted to copycat David Lane's infamous fourteen words by coining his own eighteen, which he openly spouted at close-knit rallies and gatherings: "The purity of the Aryan Race is the most precious resource nature has to offer all humankind."

He, thankfully, came in dead last out of six candidates in the Republican primary. He didn't even get a thousand votes, though the fact that he got more than twenty was disturbing enough.

PETE

Every day, working with the FBI's Fugitive Violent Crimes Task Force, I was now helping to arrest four to six major felon fugitives.

And every night I was also coming home bruised and sometimes even bloodied. It was rough work, taking on the worst of the worst.

Then there was Pete.

Pete was not a known criminal or a neo-Nazi or anything like that, but he'd gotten into a drunken argument with a girlfriend, fired a gun at the ceiling, gone outside to his truck to cool off, and when a neighbor approached, Pete shot out his own passenger window at the neighbor. The next few hours brought multiple high-speed car chases with the police. Not Pete's best day.

In the name of public safety, the police gave up the vehicle pursuit and decided to nab Pete later. I was part of the team following up on him. It had somehow been kicked up to the FBI. (Cole Bailey being kicked to death by six domestic terrorists was "small and local" but *this* case somehow had earned the FBI Task Force.)

Pete's "bad day" quickly escalated. As we surrounded him at his home, he attempted to escape again, slamming his car into one of the officer's trucks. Then he fired his gun at us. We fired back. Bullets, some from my gun, filled his truck.

Television programs can make you think police officers shoot people every day. We don't. I'd been on the force for ten years and this was the first time I had ever fired my gun during an arrest. Like *most* in law enforcement, I'd learned to deescalate things far before it ever came to that.

In seconds, we'd gone from protecting ourselves and the community to trying to keep Pete from dying. The doors were locked, and it took a nearby rock to smash out what was left of his window to get to him. Jagged glass, bullet wounds. Finally, we hauled him free from his truck, and blood from his wounds blew out onto my vest, chin, and neck—even into my mouth.

We got Pete breathing again and kept him alive until the

medical team arrived. Kudos to us. But then I was detained. A police shooting works just like any other. I was transported to Phoenix PD, where my first stop was the third-floor bathroom. I looked in the mirror, still had my black vest with yellow "Police" patch covering the front, and first saw all the blood on the yellow stitching. Pete's blood, I now realized, was also all over my arms, neck, hair, and face.

I was mirandized, photographed head to toe, and stashed in an interview room. It wasn't *my* best night either. I was filled with anxiety and dread. I didn't trust the situation, or anyone, and refused to talk.

Pete ultimately survived.

The shooting happened around 5 p.m. I finally got a ride home at 1 a.m.

I walked into the kitchen, saw Tawni, and started to cry.

"I can't do this anymore," I told her. I hadn't become a cop to shoot anybody. Of course, I'd always known it was a possibility, but I'd never wanted to hurt people. I'd wanted to help.

Tawni told me to quit the PD. She admitted to waiting for the time to say, "Let's quit." Now it was time. These sentiments had been growing for years, but she'd had been holding back because she knew the realization *had* to come from me. "I don't think you can do this and still be you," she said. "I know I can't." She said I could go back to school for something else and that we'd figure it out. But I knew I didn't have anything else I *could* do. Also, we had bills, a mortgage, and the kids needed health insurance.

As I showered, the last long red lines of Pete's blood flowed off me—but the stress stuck. I rarely got emotional, and this night, for Tawni, seemed finally like our way out. It wasn't.

The next morning, adrenaline still pumping, I simply went

back to work. I honestly didn't know what else to do. I drove to a substation in the outskirts of Mesa. Didn't want to see anyone I knew, but it didn't matter—word had spread. A coworker asked if I was Browning. When I nodded, he excitedly said, "I heard you lit someone up yesterday." Another guy congratulated me on my "trigger time."

I went home. For days. I couldn't shake the shooting. Yes, the blood was awful. Yes, hurting someone was awful. But I was reacting to it at a magnitude far beyond what I should. On my third day off, I had to see a shrink.

I knew the drill. I didn't tell him about the blood I was still tasting in my mouth (and would for years), my insomnia, the nightmares I had when I *did* manage to doze off. I didn't tell him that I wished I was an alcoholic, so I could just drink myself into oblivion. And I also didn't tell him about Cole Bailey or Swastika Hill or a neo-Nazi jamming his gun in my chest or missing witnesses or the rise of JT Ready. Or how budget concerns and jurisdictional turf wars had more to do with arrests and prosecutions than actual justice.

It was then I realized: Pete had somehow clearly become the final straw of *everything* I'd been through the past eleven years. The experience of shooting him had been traumatic enough to draw together all of my various traumas—the frustrations, anxiety of undercover work, my failures.

I, of course, didn't say any of this to the psychiatrist because when you're talking to a police-ordered counselor, your main concern is job security. I couldn't be seen as weak. I also didn't completely understand what was going on with me. PTSD was not something readily talked about in the early 2000s, at least not among cops. It was a career death sentence. Had I been truthful with that shrink, and knowing what I do now, that should have been his diagnosis. I should have been ordered into more therapy. *No shame in that, right?* Instead, I smiled and was released back to work.

CORY AND CHRIS

Cory Simpson, a leader of a newish local group, the Canyon State Skins, wanted to talk to me. He'd been picked up on a shoplifting charge and was brought into Mesa for questioning and had somehow heard from other cops that I was a guy to talk with.

I knew the name, but we'd never met. He didn't know me as Packy, only as Detective Matt Browning, a cop familiar with his world. He'd only recently gotten out of prison and was, apparently, already on his way back in again.

We met in the Mesa Police Department third-floor interview room. He sat in a chair in the corner, and I grabbed another to sit directly in front of him.

He had a shaved head, white wifebeater shirt, and Levi shorts. He was tattooed. Right above each of his knees was the "White Pride Worldwide" symbol without the words—a mix between a rifle site and a Celtic cross. His legs moved nonstop, a clear sign he was nervous. *Really* nervous. At first, I thought I was being lied to. I thought this guy is just some meth head who wanted to get off some other crime he'd committed. He'd been in prison for years, and I had no knowledge of his reputation or if he was actually a player in the White power movement.

Then he started sobbing.

He was in on a misdemeanor charge and said that if he was sent back to prison, he'd be killed by either the Mexican Mafia or the Aryan Brotherhood.

I assured him I'd help him if he'd work for me, but he refused. Needing some leverage on him, I tried to turn his misdemeanor into a felony by making it a parole violation. It didn't work out and he only ended up spending a few days in jail.

Ironically, had he gone to prison, or taken me up on my offer, he might still be alive today. A couple months after his jail stint, Cory traveled out of state to meet with some Vinlanders.

The Vinlanders Social Club was based mainly in the Midwest and is a conglomeration of the Outlaw Hammerskins (IN), Hoosier State Skinheads (IN), the Ohio State Skinheads, and the Keystone State Skinheads (PA). They were extremely violent thugs and had earned nicknames like "The Butcher."

They gave Cory the Vinlander patch, which is a tradition in the White supremacy world and a big deal. It's an actual patch like you'd get for a varsity letter in high school or the military or Boy Scouts. Feeling he needed protection possibly going back to jail, he'd aligned with the more powerful Vinlanders.

Cory had "patched over." By accepting the Vinlander patch, he was now a Vinlander. And, since he was the recognized leader of the Canyon State Skins, it *also* officially meant he'd just "patched over" *all* the CSS members to the Vinlanders.

Crew members back home in Arizona were pissed.

The Canyon State Skins had been the brainchild of a shy, bookish computer programmer named Kevin Lee who'd hoped to unite all the White supremacy groups in the Valley under the Vinlanders. They'd told Lee he needed to first build his own successful Arizona gang before being absorbed under the more national Vinlander umbrella. And he had, with Cory as their leader. Cory's getting patched over was the successful culmination of a two-year plan. He and Kevin Lee had accomplished their original goal and, moreover, Cory would have some more protection if he ultimately had to go to jail.

But members of the Canyon State Skins weren't interested in long-term plans or Cory's safety in prison. *They*, the actual foot soldiers, didn't want to be absorbed into anything and felt betrayed.

Reprisal was called for and came quickly.

Cory's ex-CSS skins (now Vinlanders) were also Odinists, and they'd planned a big party on Christmas Eve to celebrate the Winter Solstice. They met up at a house in Mesa and had a probate (someone who is new to the group and has to earn their way in) named Chris Gromberg act as security. He was a viable choice because he wasn't yet a convicted felon and could legally pack a gun. Everyone else went into the backyard and stood in a circle. Cory handed out the presents he'd gotten for his buddies: buck knives with three-to-four-inch blades.

They filled up a hollowed-out ram or cow horn with mead (homemade Viking wine) and started the toasts. One of the guys said, "I love you, brothers, because we are a family." He took a drink, and they all did a *sieg heil*. The next guy took the horn and stated, "I love you, brothers, for always having my back." This ritual progressed around the circle until it was Cory's turn.

He told everyone that he loved them, and he was glad they were now part of a bigger group.

A foremost part of Hate culture—maybe the biggest—is finding a lacking sense of identity. And being part of an exclusive group, *any* group. And by dissolving the AZ Skins, Cory had taken this identity away from his crew. They were now, instead, the lowest part of another group they *didn't* identify with, that didn't make them feel secure or superior. I believe this contributed to what happened next.

Cory was jumped and stabbed at least seventeen times by his "brothers" with the same knives he'd just given them as gifts. They then left him on the floor to bleed out.

Chris Gromberg and Cory's wife threw Cory into the back seat of a car and drove to an urgent care a mile and a half away. It was a nice gesture, but instead of bringing him inside, they rolled him out of the door onto the sidewalk and tried to drive away. Thankfully, they were detained by security while witnesses called the police. Cory was pronounced dead on the scene.

I'd been putting together a teeter-totter "from Santa" for my kids when Mesa's homicide sergeant, Mike Collins, called and told me Cory had been killed. I'd known about the Winter Solstice party and asked if Mike wanted me at the house.

He wanted me instead to go to the station and help with interviews. I entered the interviewing area on the third floor through a back door, where Mike motioned for me to hide around the corner. I ducked into the monitor room just as some skinhead came down the hall. For the next eight hours, that's where I sat.

Cory's wife was up first. Her interview was a mixture of wanting to help but knowing that, if she did, her world would end in the same manner as Cory's. She gave a few names of those in attendance but claimed she hadn't seen the stabbing because she was in the house with the wives and girlfriends letting the "bois" be "bois." She ultimately gave us nothing we didn't already know.

In the other interview room, waiting for his interview, was a heavy-set, Doc Marten-wearing, flight-jacket-still-on, legit skinhead. The locals called him "Cheeseburger," because he loved McDonald's cheeseburgers, but his birth name was Christopher Gromberg, the new recruit. While in the room, his phone was being blown up, text message after text message; it was nonstop.

And with each text, Chris's face dropped more. It was a stress, a growing panic, you could see. His brothers were already circling, warning, threatening.

Finally, he was questioned. He admitted to driving Cory to the urgent care but that was it. Chris said he was a probate with the Vinlanders and that he was simply asked to oversee security at the party.

By the look on Chris's face, he knew he'd already said too much. I like to run interviews because I'm patient and don't mind uncomfortable silences; that's when people worry about what you know and start to blabber. But because I was undercover, I couldn't be in the room. I was next door again, feeding questions to the interviewers. Even though we caught him in some lies, Chris never broke. He gave no one up and was released at 5 a.m. on Christmas Day.

"Take his phone!" I urged. "He was being blown up with texts the whole time he was in there. Take his phone!" *Who else would be texting him except the people who were involved with the murder all telling him to shut his mouth or he dies?* We could get lots of great info from it, and I was genuinely worried about Chris. "Take the freaking phone!"

They didn't take it. And there was never an explanation for why. Instead, they escorted Chris out to the front door and sent him home. I was so frustrated I ran out the doors and broke cover, confronting the new recruit in the parking lot. It was a risky and misguided move, but I was confident I could get him to talk. I told him that I knew he'd witnessed Cory's murder and pleaded with him to come back inside and talk to me. I understood how his friends operated better than he did and was concerned he'd be killed. His demeanor suggested to me that he was being threatened;

there was absolutely no ego or skinhead bravado in his mannerisms. He also knew I was right, that he was possibly never going to see the Valley again. But he wouldn't come inside.

(And to those who may be reading this who know about Cory's murder or were there, Christopher Gromberg said NOTHING; he protected every one of you pieces of garbage. He gave NO names. Not one. Not even nicknames.)

I gave him my phone number. Chris never used it.

A few months later, he was murdered in Lake Havasu.

———

Chris was found beneath a bridge in the driver's seat of his car with two bullets in the back of his head. Forensics determined another car had pulled up next to his, so the drivers were face-to-face. Then two people had gotten *into* Chris's car, one in the passenger seat and one in the back. Crime scene photos showed ample blood in the back seat of the car; the person who shot him must have been soaked. Chris's blood had even spread across the *outside* of his car because the shooter had squeezed between the two vehicles when getting out.

I first contacted a girl in Phoenix who'd been a wannabe girlfriend of Chris's for years. She told me Chris had been excited about a concert and that two guys named "Rob" and "David" were coming to Havasu to meet him. The plan was for the three to all travel to Long Beach together for the show. He'd *also* told her in instant messages that he was scared and nervous about seeing the guys but felt it had been long enough since Cory's murder and he would be OK. Chris also told her he'd been asked to finally return to Mesa for a private meeting with the crew to discuss things but couldn't because his car was broken and wouldn't make the five-hour trip back. The night of the concert, Chris was to meet Rob and David in the parking lot by the London Bridge.

I already knew David and Rob.

David Bounds was a skinhead who'd just been arrested for an armed robbery of a TGIFridays in Lake Havasu days after Chris's murder. I got his cell phone records, which revealed his signal had bounced from Queen Creek to Lake Havasu and back again the day Chris was killed.

Rob Strong was now an active Vinlander and former Volksfront member who'd moved in and out of other supremacy groups over the years. He'd been the very guy the National Alliance and Jerry Harbin *almost* got into the police station as an employee! He and David were inseparable. With the girl's testimony, cell phone records, and a couple hours of questioning, we'd have them. Guilty, done.

We were putting all this together when I was told that the City of Mesa was not going to investigate or assist anyone in this murder case. I couldn't pursue Chris's killers.

Lake Havasu was three hours away; another city's problem, another city's time, and budget. What did it matter that one more skinhead was gone?

On top of that—and I would swear this was an even bigger reason—Mesa *already* had one notorious Hell's Angels group in town and didn't want to be known for also having a "White supremacy problem." Without an investigation, how could anyone in the press or public ever learn of a "problem"?

I was ordered to drop it. I did.

Chris, truthfully, is one of the ones who visit me in my dreams.

———

My desks at work and home were both covered in pictures of Tawni and the kids. They kept me grounded. But I also needed to know who the "bad guys" were that I was chasing, so I slowly began to put *their* photos around me as well. Over time, the bad guys on my desk began to outnumber the good until eventually, the pictures were almost all of bad guys. I'd gotten so focused on putting people away that my home life was now coming second.

SKINHEADS AFTER T-BALL

After T-ball one day, my son and I decided to get some ice cream. The ordinary outing ended in a high-speed chase with skinheads.

It was his first year playing. I'm not a huge baseball fan, but Tawni encourages opportunities for our kids to try a lot of different things. Since it was his first T-ball practice and he'd been giving it his all, I thought some celebratory ice cream made perfect sense for both of us. As we went into the store, I'd lifted him into the grocery cart. We looked kind of ridiculous, a bigger kid all in his baseball gear, sitting in the basket like he was the king of the store, but I loved it; it was a needed reprieve from the seriousness of what had been going on at work.

Walking in, I went left, looking at the bakery and cupcakes first, then made my way to the back of the store, heading for the ice cream aisle.

In front of us, every step bringing them closer, were five twenty- something neo-Nazis. Guys I knew, who knew me. It was Walmart all over again.

"Oh…shit," I unapologetically said, even as my son looked at me, shocked by my unusual language. "Listen to me, little man,"

I said. "I need you to look at the floor. Don't say a word and, no matter what happens, we'll be OK."

I felt the threat, and I'm sure I handled that all wrong. Without any context, it was probably a lot for a newly christened T-ball player to grasp. He's a pretty relaxed kid, and, completely ignoring my directions, he just kept looking around and swinging his feet with no care in the world.

By this time, I had made eye contact with one of the guys, a two-hundred-pound, stocky, big, shaved-head skin I knew, Rob Strong.

The same guy connected to the Chris Gromberg murder.

In a normal situation, I'd go up to him as Packy: *"Rob! What's up? What the hell you doing out here?"* And then I would figure out how to play it off as I went along.

But this time, I had my son.

Rob and I were now ten feet apart. With Rob was Brent, his extremely loyal side kick, a known Hammerskin, and two more guys I'd never seen or met. Just as Rob was about to say something— that whole "I know that guy from somewhere" vibe but not quite knowing how to process exactly who I was—I quickly turned down the beans, rice, and hot sauce aisle and made our way back toward the front.

As I've said before, no undercover cop does everything right all the time. I'm not proud of what happened next. Instead of walking straight out the door, I decided to try to get pictures of those new skins so I could identify them if anything went south. My phone then wasn't great, so I needed to get close enough to get a good picture. I made a quick left turn down the baking aisle, hoping to come up behind them around the cheese and liquor aisle just long enough to get a picture. They were gone.

I made my way around the store with no luck. Thinking I was in the clear, I grabbed the ice cream, paid, and headed out. It had all become so normal.

But it wasn't.

We got back into the truck and, after scanning the lot, I thought, *OK, we're good.* As I geared into reverse and looked behind me for traffic, I saw it—their white Ford Ranger. Nothing really to look at except for the five shaved heads jammed into it—all staring right back at me. My cover story had always been that Packy has no family. As I rolled back, the doors to the Ranger opened, and Rob was struggling to get out of the cab.

It was the second time my son heard me swear. "Damn it!" Forget reverse, I went straight, weaving through cars and out to the road.

Behind me, Rob had jumped back in the truck, and they quickly followed me. The chase was on.

We lived in a rural area, dirt roads, not much traffic, and no stop lights. The little Ranger was quickly gaining on me. I made a quick right turn, followed by an abrupt left, dirt and rocks bursting behind us. My son twisted to look back over the seat at what was going on.

They were still there. Another left turn, this time a little too fast. I fishtailed, even more dirt flying, and then I was back on the main road, asphalt. After the dust had gone down, still three to four car lengths behind me was that white Ranger. I must had passed our street turnoff four times, once with them behind me, but no way was I taking them down my actual street. I started thinking that now would be a good time for a show-down. *Just do your thing, Matt.* No cars around, a quick stop and deal with it, but that quickly left my mind when my son said, "Faster, Daddy. Faster!"

That was all I needed to hear. A stomp on the gas, more turns and dust…and they were gone. We'd lost them. It took me thirty more minutes to get home. Pulling over, pulling around corners, going through different neighborhoods, all to see if I was still being followed.

I finally turned down our street just as my phone rang; it was Tawni. "Hey, isn't practice over yet?"

"Yeah," I replied as I pulled into the driveway. "We should probably have a talk." I told her the broad strokes of what happened.

"Matt, what the hell?" I don't know if that was because I ran into these guys by our house or because our son exited the truck and said, "Hi, Mom. Daddy said 'shit.'" The hundred-mile-per-hour trip home from the grocery store was only second on his list of things worth talking about.

Inside the house, I finally had time to realize that these guys had been shopping at our neighborhood grocery store. They lived out by us.

I was slowly being outed—being Detective Browning for *this* case and Packy for *that* outing. *How much longer could I keep my two worlds separate?*

As we ate our half-melted ice cream in uneasy silence, I conceded to myself that bridge had already been crossed long before. And, if there were any doubts, that same bridge was soon about to be forever burned to ashes.

David's supremacy politics begin after attending a meeting of Citizens' Councils of America (sixty thousand members across the southern United States founded primarily to oppose integration of public schools) and reading pro-segregation books, which detail the belief that Black people are inferior and the races must remain separate. He is only fourteen. David joins the Klan before he graduates from high school. In college, he forms a student group called the White Youth Alliance, holds parties on Adolf Hitler's birthday, and becomes known on campus for wearing a Nazi uniform. He's arrested in New Orleans for inciting a riot during one of several racial confrontations in the city. Shortly after graduating, he creates the Louisiana-based Knights of the Ku Klux Klan and, two years later, becomes the youngest-ever grand wizard. He insists the Klan is "not anti-Black" but rather "pro-White" and "pro-Christian." He founds the National Association for the Advancement of White People and adds Holocaust denier to his calls for racial segregation. At twenty-five, he first runs for office as a Democrat, winning one-third of the vote for Louisiana State Senate. He later runs for president of the United States and collects more than forty-five thousand votes. Switching parties to Republican, David wins 46% of the vote for the U.S. Senate and, later, 39% running for state governor—narrowly missing both jobs. He runs again to join the Louisiana House of Representatives and, in a close special election, wins. He represents the state from 1989 to 1992. Three years later, his ex-wife cofounds an online bulletin board called Stormfront, which becomes the largest online White power community in the world. He lives in Moscow for five years but returns to the United States, where he still considers running for various offices and endorses various bills and politicians from Democrat Tulsi Gabbard (whom he'd deemed as anti-Israeli) to former president Donald Trump.

---

*David: "David Duke," Southern Poverty Law Center, www.splcenter.org/fighting-hate/extremist-files/individual/david-duke. .

MR. HITLER GOES TO WASHINGTON

To Serve...

JT Ready, avowed White supremacist, was now running for city council.

This man who'd passed out racist propaganda dressed in a Nazi Gestapo uniform, who'd hunted Mexican nationals on the border and organized Hitler birthday celebrations. A suspect in multiple shootings. His most public affiliations were with nefarious militia groups, like the Ready Rangers and U.S. Border Guard, or the National Socialist Movement—an actual, full-blown neo-Nazi organization.

I spent most of every day angry. Disgusted. Flattened.

JT's run for state representative had been revolting enough. But he hadn't remotely made a blip in the primaries. We thought that'd be the end of it.

This time, however, he was polling in the top two in a ten-person race. This time, he'd collected support from a state senator (Russell Pearce), an Arizona U.S. congressman (J. D. Heyworth), and several local legislators serving Mesa.

It was support he would need.

During the campaign, JT Ready fired a pistol at a Latino man in "self-defense"—the third time this had happened to Ready. But no charges were pressed; it was, instead, deemed a misdemeanor and the report wasn't clear enough to ever properly adjudicate. He'd then volunteered to act as master of ceremonies for Mesa's annual Veterans Day parade, but his Marine court-martial finally came to light publicly and he was replaced.

Yet, neither of these two events affected his polling numbers or support in the local papers. Not with the high-profile backing he had garnered.

I'd like to write something simple here like "Tawni and I couldn't believe it," but that'd be a lie. For decades, politicians have gotten into bed with White power groups and individuals for votes, funds, press, volunteers, and, sometimes actually, because of similar beliefs. Examples of this range from Southern Democrats connected to the KKK and Jim Crow laws well into the 1970s to Republicans now linked to race-based militia groups or far-right factions like America First, which are both attracting younger Republicans and supporting politicians like Paul Gosar, the *very-far-right* U.S. Representative for Arizona's 9th congressional district since 2013.

Getting elected and staying in power ain't easy, and "strange bedfellows," or even reprehensible ones, are sometimes necessary to play the political game. To that end, JT Ready's strongest supporter was Arizona state representative and president of the Senate Russell Pearce.

It can be advantageous to have one in a lower position like JT, a foot soldier, taking on some of the tougher assignments. JT Ready would later admit as much, claiming he was able to protect Pearce by becoming the outspoken, less-powerful lightning rod for their shared ideologies. "I can be the voice box," Ready said. "I can also be the bellwether to tell how much resistance we are going to get... how much will they take? How can we push the bar a little bit further? Keep him [Pearce] in the safe zone…and I take all the hits…kinda like I'm doing all the blocking…kinda a pincer strategy."[i]

Ready and Pearce were attacking decency, justice, *and* humanity from both sides.

PEARCE

Pearce had come up from deputy sheriff to chief deputy sheriff in Maricopa County, which includes just about every city you've ever heard of in Arizona. His career developed under the wing of Sheriff Joe Arpaio, the "toughest sheriff in America" who'd become nationally notorious thanks to "Tent City," which he started in 1993 as Korean-era military tents erected in the middle of the desert as a solution to overcrowding in the jails but, by 2007, had become emblematic for housing thousands of "undocumented immigrants." Sheriff Joe dubbed Tent City his "concentration camp."[ii] *This* was Senator Pearce's mentor.

After twenty years as a street cop, Pearce had retired and become a judge in Mesa for a year, then went into professional politics. His focus had always been on immigration as he pushed rhetoric about race and "illegals" on the southern border. He would later make national news after pushing through new Arizona laws that required police to question people about their immigration status if the cops had "reasonable suspicion" they were in Arizona illegally. Stop-and-frisk, Latino style. Plenty of new guests for Tent City.

Cops would be *required* to document just about every Latino we came in contact with. Racial profiling at its most vile. In Arizona, the Latino population makes up more than 30% of the demographic. It got so ridiculous that even John Meza and some of my other Latino coworkers were getting nervous about driving around the city. Unless you "looked White," you were going to be a target.

The new law, justifiably, sparked protests, boycotts, and lawsuits across the nation—as well as several copycat laws in other states. (Ultimately, three sections of the Arizona SB 1070 bill were shot down by the Supreme Court and never really took hold. And in 2016, an immigrants' rights group won a lawsuit that essentially made the bill lose whatever teeth it had left.)

Pearce also advocated bringing back a 1950s militaristic mass roundup and deportation policy for Arizona immigrants *officially* known, then, as Operation Wetback. Thanks to Pearce, a state-funded border militia had also been in the works since 2007, and one 2012 bill would have formed a three-hundred=member volunteer force, Arizona's Special Missions Unit, to guard the border.[iii] The bill was eventually shot down. But it'd gotten close. *Real* close.

Pearce's next bill was going to be an "anchor baby" bill written essentially to overturn the Fourteenth Amendment and disallow legal status to children born in the United States by non-U.S. citizens. Pearce announced it was "time to target the women" because Latino men don't "drop anchor babies."

He liked to deny being racist, cloaking his beliefs in border security policy, but there was more than enough evidence to the contrary.

For example, he'd once emailed an inflammatory article by the National Alliance to all his supports. Titled "Who Rules America? The Alien Grip on Our News and Entertainment Media Must Be Broken," it railed against the "Jews ruling the world."[iv]

The Anit Defamation League brought the letter to the media's attention, and they ran the story, but the gravity of the situation never truly sank in with the public. Pearce apologized with a standard "merely forwarded the email without fully reading it" statement, and all was forgiven or forgotten.

He'd been considered a kook until he wasn't... Now, politicians had grown afraid to cross him. It you didn't agree with him, you were a traitor or coward. He'd became a "king maker" in Arizona politics, and conservative politicians routinely sought out his endorsement.

And now he was endorsing JT Ready.

Pearce had said, "The thing I appreciate about JT is the fact that I think he's committed and a true patriot."[v]

Ready, in return, openly called Pearce a "surrogate father" who'd "enlightened him."[vi] When JT Ready was baptized into the Mormon church two years earlier, it was Senator Russell Pearce who'd proudly stood by his side. And when Pearce's twenty-something son, Josh, got new tattoos on his neck and chest, an iron eagle with a swastika, it was Ready standing by *his* side.

A TRIP TO THE STATE CAPITOL

Russell Pearce and I had met before.

But I hadn't been invited to this meeting. I'd crashed it.

A narcotics detective came into my office one morning and handed me a printout of an email he'd received. "You want to go to this?" he asked. "I have no idea why it was sent to me. I know nothing about gangs."

After reading the email, I could only see that it was a meeting with Russell Pearce in regard to GITEM—Arizona's Gang Intelligence Team Enforcement Mission. The team, established a

good decade before Pearce was a senator, consisted of law enforcement from twenty-two different agencies and cities from across
the state in a coordinated effort to better thwart street gangs.
But, following 9/11, budgets and attentions moved elsewhere and
GITEM mostly faded away. Mostly.

Now Pearce was calling the "top minds" in gang work to the
capitol for a special GITEM meeting. Since my specialty was
"White-boy" gangs, I wasn't surprised I hadn't been invited. In rec-
ompense for the slight, I figured I'd attend anyway, listen quietly in
the back of the room, and maybe get a better sense of JT Ready's
big ally and the developing language of anti-Latino rhetoric.

"Why not?" I said.

"Great," the narcotics guy said. "I'll email the guy back and tell
them you'll be coming instead of me."

What could possibly go wrong?

———

The meeting was at the state capitol building. I was directed into
a big, open reception-type area where there were already a dozen
cops I recognized from around the Valley. Terry, a Gilbert gang
detective and one of the best cops I know, was one of them.

"Do you know what this meeting is *really* about?" I asked.

She had no idea—some new gang technology for GITEM,
she thought—but, since it involved Pearce, we agreed it was going
to prove interesting. As we chatted, a professional-looking guy
came out and asked us all to come into a conference room.

It also proved to be a suit-and-tie crowd inside, and I was entirely
underdressed. Terry was clad even more casually than I was, and
another detective was just wearing a T-shirt. There was a long table

with sixteen chairs set up around it, and everyone else had already taken their seats. These guys in suits and ties were not detectives.

Across from me were the head of the U.S. Marshals office, the heads of the DEA and ATF next to him, along with Phoenix PD bosses and some other major Valley guys. A lot of biggies.

This wasn't, I now fully grasped, a meeting about new software.

Senator Pearce marched into the room with an aide. Pearce was an older, heavy guy and started with the typical "Thanks for coming, and added that we were all the "premier law enforcement in the Valley and that's why I invited you."

Well, about that, Senator... "Invited" in broad terms.

He then talked about GITEM and its importance and about how he oversaw funding for the program and was going to "make some changes." You could hear the room take a collective breath and switch fully into poker-face mode. All we could do now was listen and wait.

He began with a long rant on undocumented immigrants creating a major problem, focusing on their relation to gangs of Arizona. Then came the big announcement...

He'd added a *second* "I" into the team's objectives.

GITEM was now GIITEM, and the new extra "I" was for Immigration. The responsibilities of this special state-wide unit would now include deterring "border-related crime." He wanted GITEM to become an elite squad targeting...*undocumented immigrants.*

"So, what I want now is to get everyone's opinions on how we can make GIITEM an even better, more rounded organization. Because remember, I'm in charge of the funding... and want to make sure we use the money appropriately."

Nobody in the room responded. It'd been a monologue, and everyone was still processing the new "I."

Pearce's message was clear: If he wanted to add another "I" to GITEM, he would. Refuse, and he'd cut all funding for *all of it*. It was bullying politics at its best, and the man known for distrusting "Jews" and "Arabs" and fearing a "more Latino America" was now threatening *all* budgets to shore up law enforcement along the border.

When the conversation finally turned to the *actual* gangs, he only spoke of the Latino gangs. I took it as an opportunity to bait him.

"Mr. Pearce," I said, raising my hand, "I've worked a lot with GITEM and they *are* great... But they only work Latino gangs. Or Black gangs. If we are adding objectives to the unit, why not add a squad that specifically works White boys. You know, skinheads and vigilante militia members?"

The room went silent, except for Terry, who whispered beside me, "Oh fuck, Matt. No."

It was like watching one of those slow-motion ballistics test firings, the bullet approaching so very slowly until it finally hits the rubber block and the whole thing explodes out in every direction in a matter of frames.

"What... did you say?" the state senator, or rubber block, asked.

"A squad made for neo-Nazis and skinheads. And for those militias committing serious crimes on our border."

"'White boys' and 'neo-Nazis'? Our problems, my friend, are *not* with White boys and skinheads. Or the militias. They are with these illegals coming across and killing our officers. GIITEM is here to arrest Mexican gangs and illegal aliens." He'd already moved on.

"Excuse me, but..." I held up my hand again. "I thought GITEM was a state task force created to combat gangs. *All* gangs. A White-boy squad *would* take some very violent individuals off the street, sir."

"GIITEM is not, and never will be, the thought police," he said. "It will never investigate these so-called skinheads."

"Matt…" Terry whispered again next to me. "Maybe let's not."

I kept going. "I've worked three homicides recently," I said. "Within the same local skinhead crew, sir. These are not merely 'thought crimes.'"

"White gangs, if there are any, don't do nearly the damage illegals do."

"Again, sir. I can show you the morgue pictures of those who'd disagree. And what about the unsolved murders on the border? The militias who hunt illegals?"

"Who are you?" he asked.

"Me? I'm an Arizona detective who was invited here to share my professional opinion on our gangs." *OK, not entirely true.* "And that's what I am doing. But let's get this clear, as I've taken enough of your time. You're telling me, in front of all these people, that White gangs, in whatever form, are not a priority and never will be as long as you're a part of GIITEM?"

His response floored me. All of us, really.

"GIITEM is my baby," Pearce said.

Huh?

"And we *will* be focusing on immigration," he reminded us all. "Thank you all for coming. This meeting is over. 'I' for Immigration!" He grinned and raised a fist jocularly.

"How 'bout 'I' for idiot, Mr. Pearce?" I grumbled.

There were many smirks but dead silence throughout the room. I looked around and surveyed all the guys in suits. They had to know I was right, but I also had to admit it was probably a reckless thing to say. Pearce moved about the room and shook some hands.

"Dude…" Terry pulled on my shirt. "You'd better go." She could see I was getting mad, and it wasn't a look she'd often seen. But, at this point, I was tired of being the invisible guy who only took it all in. White crimes and vigilante crimes were "my baby" and people needed to start listening.

Clint, an officer from Phoenix, sidled over. "I totally agree with you, Matt." Then: "Good luck."

I finally decided Terry was probably right and made for the exit, but then Pearce walked up to me. "Who are you?" he asked again.

"Matt Browning. An officer who's spent a lot of time in these organizations. Undercover. And you're dead wrong about them not committing crimes. Real crimes."

Pearce moved closer, inches away, trying to intimidate me.

I wouldn't allow it. "You're no different from a lot of people, Senator Pearce," I said. "You don't look at the problem in full. You look at only what *you* want. And so, you're wrong. These White guys are *also* a real threat."

His face was beet red, spittle collecting at the sides of his mouth. His assistant stepped between us, his back to me so he was facing Pearce. "We need to go," the aide said. Terry jerked on the back of my shirt, trying to pull me away also.

All I knew was that any more of this conversation might get me into *real* trouble, so I thanked Pearce for inviting me to his "immigration meeting" and left.

Part of me had still thought politicians were middle ground, wanting the best for everyone. Russell Pearce wiped out whatever youthful naivete I'd had left. Before I'd even returned to the office, my commanding officer had already been called. I was told never to return to the capitol building again. *Ever.*

THE VIKING SON

JT Ready finished in second place, one shy of claiming the open seat on Mesa's city council.

With each political loss, JT's rhetoric grew more hostile and direct, including advocating a third U.S. political party known as "White People's Party."

That spring, he organized and led an anti-illegal-immigration group, America First, in a protest held in front of the Mexican consulate in Phoenix. There, he told *The Arizona Republic*, "We are advocating that the government of Mexico should be designated a 'threat nation' because they are openly subverting our laws and sovereignty."[vii]

Months later, Ready finally landed a spot in mainstream politics.

He won a post as GOP precinct committee person in a west Mesa district—running as the only candidate in a primary. His duties now included helping local GOP candidates with marketing efforts, organizing fundraisers, and assisting with voter registration.

During this time, Ready also distributed racist and anti-Semitic materials throughout Mesa Republican Party meetings. He also visited Omaha, Nebraska, to march beneath swastika banners beside brown-shirted members of the National Socialist Movement (NSM), a neo-Nazi group he'd soon join. In Omaha, Ready, billed as an "Arizona Republican activist," gave a speech proclaiming America was a "White, European homeland" and "That's how it should be preserved if we want to keep it clean, safe, and pure."

He'd also created an online profile, "VIKING SON," on a neo-Nazi social networking website—New Saxon, run by the NSM. VIKING SON's profile pics featured Ready wearing a kilt, bulletproof vest, and him "hunting illegals" through a pair of binoculars. His listed "turn-ons" included "a woman who loves our Race," Kultur (which is German civilization), "Heritage, History and Future." He'd listed *The Turner Diaries* as his favorite book and Prussian Blue—a neo-Nazi pop duo made up of two blond-haired, blue-eyed fourteen-year-old sisters—as his favorite band. (The girls have since renounced the movement.)

A typical post on this profile could read: "The jew [sic] itself knows it is a parasite. I have had them admit as much to me and laugh in my face… But a parasite cannot carry on in its parasitic nature if it is exposed for what it really is. Their whole house of cards comes tumbling down for all to see. Like in 1933 Germany. Just because it has two legs does not change its nature any less than a six-legged parasite stops sucking blood. There have been many pogroms when the host people stop being victims of these vampires. Another pogrom is approaching." [viii] (A pogrom is defined as the "organized massacre of a particular ethnic group, in particular that of Jewish people.")

Ready next attended the National Vanguard's Winterfest gathering in Phoenix in December replete with mead, lit swastikas, and shouts of "Valhalla" and "White power!"

At long last, Ready's actions finally bubbled up to the radar of Arizona U.S. Congressmen John Shadegg, Trent Franks, and Jeff Flake. All three beseeched the chair of Mesa's Republican Party to expel Ready immediately.

Yet Ready retained his office until his term ran out later that year.

PACKY EXPOSED

Despite warnings to keep away, I was eventually invited back to the State House. With my chief's blessings, I'd been asked to participate on a panel called "Improving the Tone of the Immigration Debate."

State Representative Kyrsten Sinema (now a U.S. senator) was then sponsoring a legislative meeting on the topic of how hate fuels violence at the border and asked me if I would lend my expertise to the discussion.

Arizona did have more than four hundred and fifty thousand undocumented immigrants at the time;[ix] there was clearly a need for real discussions and solutions, but ones decidedly less inherently prejudiced and, ultimately, more humane than what JT Ready and others like him were putting forward. It'd been more than a year since my run-in with Pearce, who'd been invited to the panel but had decided he wouldn't attend. Pity. In attendance, however, would be other state legislatures and representatives from the Anti-Defamation League.

My only goal this day was to get people to talk and think about what was going on so real changes could be made. I planned my remarks carefully and even wrote down notes, which I almost never do. Tawni got me a new tie to wear, and when my mom heard what was going on, she got invited to come along also.

It sounds a little ridiculous now: my mom tagging along, a new tie. But I was excited. Inspired by my previous encounter in the State House, I even thought I could make a difference. I'd also be back in the same building my great-grandfather and great-uncle had served in, in state/territorial legislatures. After all, I was still a fifth-generation Arizonan, still proud of our state.

When I arrived, the lawmakers were in attendance as expected. But the gallery was also open and there were close to sixty people, regular citizens, in the audience. I'd been told the meeting would be closed to the public and all media would be outside, so there was no chance I'd appear on any news shows and blow my cover. I strongly debated leaving but figured this was a rare opportunity to talk directly to many lawmakers and pushed through.

I could tell most private citizens in attendance were anti-immigration, close-the-border types. Some even had signs: "American Jobs for American People" and "Invaders Go Home," or "Return to Sender" or "Return Them Back with Birth Control." There was also a smattering of "We are ALL Immigrants" and "No Human Being Is Illegal" mixed within the signage.

I thought to myself: *I hope this will be something* I'm *proud of.* Then looking at Tawni, who smiled and gave a quick wave, I knew Matt—no matter what happened next—would be all right.

Now, Detective Browning and Packy Von Fleckenger?

Those two guys, I was soon to learn, were on borrowed time.

———

My presentation was a short talk about how hate groups and anti-government extremists were fueling the fire of hate along the border and how they'd infiltrated the border militias. Throughout the speech, I had zero political agenda. I just knew what was happening was wrong and that some violent people needed to be stopped. I discussed a few homicides and how the rhetoric and provocative language of the far right were being used as a battle cry for racist-minded individuals to harm Mexicans.

I started to—

Then everything changed. The door opened, and in walked Jerry Harbin and four other members of the National Alliance. With them was JT Ready.

It was the end of Packy Von Fleckenger.

———

All those years spent standing beside these same men, drinking a beer, folding flyers, pretending to be one of them. Now, they would know me for who I really was.

I paused, took a deep breath, and then just kept going. What else could I do? Years of undercover work had taught me to always just push through. *Just keep going and you'll figure it out.* So, I kept talking, taking questions, and doing what I was there to do: speak truth, hoping someone who could do something would finally listen.

JT stood at the back door, glaring murderously at me. His face was an angry red, his breath coming in short quick bursts. Jerry, in contrast, didn't move at all, as if he was still stunned and still trying to process it all. They both knew they'd been had. An undercover cop had worked beside them for years, had been included in their most-inner circle. Eventually, both men turned and exited back outside through the double glass doors.

We finished our panel an hour later. The crowd cleared out, many visibly unsatisfied, as if their concerns had been ignored. Others openly grumbled about the things I'd said. The legislators themselves proved more contented, excited about how well the seminar had gone and even hopeful for the future.

"How do *you* think it went, Detective?" Representative Sinema asked me.

What was I supposed to say? That I'd just ruined years of work and probably put my life at risk because I didn't know this was an open meeting? "Thank you so much for doing this," I managed. "It was great."

Tawni knew I was nervous. I didn't want people there to know we were married, so she went outside with my mom.

As I walked out, the media gathered around, but I walked right past them to my truck on the other side of the park in front of the capitol, looking behind every tree and car as I went. I made it to the truck and drove the longest, slowest cruise I could back to my office.

There, my commander was standing outside my office waiting for me. "We need to talk." He dragged me into his office.

Apparently, news of the meeting was already spreading across town. Websites, news articles, talk radio. The media attention was immediate, and it was—shockingly—focused on me. I didn't get it. I thought I was the least important person there.

But JT thrived on media attention, and journalists were quick to oblige. This militant neo-Nazi accused me of spouting my own political agenda in support of undocumented immigration and argued I'd overstepped my badge. Summarizing: *"How dare Matt Browning label American patriots concerned about our borders as domestic terrorists?!"* It was this take, *his* take, that went out to the Valley that day.

The result? Within a matter of hours, half the city was mad at me for implying *any* border activists were connected to hate groups and that Arizona had a neo-Nazi problem. I'd only spoken the truth, but it was one that didn't fit *their* narratives—so, truth be damned.

———

After work, I headed to our oldest boy's lacrosse game.

Tawni called. "You may want to turn on the radio." She gave me the channel. They'd somehow gotten audio from the meeting and taken two phrases of mine—"Arizona has the most violent, racist skinheads" and "It *is* terrorism; it's domestic terrorism"—and kept looping it like some kind of rap song with booming voices.

"It is terrorism; it's domestic terrorism…"

"It is terrorism; it's domestic terrorism…"

"Arizona has… Arizona has… Arizona has the most violent, racist skinheads."

"It is terrorism; it's domestic terrorism…"

Someone on the radio staff, maybe the host himself, had taken the time to make this. The host had completely joined in the camp of me being a Chicken Little, grossly exaggerating the existence of White pride adherents in the Valley.

Tawni called into the radio station posing as a random concerned citizen in support of me. "When was the last time you saw a cross burning on the streets of Phoenix?" the show's host challenged. "When has there been a lynching in your neighborhood?" As if these were the only two manifestations of racism. But the more the host pushed back, the more Tawni had an answer. She knew her stuff; he didn't. After their call, the announcer was flustered and, to his credit, said as much.

JT then used the power of the internet to claim that I promoted the lie that "all" border activists, constitutional study groups, tax protesters, and White Heritage Club members were "domestic terrorists." What I'd argued was that the anti-immigration movement was attracting extremists and domestic terrorists. That I'd seen it firsthand. That the movement had become a battle cry for extremists and neo-Nazis now in the ranks of the Minutemen; that the National Alliance and skinhead crews were heading to our southern border. And that such forces were "domestic terrorism."

All that day and into the next, Tawni lived online, tracking all the comments on a dozen different sites and chat boards. Newspaper articles and the comments that followed were written by regular folk, extremists, and law enforcement members alike.

Some of the hate-filled comments began to get into my head, and Tawni begged me not to even read them.

Eventually, though, she called me in to look at her computer. JT was online, openly asking people to "take Browning out to the desert" and "bury him."

I called my chief and the next morning was in his office with a stack of printed-out threats being made toward me. He already had his own stack in hand. "You're done on the street," he said. "For a while. Grab a different car, anything you need, and you can do my intel work for me directly. Can't have you getting hurt."

In a career driven largely by ego and the desire to do your job better and faster than the next person, being pulled off the road was torture. I stood, furious, and left. I needed *more* manpower, and with me out of commission, we now had less. I swapped cars and went home, wishing I had eyes in the back of my head. Awaiting the trigger man.

It never came. At least, not in the way I suspected.

The next morning, I was called back in. The chief was on the phone. He cupped the mouthpiece and said, "You have thirteen new IA complaints made today against you."

I'd never had one complaint in my entire career. "For what?"

"Overreaching your authority as a police officer."

Within the month, there were seventeen complaints filed on me and an investigation was opened for each. To his credit, the chief told me later that it was all a formality, but we had a duty to the public to be transparent and each complaint would have to be investigated completely.

For fifty-plus years, supremacy hate groups have used the legal system against itself via frivolous lawsuits, loopholes, teams of lawyers, and a thoughtful and systematic understanding of legal procedures and their "rights." It was the Sovereign Citizens play-book all over again.

The complaints against me came from the likes of an online columnist who vowed I would "pay for my participation with my blood."The rest were from people who didn't even live in Mesa. My supervisors recognized they were frivolous but were still required to take each one seriously as all of this blew over.

But if there was any hope of any of this ever blowing over, it ended with Mike.

———

Mike, a cop in a marked car and in full uniform, flipped off a bunch of Open Border protesters downtown—not once, but twice. He'd taken a stand for the Border gang and, in doing so, somehow dumped fuel on *my* little fire. Now, the two events were in some way linked, and the entire Valley was debating undocumented immigration, border issues, and police work in general.

Throughout, JT and his local buddies blasted me with an organized multipronged attack while my allies were too busy with other matters to help much.

All I really wanted to do was regroup and mourn the "death" of Packy and the undercover career I'd worked so hard to develop. I was interviewed by Internal Affairs to deal with all the complaints, waiting for them to make a decision on whether or not I had done something wrong, whether I was still a detective.

For Tawni, it was surreal. The controversy had taken over our entire life, and it was everywhere in the media. But most people in our lives didn't even know what was really happening—only that I'd "done something."

This is where it started to get genuinely dark for me.

What was the point? I thought. *No good deed goes unpunished.*

Meanwhile, the city of Mesa also suddenly decided I was "no longer able to give media interviews" because I was "making Mesa look like the White supremacist capital of the world." Their wishes trickled down through my supervisors in law enforcement.

My cover blown, pulled off the streets, I was also now muzzled.

HITLER'S BIRTHDAY

As this was all happening, I heard JT was having a "birthday party for Hitler" at a park in the far northeast valley called Usery Park. (Somehow, not all of the skinheads had yet heard that Packy turned out to be a traitor.) JT had reserved the largest camping spot in the park. With all the buzz and talk in town, I knew the party would be a gathering of all the local neo-Nazis who, like JT, wore ties, had white-collar jobs, and even worked in government. The event would prove a smorgasbord of intel.

My supervisors told me to forget about it.

They warned me to leave Ready alone. They had no interest in this gathering and, more to the point, still wanted me on the sidelines.

That wasn't going to happen. My reputation was under attack, my career endangered, all my work as a detective suddenly being brushed aside by friend and foe alike. Standing aside would have been—no exaggeration—suicide. I was humiliated and defeated. I had to do *something*.

Tawni and I decided we'd investigate this Hitler birthday ourselves, as private citizens. Forget the Mesa Police Department. Forget my commanders. Forget the law.

"Whose birthday party is this?" she asked, confused.

"Adolf Hitler," I said.

"OK, so…heels or boots?"

"Boots," I said. "Old jeans and a warm hoodie. We're going to get dirty."

She lined up a babysitter and we drove out to the park loaded with a camera, binoculars, and an extra little .25 auto for Tawni to carry. We parked a distance away and began to walk in at dusk. It was April and got cold real fast after the sun went down. As we got closer, we crawled on our elbows and bellies in the Arizona desert to get within fifty yards of the camping spot.

Torches were lit, music playing with an occasional "*Sieg heil*" being shouted across the dark desert. It was, actually, a fairly small group. Maybe fifteen people, but from all over the valley. We could smell the smoke from the fire and the burgers on the grill and could occasionally hear JT complaining *he* was in charge of the hamburgers. "Who has the buns?" he'd yell. Multiple times, he'd moved something around the trunk of his car, invited others for a look. But we couldn't get close enough to see what he was showing off.

Otherwise, it was a typical White power event. JT, now donning his White German soldier hat, gave an impromptu speech on his "hero Adolf" and ended it with "Heil to Hitler. A great White civil rights leader."

Tawni and I were filing away faces and cars. My undercover work had always been intelligence based—linking people and activities together so we'd know where to turn when we needed information. This night was no different. I knew that if JT tried to run for office again, I now had enough intelligence on him to at least let the public know what he was really about.

We were trying to keep comfortable lying on rocks, attempting to stay quiet in the bushes, only to have an enormous Arizona black beetle crawl over Tawni's leg. "Can we go do what I want to do now?" she finally asked. "What *are* you hoping to get here?"

I asked her to wait just a few more minutes. I couldn't leave just yet. But I knew she was done with being cold, bored, dirty, and crawled on by bugs.

I finally put down the binoculars. "OK, let's go," I said.

As we edged back away toward the truck, we heard them:

"Happy birthday to you!
Happy birthday to you!
Happy birthday, dear Adolf.
Happy birthday to you!"

Back at the truck, I called and let a few of my law enforcement friends know the party was happening so they could keep an eye on things if they had time, not knowing if anyone would take me up on the offer.

———

Only days later, I got intel that JT possessed illegal explosives.

Lance, an old intel partner of mine, called. "Hey, stop by when you get a chance; might have a big one." A woman source of his had been having issues with none other than JT Ready—a feud about something, she claimed to not remember what, that had escalated—and believed JT was planning on "blowing up" her car. On the night of Hitler's birthday party she'd heard that JT actually had the explosives for the job in his trunk.

It wasn't that out of question. JT often talked about putting homemade mines along the border and habitually bragged about all the explosives he had. He was also good friends with the son of

Jerry Harbin, a twentysomething who was arrested years later for having a dozen homemade grenades.

"Do you trust her?" I asked. I knew a trap wasn't out of the question.

"Very much. She's always given me solid info. And something else... Guess who got arrested after Hitler's birthday?"

I could tell from his look who it was. "You're kidding. Why did no one tell me?"

"It was done quietly. I just happened to notice it on the booking website. But one 'Jason Todd Ready' was arrested for possession of a 'street-light changer' and fictious plates." His possession of a 9-millimeter handgun went uncited but had been noted in the arrest record. Apparently, JT had a box on his dash that he was able to use to change red lights to green—obviously illegal unless you're in a firetruck. Some Department of Public Safety guy had booked JT, and his car was impounded.

"Wait," I asked. "Where's his car?"

"The tow yard in East Mesa."

"You trust your source. Let's do a warrant on his car and nail this guy."

We thought it best, given the heat surrounding JT and me, that Lance take the lead. But I took the pleasure of writing the warrant, got it signed by a judge, and had JT's car taken from the tow yard to the Mesa PD evidence garage. We took the carpet out of the trunk of the car and had it sent to the ATF for the testing of explosives residue.

In the midst of all this, JT started to call, wanting his car back. In fact, he went inflamed, incessantly calling, even arrived at the police station decked out in his suit, notified the local media, and continuously complained about *me*—somehow, he knew I was on the case—for "seizing his personal property."

Lance explained the situation to Ready and told him that as soon as we were done with his car, we would call him, and he could come and get it.

My original plan was to be standing there when he arrived.

"Matt," Lance said, talking me down, "it's not a good idea for you to return this car. Why don't you let me take care of it?"

As much as I wanted to see JT and confront him directly, I knew Lance was right. It was a smart way to distance me from the Ready/Browning shitstorm.

It didn't matter. The shitstorm was just getting started.

———

Inside, sitting at the small round table, were the chief, the city attorney, and the two assistant chiefs Lance and I had spoken with to get the car impounded. Behind them stood John Meza. He wouldn't even look at me. This wasn't good.

"Sit," Chief said, and then I was bombarded with questions for half an hour. *Why did you do the search warrant? Who approved it? Why is JT Ready making claims against the city?*

Before I could say much of anything, both assistant chiefs physically turned their chairs, so their backs were to me—just like my little sons did when they thought they were in trouble. Not even looking at me, they denied I'd told them anything about Ready— only that I was doing "a warrant." I felt like I was in *The Twilight Zone* and asked if we could call Lance to verify my version of the story. He got there quickly and confirmed everything I'd just said.

Still, we were both dismissed with the warning that I was no longer allowed to track or monitor or concern myself with JT Ready.

"Give him all his property back and close the case," my chief said.

A few days later the test results came back on JT's trunk carpet. No trace of gun powder or explosives had been found.

Why was everyone afraid of JT? Where was his power? Was it just Pearce, or did he have something more?

Later, I would hear from law enforcement and those in the White power movement that JT was an informant, a snitch for someone above my paygrade; that he was protected. There was no way else to explain how lucky he was. Always one step ahead…

I would—at the threat of my job—leave JT Ready alone.

He, however, was not yet done with me.

TOWN HALL

Weeks later, JT tried to take over a city council meeting in another effort to end my career. He claimed I'd "unlawfully seized his personal property" and that Mesa wasn't doing enough to punish me.

The Mesa City Council has their meetings open to the public for comments and gripes, and Tawni found info online that JT was planning to verbally attack me in front of the city council. He was also urging his supporters to show up and voice their complaints of how I'd overstepped my duties during the panel at the capitol.

I passed this info on to my chief, and he ordered extra security, including the SWAT team and plain-clothes intelligence officers to be there. I was ordered not to attend.

Tawni went in my place, but I made her promise not to say anything to JT or bring attention to herself. A friend of hers volunteered to go with her. The hall was filled with armed law enforcement inside and out. I stayed back at the main station, watching it all unfold on a monitor.

The formality of the meeting was boring; however, the room

chambers were filling up. Perhaps on purpose, the lengthy dialogue between the counsel was entirely about nothing but ordinances. JT stood in the back of the chambers, Jerry Harbin right beside him, along with other members of JT's organization, United for a Sovereign America, which was getting to be an enormously powerful group in town.

The meeting finally got to the community comment time. The council opened it up to the public, and there were several commenters, none having anything to do with me.

Then, the mayor adjourned the meeting, saying no one else had signed up to speak. Ready's name wasn't on "the list." He'd forgotten to sign up to make a comment. JT Ready went ballistic: "Mayor Keno! Mayor Keno!!!"

But the mayor wasn't having it—rules were rules—and JT just started yelling: "Matt Browning is corrupt and dirty! Matt Browning is a rogue cop! Fire Matt Browning!" His associates started yelling my ID number: "Nine two nine one! Nine two nine one! Fire Matt Browning!" The council told JT to calm down.

"Why the increase in security, mayor?!" JT shouted. "Just for a citizen to voice his complaint about a rogue cop?! Nine two nine one!"

It was chaos. The mayor ordered JT to be removed and he was abruptly escorted out of the building, bellowing at the council the entire time. Tawni later told me it was all she could do to not confront JT, that she'd physically had to sit on her hands while her friend talked her down.

———

When I'd graduated from academy, the veteran officers' wives invited all the new officers' wives to a meeting. In a nutshell, they warned our wives that their husbands were going to get "fucked up" mentally because of their job and that these women should make a support group to help each other. Then they passed out some cookies. Tawni couldn't believe that would ever become our life. *Not Matt, not us*, she thought. By now, she'd realized how naïve she'd been.

Cops are human. We have baggage and biases, just like in every other profession. The stressors of the job just add to what was already there, and cop culture does not entail talking things through. Any building pressure has no outlet... so it just simmers, then boils.

"Choir practices" (no clue why they're called this; just ironic tradition) were a regular occurrence. Beer was bought while the cops were on duty and iced down prior to end of shift. The squad, and others nearby, would gather at some hangar behind the station. Tailgates down, beer guzzled, and off-color jokes told. And the next day, no one talked about what was said, or felt, the night before. The violence encountered, frustrations with an imperfect justice system, the everyday pressure of not getting killed...all of that was locked away deep in the cops' minds again as they got ready for a new day.

When your stress is only relieved by your vices, Choir Practices don't suffice after a while. Beers become whiskeys; strip clubs become sex clubs.

Aside from a stint where I'd abused RipFuel to stay awake, I didn't have any of those kinds of addictions. None. I genuinely wished I *were* an alcoholic, to drink myself into oblivion each night. But I didn't even attend "choir practices," which meant I was sober whenever an after-shift call came through; I usually took the call solo because many of my fellow officers were already drunk by then.

I now envied them.

It took over eight months and a 100-page report before I was told, "You did nothing wrong." I found out with a simple phone call and called Tawni right away. But, by then, for her, it was old news, and she was more worried about me personally than any fabricated complaints.

She was right to be worried.

I was a mess. Paranoid. Indignant. Drained.

But the only thing I knew to do in response to all that was throw myself back into work.

But, how? Packy and my backdoor into the neo-Nazi and supremacist world were now gone. Maybe, though, it was for the best.

Hate had clearly moved to the borders, to the militias.

Fine. Then that's where I was going.

Alan Berg is a Chicagoan transplant with a successful talk-radio career in Denver. His contentious program is now broadcast into more than thirty states. Alan, who is Jewish, holds liberal social and political views and uses his program to openly target and mock individuals and groups who promote hatred of Black people, Jews, leftists, gay people, Latinx, and other minorities and religious groups. He specifically focuses on the beliefs of the Christian Identity movement, whose members claim Jewish people are descended from Satan. He routinely receives death threats from these groups. Returning to his Denver townhouse after a dinner date, he steps from his black Volkswagen Beetle, and gunfire erupts. He is shot twelve times and killed. The murder weapon is later traced by the FBI to The Order—a White supremacist terrorist organization connected to multiple bank robberies and murders. At the trial later, a founding member of the group admits Berg was targeted because he was "thought to be anti-White and he was Jewish." Four members of The Order, including David Lane (of the infamous fourteen words), were indicted, but only two, including Lane, were convicted—neither of homicide but instead of racketeering, conspiracy, and violating Berg's civil rights. Later, Lane said: "The only thing I have to say about Alan Berg is, regardless of who did it, he has not mouthed his hate-Whitey propaganda from his fifty-thousand-watt Zionist pulpit for quite a few years."

*Alan Berg: Stephen Singular, "Talked to Death: The talk show host made listeners deathly angry until he was taken off the air—forever," *Rolling Stone,* January 31, 1985, www.rollingstone .com/music/music-news/alan-berg-talked-to-death-71920/;   https://www.history.com/this -day-in-history/a-radio-host-is-gunned-down-for-his-controversial-views.

BORDER SONG

The Coyote

It was Saturday night in Pinal County, a rural area between Phoenix and Tucson. Quiet, dark, and even peaceful. A couple of local kids rode their bikes along the irrigation ditch when a van with a flashing blue light pulled up next to them. They assumed it was the cops, so, being kids, took off and were chased along the road and down the ditch until the van finally turned away. The kids weren't sure exactly what had just happened but were glad they'd lost them because it was "scary." Later that same night, the van was seen by multiple witnesses parked on the side of the street in the dark.

Around midnight, an old Chevy pickup glided slowly along that same irrigation ditch road. The pickup was known as a "coyote truck" and had been used countless times to move undocumented immigrants deeper into the state. This night, the pickup carried five people.

It was precisely what those in the van were waiting for. They first turned on flashing blue lights, then the headlights, and then gave chase. As the van caught up to the Chevy, its side door slid open, and three different shooters leaned out of it and began firing into the truck. AK-47, .223 and 30.06 rounds were all used. Everyone in the pickup was hit.

The driver lost control and the truck careened off the road, jumped the ditch, and finally lurched to a stop in a dirt field as the van sped back off into the night.

In the bed of the pickup lay a fourteen-year-old boy who'd made it up on foot from Mexico. He'd been struck multiple times in his legs, and one round had broken through bone, nearly cutting the leg off. Everyone else was already dead as he bled in the dark for another hour before someone discovered the truck meant to carry this kid to a more promising future.

I got this lead from the Anti-Defamation League, who'd called for help. I'd now worked closely with them many times before, and—as I was basically sidelined on my real job—I appreciated getting back in the game.

The lone survivor was not able to give an interview yet, but we'd found the kids on the bikes, and they provided a composite sketch of the "cop" they'd seen that night.

What they described was a face and a beret I was sure I'd seen before.

———

Chris Simcox had been a kindergarten teacher for thirteen years at a private school in Los Angeles and a newspaper editor with the *Tombstone Tumbleweed*. For several years now, though, he had been one of the country's most powerful border militia organizers and cofounder of the Minuteman Project and later the Minuteman Civil Defense Corps...with, yes, one JT Ready.

Appearing on CNN, Fox News, and the documentary *BORDER* (2007), Simcox brought in people from all over the United States to patrol along the border. He and his crews often drove the back desert roads between the farmlands of Queen Creek and deserts of Tucson looking to make "citizen's arrests" in the name of border security.

We also knew those "arrests" often became target practice.

The Minutemen—specifically JT Ready—were under investigation for forcibly detaining immigrants, and the FBI were finally looking into immigrants found shot to death in the desert. And it had been Simcox and the Minutemen who'd come up with the plan on the U.S.-Mexico border to start a war and who'd put the call out to neo-Nazis to help.

Still, in 2010, Simcox ran for the Senate as a Republican, dropping out only when it appeared that J. D. Hayworth (a former congressman and fellow nativist) had the best chance of unseating John McCain.

As Packy, I'd met Chris Simcox many times.

And the first time, he'd been wearing a ridiculous red beret.

He was down south at the Southern Arizona Bible College in Hereford, promoting his Minuteman stuff: border security—the Mexican "rapists and drug lords" now filling our southern towns. There'd been a dozen men around him with heavy assault rifles slung over their shoulders. He was equally surrounded by media and militia men turning in their reports from the day guarding the border.

Over the next few years, I'd seen or been around Chris Simcox a handful of other times. He had no idea who I was or what I was about and just assumed I was one of the many followers he'd managed to collect.

BORDER MILITIAS

Militias, an idea in America since the 1600s, reemerged mostly in the early 1990s with the election of President Bill Clinton and a

Democratic Party who favored bigger government *and* tougher gun-control laws. Conservatives across the U.S. feared an expanding federal government would overstep its authority. Then came Ruby Ridge ('92) and Waco ('93), as if, for many, to confirm the concerns.

By 2016, the Southern Poverty Law Center had identified as many as 165 armed militia groups within the United States.

Undercover, I'd attended meetings with Constitution Rangers, 4th Judicial District, Ranch Rescue, and Arizona Border Recon. I found myself in a web of antigovernment groups with ties to anti-immigration philosophies that, naturally, often led to genuine racist ideologies. (The KKK, for instance, started *their* own border patrol, the Klan Border Watch, as far back as 1977.)

No, it wasn't very hard to draw a direct line between a carload of skins going on a "hunting trip" in Sunnyslope to the guys driving into the desert with rifles. Hate is hate is hate, whether it wears boots and braces or camo or khakis.

However...

Tying militias directly to White pride or the supremacy movement is oversimplified, inaccurate, and, ultimately, dangerous.

Of the three main suspects in the Oklahoma City bombing, for instance, only one (McVeigh) had a genuine connection to the White pride movement. None of the Wolverines in the Michigan kidnapping plot have known connections to supremacy groups; in fact, one suspect reportedly joined because he was outraged at the killing of George Floyd and wanted to hold cops and government more accountable; another thought Trump was a tyrant.

I wish I could say there was one identifiable set group of people within these militias. But a genuine variety attend any given event. In border militia meetings, I'd stood beside a Black man talking to a Jewish guy. There were soccer dads and professionals. Bank tellers, insurance salespeople, a land surveyor who owned her own company. Latinos who'd immigrated legally, or been in the United States for generations, often attended hoping to better secure the border.

Are some of these militias attracting racists? Yes.

Do some promote White supremacy? Yes.

(Let's face it: when the Minuteman Project needed bodies on the border to start a war with Mexico, they'd called the National Alliance, known neo-Nazis.)

But most militia groups and members, in my experience, are more concerned with the influence of an expanding federal government, Second Amendment rights, and border security.

This is the same language I'd used at the capitol the day of the panel, and I understand how many were troubled, even outraged, by my professional opinion on the matter. It was not the cookie-cutter answer any "side" wanted.

But the matter is complicated.

And it's getting more muddled every day.

"I'M YOUR HUCKLEBERRY"

During one of my last encounters with the Minutemen, two years before the shooting of the immigrant pickup truck, I'd gotten word they were organizing a border watch and recruiting event in Tombstone. *Tombstone*, I marveled—*like Wyatt Earp and Doc Holiday Tombstone?* As an Arizona kid with family roots steeped in the state's history, I was both disgusted and ready to work in this old cowboy town I'd grown up hearing stories about all my life.

I made it to Tombstone just as the sun was coming

up. Thirty-odd motorhomes and more trucks than I could count were already in the parking lot and lining the streets. I looked at the plates; almost every one was from out of state, some from as far east as Michigan and New York, Florida even.

The building where the meeting was held—and the town's newspaper, *The Tombstone Tumbleweed*—was owned by Chris Simcox. I entered the small office and was greeted by a sign directing us to wait in the courtyard for "ORIENTATION." I found an empty metal chair and sat beside twenty other people, all men, ranging from forty-five to sixty-five with a few outliers. I was clearly one of the youngest there. Another dozen men soon filed in.

An older guy in his early sixties unfolded a lawn chair like he was going to watch his grandkids play soccer and sat down next to me. He wore a Hawaiian shirt, khaki shorts, and flip flops. "I thought I'd never make it," he said.

"Yeah? You come a long way?"

"Not too bad. Just from outside of Los Angeles. Thought I'd try out the new motor home I got for when I retire. In another year or two or three…" he chuckled.

"What do you do?" In law enforcement and the military, the phrase "When I retire" is code for saying "I'm a cop," so I'd already perked up.

"Oh… I'm the chief of police in a small city outside of Los Angeles." He gave the city's name, and I really couldn't believe he was there. It validated tenfold that I needed to be here and pissed me off at the same time. Not just a cop…but a chief. And, in one of the most famous areas in LA, besides Beverly Hills or Hollywood. *Are you freaking kidding me?*

"Heard of it," I said. "I have to ask, though…why do you want to be here?"

"Tired of all the Mexicans," he said simply. "Destroying my city. Sitting on their couches, throwing beer cans in the street. They *are* destroying my city. The loud Oompa Loompa music, smoking and selling marijuana instead of working real jobs..."

Just as I was about to get more info, in walked a burly man, dressed in a long-sleeve brown shirt and black military-style pants.

I pulled my ballcap down even lower and skulked down into my chair.

It was JT Ready.

Across his chest, in the ugliest holster I'd ever seen, was an old western-style revolver. In a very controlled and commanding voice he said, "Welcome, everyone. My name is Jason. If I could get everyone to look up here, we have a lot to discuss. We are having a shift change now and it's running a little long, so Chris will not be able to make it. What we are doing here is protecting our country from illegals, drug cartels, and gangs. This is a non-confrontation deployment where all firearms should be kept in your vehicles or not brought in at all." All of this was said as he tapped the revolver strapped to his stomach.

"We are to only find the illegals and report them." *Tap tap tap* on his gun.

"If you see something, first call Border Patrol..." *Tap tap tap* on his gun. "Then, call the Minuteman hotline..." *Tap tap tap.*

"Now..." He surveyed the room as I dipped my head. "What we need is to have everyone fill out this paperwork, so we can get you to work."

All I could think was (a) how to get out of Tombstone as quickly as possible (b) what I would give for a copy of all those papers being turned in. If JT hadn't been there, I probably could've been honest with my paperwork and said I was a cop, fast-tracking me up the militia hierarchy ladder.

"Good luck out there," my new chief-of-police friend from California said to me. "Stay safe."

Driving to my own assigned post, I passed my new friend and his motor home, parked along the border wall, only about thirty yards away from Mexico with the same chair, same flip flops, binoculars, and a shiny new AR-15 across his lap.

Another there had on his brown BDU (battle dress uniform) pants, a load-bearing vest on that read "SHERIFF" with the actual county sheriff's badge, standing guard over Mexico with *his* AR. Off-duty, that is simply not allowed.

I did my "shift" long enough to not attract attention and then started my way back home, probably a good three-hour drive after a quick drive along the border for some much-needed recon.

Some of the darkest country you'll ever see is along the southern border, absolutely no light anywhere except the headlights on my truck. I crept down the border road, the tall fence to my left, and open desert to my right. As I made my way down the road, my attention went from the left to the right. *What in the world are all those red bugs flying around?* Almost like fireflies. But they were red.

I drove down into a dry riverbed then up the other side and, as my headlights pointed up and then back down, for just a brief moment, I could see what it was. It wasn't some weird southern Arizona bug.

There were people hiding, posted, all along the U.S. side. Sitting in chairs, waiting in the dark, wearing night-vision goggles. The red dots were the laser sights of rifles being pointed at the windshield and windows of my truck.

Did these people assume my truck was carrying drugs or "illegals?" And what would happen if it actually was?

Miles and miles of red dots.

I couldn't get out of there soon enough.

———

The deserts of Arizona, Texas, and New Mexico are littered with bodies.

Thousands of unsolved deaths. And they're not just from exposure or lack of water. And not from cartel coyotes who "changed their minds" on the U.S. side.

They're from American vigilantes stalking the border. Men like Chris Simcox.

And we had him. Simcox and his Minuteman Project were done. We had multiple eyewitnesses, including a survivor of the attack. All we had to do was wait and interview the teen, the only surviving victim.

It never happened.

The boy was deported—both his legs in casts—back to Mexico before a complete interview was able to be done. *How does that even make sense? Why were we letting this happen?* This was a real crime. It was murder.

Whatever your stance on immigration, there is no place in the world for such injustice and inhumanity.

The case was closed. Five murders forgotten.

VIOLENT OFFENDERS

With my chief's blessing, I was excited to form and direct a Major Felon Squad within the Mesa PD. Tawni and I wrote the

proposal together. It was everything I wanted to do as an officer. We went after fugitives, parole violators and gangsters, and
did surveillance on homicides. We set it up, so it encompassed
White supremacist and border groups as well. (Now renamed
the Violent Crimes Unit, it's still the most coveted and successful
squad on the Mesa PD.)

It was a perfect opportunity to rebuild my career, forget about
the past some, and maybe even get my head back together a little bit.

This squad had been up and running for a few months when, out
of nowhere, I was suddenly informed I needed to pass the sergeant's
test to lead it. The timing was...*curious*. Apparently, I was still very
much in the doghouse. I'd never been interested in this badge—I'd
wanted to work, not supervise other officers—but, if this was what
was required to head the unit we'd created, I was willing to play ball.

With help from Tawni, I studied for weeks, passed the test,
and was excited to get back to work. In the end, however, they
wound up giving the Major Felon Squad to a guy who had "more
supervisory time"—a guy I'd helped train. In consolation, the city
offered me sergeant of graveyard shifts, or of late swings to help
build up my "supervisory time."

It was a job for young sergeants and guys being nudged out
the door. And I wasn't young anymore. I'd built the Major Felon
Squad from scratch and was by now a nationally recognized expert
in hate gangs and militias. But driving around during the night
shift was now being presented as my best career path.

I rationalized that taking the shift meant I could still see my
kids before and after school and go to their games. And I also knew
that some of the White supremacist guys lived out east, which this
assignment covered, so I felt I could keep an eye on them. I started
my new job.

On the outside, I was "great." An A+ employee trying to work himself out of the doghouse. I'd complete my paperwork quickly and hit the street. I was teaching my guys about skinheads, about reading tattoos and runic writing. Teaching them who the militia guys were and where they liked to hunt.

However, moving to graves proved to be the beginning of the end.

These shifts are not for older guys—which I was (at least by law enforcement standards—it's a young man's game) by this point. You end up running on no sleep and it starts to mess with you. I was just now getting past the Internal Affairs complaints and public attacks from JT Ready, and driving around alone at night became disconcerting. For the first time in my whole career, I wasn't the relentless guy looking for action. As best I could, I just trained my guys, bided my time, and collected a paycheck. I became more isolated on my shifts, and my fuse was getting shorter. I knew to keep away from other people.

If I didn't, there was no telling what might happen.

———

One night I rolled up on a stop my guys had done. Four of them were struggling to get one guy out of the car. As I stepped out of my car, one said, "Hey, Sergeant, I think this guy may be one of your White boys. Wanna give him a look?" I walked to the stopped car but didn't recognize him.

"Get out of the car, please," I said.

"Fuck you," the driver said. "I don't have to do shit for you."

That's all I needed and said some things that caused my guys to stop in their tracks. The guy stepped out. He had a shaved head and wore black shorts, no shirt, and Doc Marten boots with red laces. "Who the fuck are you to talk to me like that?" I bombarded him with questions. "Do you know who I am?"

"When did you get out?"

"Who do you run with?"

The guy puffed up his swastika-tattooed chest. We were now standing nose to nose, and I braced myself for the first blow. My patrol guys stared on, in shock. "You're Browning, aren't you?" the skinhead said.

"Yeah," I replied. "I am. What's it to you?"

"It's nothing to me... Except that *they* have paper on you."

I glared at him. "Who ordered the hit?"

He didn't answer.

"Well, here I am. You want to carry it out...or try to?"

The guy shook his shaved head. "What *they* want, *they* want." He held eye contact. "Not my thing, man. I'm done with all that... I just want out."

After his claim, we began talking more like human beings, but he refused to tell me who had green-lighted me. I took a picture of him, and he got back into his car and left. I turned and looked at the younger officers. "If you do your job right and put these guys away, this may happen. Someone may put a hit on you. This is the fifth one I know about."

I got back in my car and pulled away. I'd played the big, tough supervisor that night, a part I knew well, but later, as I sat alone in my car, anxiety crept in. It was the fifth such claim I'd heard, but it was the first one I was worried about. I stared at the guy's photo and thought, *Who put out the hit?* JT, obviously, was my top candidate. Would Jerry Harbin dare? Chris Whitley, David Bounds, Josh Fielder, Sammy Compton, anyone of the Unit 88 skins, Brian Wallace, Toby Gaspard, the recruit who had been fired and came to the house—there were so many. I had been undercover for so long and met so many people. Take your pick.

My mind started to go. It told me nobody could be trusted. Even my brothers in blue would give me up if it helped their careers. I grew increasingly more paranoid and anxious every hour, every night.

A "paper" on me? Someone wanted me dead. It was kind of… amusing.

I, myself, had already started figuring out ways to take Matt Browning out.

———

From two until four in the morning is the worst part of a graveyard shift. No one is on the street; the bad guys have gone to bed or aren't up yet. It's very lonely, dark, and isolating. Too much time to think if many of your thoughts are dark. I had those.

Some nights, I sat in my car thinking about putting my gun in my mouth. It'd been building for months, years. Always looking over my shoulder, the hate, the bureaucracy, the hopelessness, the questions… the *whys*? Why am I doing this—just to be kicked in the nuts and pushed back ten steps for every step forward?

JT's campaign had worked. My undercover role as "Packy" was blown; my bosses were pushing me more and more to the sidelines. *Why?* I was a wreck. And each day, I looked at Tawni and lied that everything was fine.

She knew better.

Weeks earlier, I'd assisted on a call involving an intoxicated Native American, and images of skinhead boot parties and beatings kept flashing through my mind. I'd wanted to beat the guy and leave him in the street, drive away just like the crews I'd worked had done. I was filled with rage, with the desire to hurt…someone. Did the fact that this man was Native American have any effect on that impulse?

The imaginary wall between cop and White supremacist had finally fractured. I didn't even know the man I had become. This wasn't me. I wasn't me. I'd become everything I hated: Prejudiced. Filled with hate. A bully.

Everything I had fought so hard against.

What chance did a twenty-year-old with a fraction of my advantages have? Good childhood, great marriage, a kindly religious upbringing, a meaningful career. Even with all that, over fifteen years undercover, all that hate and anger and resentment had finally broken every levee I'd carried into undercover work.

How much of a monster had I truly become? Nietzsche's warning about those who "fight monsters" was right, and I wanted out.

But if I was going to go out, I wanted to go out a hero. Suicide doesn't bring that, and cops who just walk away are forgotten. So is their work. If I died in the line of duty, I'd become a martyr. I'd receive a policeman's funeral with thousands from around the nation, even the world, attending. "Death at work" started to seem like the best way out. My family would be taken care of. My kids would go through life thinking their dad was a hero, not knowing my job had ultimately messed me up.

I'd begun looking for a transient to shoot me. I cruised around on my shifts, trying to find someone who was hyped up enough on drugs to do the job. I looked for cameras on buildings, people sleeping nearby, anything that could be a witness to me negotiating my death. The plan: I'd be sitting in my car with my backup gun on my dash. A transient guy would walk up, get the gun through the open window, and shoot me in my head. Then he'd take the gun and the $200 cash from my front pocket and leave me for dead.

It was a good plan.

But I was transferred out of graves before I found my guy.

I'd been reassigned back into a Gang Unit; I had regular hours and work I was used to. I lived for my team, had their backs. They were learning quickly how to be solid, aggressive, and fair cops—everything we needed then and today. I found some gratification in that. But I was in a constant struggle with my new commander. Our unit had the most field interviews of any city in the state, yet we weren't arresting enough people. I was lucid enough again to stop actively looking for a late-night executioner, but I remained a broken cop with a short fuse.

It was only a matter of time…

—

I've always hated bikers.

The lifestyle, the lack of decency they show to anyone. The bike gangs, I mean, not your weekend road warriors.

The Hell's Angels are the biker club who rule Mesa. JT Ready notoriously asked for, and got, their support when he ran for office, which probably made me despise them more.

One night, I drove through the parking lot of a bar riddled with them. As I passed, someone yelled, "Fuck you, pig!" and continued, "That's right! Keep driving before I rip your head off and piss down your neck."

I stopped my car, got out, and walked toward the three-foot fence that surrounded the bar deck. There were forty-plus bikers on the other side of that fence. This was my chance. I got out to provoke the biker gang and, I genuinely hoped, to die in the effort.

"Which one of you wants to 'rip my head off?!'" I asked.

No one answered.

I started shouting. Lots of words and taunts you'd maybe expect. "Cowards" is the only one I'll share now. I'd found my triggerman—forty of them. All they had to do was take the bait. Matt Browning, cop hero.

A Gang Unit partner, Dwight, arrived on scene. "I think we should go before we both get killed," he said. I didn't agree. He pulled me back to my car as I yelled to the Angels, "You have *ten minutes* for the bitch who said it to come forward so I can deal with him! Ten minutes!"

The ten minutes passed, and the Angels all vanished. I didn't feel anything.

I went home, walked into the kitchen, and looked at my wife. I can't imagine what she saw in my face. I told Tawni what'd happened.

"You're done," she said. "Or I am."

I was done. I never went to work as a cop again.

———

After the biker incident, I took a long vacation.

First, Tawni and I went to a local hotel and talked and decompressed for a full week. I then requested a second week off and was told to take "as much time as I needed." I did and burned through all of my remaining vacation and sick time. Eventually, I got the calls and letters informing me I was close to being fired because I was abandoning my duties.

I'd checked myself into an outpatient facility and was diagnosed with extreme PTSD. Even writing it, I know how it might sound. We've come a long way, but I know some of you just thought, "Boohoo, Matt... People have been through or seen much worse." I know. If you think your disapproval of me is any worse than my own was...you're very mistaken. Like so many, I had been taught to "cowboy up" since birth. My entire career as a cop was based on showing aggressiveness and bravado and always moving on to the next case. And in my own defense, there was much more I saw and did than can be written in a single book. Still, I struggle with how it went down. But it is what it is. Everything pushed down and put in a box—I now know there is a much better way.

But now I was looking for someone to kill me.

The retirement board wanted a second opinion and sent me to a city-approved doctor. My new shrink met me in his reception area. He wore a wrinkled shirt, rehearsed smile...and a yarmulke, the caps worn by Jewish men.

I tensed. Paranoia and anger filling my whole body.

Throughout my life, I'd been friends with, or worked beside, Latino, Black, and Jewish people and never once thought of them as a "threat" or "inferior" or... But now, as I looked at this doctor, everything I'd heard from my White supremacist "brothers" for more than a decade flooded my whole mind: *The Jews own the banks; they own the media; they start the wars; they want to control the world...to control everything."*

It's unthinkable from the place I sit now to even admit or write that, but back then I knew in my heart this particular "Jew" now wanted to control *my* life, my retirement, my family, and that he'd protect "his" government, by working against me, lying in his reports. I'd totally gone into "fight mode"…figuring out ways to overcome *his* bias and lies. I saw his lips moving, but all I could hear was ringing in my ears. I shook my head. *What is going on?*

"Mr. Browning…Mr. Browning, can I help you?"

These words jolted me. Finally cut through…

"Can I help you?"

I now stared at him, his eyes sincere, his voice concerned. Fortunately, the "real" Matt somehow pushed through then. I nodded.

"Yeah," I said. "I need help."

It took time, but I got the help I needed. I was also now officially retired.

And, apparently, my work fighting White supremacy was only just getting started.

The Aryan Republican Army (ARA) has been nicknamed "The Midwest Bank bandits" by the FBI and law enforcement and has robbed twenty-two banks in the Midwest in just two years. The money is being gathered to support the White supremacy movement and to stockpile weapons and ammunition to help start a race war. The group was founded by two friends from high school in a Maryland suburb of DC. After filming and producing right-wing propaganda videos, the group grew and recruited bank robber affiliates to increase funding. The group begins to fall apart quickly as members are arrested when former members become informants as part of various plea bargains. One is arrested in Cincinnati after a two-hour chase by Bureau agents. Another is arrested after a siege and fifty-round shootout in Columbus, Ohio. Later, several witnesses and accounts have linked the group to the Oklahoma City bombing. Multiple witnesses claim ARA members met with McVeigh days prior to the terrorist attack and, still others, that McVeigh participated in several of the bank robberies.

*ARA: Richard Lei, "The Saga of Pretty Boy Pedro," *The Washington Post*, February 13, 1997, https://www.washingtonpost.com/archive/lifestyle/1997/02/13/the-saga-of-pretty-boy -pedro/32910dec-daf8–4f75-b6f3–14a27910885b/; John Solomon, "FBI Tied McVeigh to Supremacist Plotters," February 13, 2003, https://www.seattlepi.com/national/article /FBI-tied-McVeigh-to-supremacist-plotters-1107464.php; Declaration of David Hammer and Paul Hammer, filed in United States District Court for the District of Utah by attorney Jesse Trentadue on February 16, 2007.

SMALL WORLD

SIN

As early as 2002, I thought it'd be a great idea to share the information I'd gathered on hate groups with the other "Matt Brownings" out there. Those men and women in other cities and agencies working White gangs usually only part-time and with limited resources. And there were no formal communication lines connecting us all.

Tawni and I founded the Skinhead Intelligence Network (SIN) in 2005 so law enforcement and analysts could talk freely and share all we knew, sans politics or jurisdictional concerns. It began with some emails and phone calls to contacts I'd already made across the state and country, from local sheriffs to agents in the FBI.

Our first meeting had been only six people. By the time I retired, we were up to forty-five official "expert" members. We kept the group small on purpose to only include those who'd been vetted extensively for their knowledge and expertise. The group began holding national conferences and was directly responsible for putting dozens of people in jail.

We'd also begun speaking with members in Canada, the UK, Germany, Australia, Spain, and the Netherlands. Now, if a White power hate band was traveling from New York to Sydney, I could call my SIN contact in Sydney, who then called their border security folk. Within minutes of landing, the band would be detained at the airport and sent back to the United States on the next flight.

I was off the streets, but—after eighteen years in the business—I still had intel resources across the country. Information still came in daily.

Much of it, in these years, came directly from Tawni, who'd never stopped working her own sources and her own computer investigations. She'd learned to look for intel in photographs, and come to understand that what was in the forefront was rarely as important as what was *behind* the photo's subjects. More important, Tawni had built her own connections. And she'd done it *her* way, always looking at the people as people... not just sources (as I still, admittedly, did).

They'd responded overwhelmingly. Leads and material kept coming in.

Her work was about to open a whole new world for us, and an eye-opener for law enforcement and politicians across, literally, the entire world.

VOLKSFRONT

Volksfront was one of the most active, violent skinhead crews in the world. It'd been formed in prison in 1994, while founder Randall Lee Krager was serving two years for putting an African American man into a coma. Krager maintained, "It ain't that I'm that cold blooded. It's just I look at a little White girl and I look at a, you know, a baby Black or whatever and I'm like...there's no comparison. If there's *any* threat to the White, we'll kill the fucking Blacks... I don't like what I do really, you know, I just do it because it's what's right."[i]

Not surprisingly, then, his group was known for highly visible violence as they expanded. And expand they had. Volksfront now had at least seventeen U.S.-based chapters and also chapters in Australia, England, Germany, Portugal, Slovakia, and Spain, with probationary chapters in Canada, and with members in Croatia, Italy, the Netherlands, Poland, and Scotland.

During this growth, Krager had methodically rebranded his organization. Positioning Volksfront as the pro-America champion of the working-class White man, an organization that offered an alternative for those supremacists who wanted to be amongst skinheads and the White power movement but who *also* wanted to strive for more than being the garden-variety, tattooed, beer-soaked hooligan. Krager now openly made fun of the "Nazi idiots" who recited the 88 Precepts and "meaningless slogans," and those who "glorified Hitler" and wore flight jackets that "look like Third Reich Christmas trees." In some ways, it *did* make his outfit that much more dangerous.

In an email we got from a source, Krager argues: *"I'm not a goddamn 'neo-Nazi' any more than you are, dude. I'm a patriotic American, a proud member of the working-class, and simply a guy who has the balls to stand against the social, cultural, and biological destruction of his Folk. I don't want to see our people and the country we've built disappear, man. That's it! Is it wrong or 'hatred' to think that White people should have the right to defend and celebrate their racial identity in the same ways that Blacks and Hispanics do?"*

VF's new course was to sweep aside the old skinhead clichés in favor of a more palatable narrative—"Nationalists" instead of neo-Nazis. "Proud" of their White heritage as opposed to claiming it made them superior. And, at the time, VF was doing a fairly respectable job of it, attracting more-educated millennials *and* members of the armed forces.

But it was all still there. That toned-down façade was just that: a façade. Some of the most guttural human beings I've ever met (which says a lot considering the years I worked the streets) were in the ranks of VF.

I'd started teaching about Volksfront in 2003 to anyone who would listen—gathering names, crimes, pictures, and addresses. I knew they were going to be a problem for the Valley if law enforcement didn't strike fast and first.

Chased out of the U.S. Northwest following a murder case, they'd been moving steadily east into Arizona and other states. By this time, I had "brothers" inside VF all over the country. I'd attended the most recent Hammerfest vicariously via photos and reports days after, as I'd been outed in the months prior. Tawni had a source there as well. She received a lot of pictures I was later able to show at a Domestic Terrorism Conference in Spokane to the amazement of my peers there since the event had only happened days before.

VF had been on her radar for months now, primarily because it'd been a local Volksfront member who'd followed me and our son home from the grocery store that day years ago. Protecting home base was still a driving purpose of Tawni's ongoing involvement.

Also, Volksfront's open-ended war with the Hammerskins had recently escalated and taken center stage of the White supremacy world.

This would prove a terrific opportunity for us both.

———

Though VF and the Hammerskins had been friendly just the year before, small disagreements had grown into an ongoing conflict.

What had truly started as a dispute of words between the

Portuguese Hammerskin Nation and Portuguese Volksfront jumped quickly to Spain and then across the United States, England, Canada, Germany, and Australia. Other groups such as the American Front and C18 allied with VF or HSN to join the fight. All of this played out in various home invasions, stabbings, and beatings with baseball bats. In Florida, one VF member was jumped by a Hammerskin in the lobby of a hotel where David Irving, an English author and Holocaust denier, was speaking; the VF member pulled a knife and stabbed multiple Hammers. Police arrived, transporting the injured to hospitals; no arrests were made.

What White power problem?

The ongoing battles between these two groups proved to be fantastic for intel. Members on all sides were bragging, tattling on others, and also quitting these clubs, ready to share on the way out about all "those who'd done them wrong." People were pissed off and ready to talk, and that's always the best time to get info. It was a movable feast of information.

Tawni and I worked sources separately and then compared notes, vetting what we'd learned. There were stories these guys would tell her (as one of her online or in-person personas) and things they'd tell me.

We were busy putting together the stories, timelines, and international organization link charts, and what these guys were actually getting away with in the States and abroad. VF's reach was deeper than we had ever known. *Which of the VF guys in Kansas City is a firearms dealer? Which member is a TSA airport security screener? Who, in Australia, funded the latest operation in Florida?*

It was like tugging at a loose string, or maybe finding the right puzzle piece that revealed where two more pieces went, which revealed where...and so on. Exponentially growing more every week. For more than two years, we interviewed, listened, discovered, and ultimately even untangled a knotty, ongoing chronicle of Volksfront and Hammerskin members spread across multiple countries and dozens of criminal accusations and operations.

It was truly an international hate group.

We took it as far as we could and then went to some trusted associates at the Southern Poverty Law Center (SPLC) to ask if they'd be interested in helping fund some things. They were floored by the intel we had, including the names and locations, the funding and leadership trails. But the SPLC only wanted to focus on the United States, jurisdictional concerns weighing in again. (To be clear, however, the SPLC was great throughout and helped us in many other ways.)

Still, we passed all of this along quietly where we could and continued to acquire more as we did. If they traveled, law enforcement was there first. If there was to be some type of altercation, we had police there first to stop it. More than ever, my focus changed from the relentless, reactionary police work that I'd always hated—waiting for a crime to be committed or believing that a case was *only* successful if everyone goes to jail instead of *preventing* crimes.

We put together our presentation, got it down to one hundred slides, and presented it all at our next SIN conference.

———

We'd brought in investigators from across the U.S., Canada, the UK, and Australia. Tawni had been at the conference two years earlier and stayed in the background as an organizer. Today, she was in the forefront. She'd been so entrenched in the investigation, there were times I just stopped talking and she took over the presentation. I beamed knowing law enforcement and the confused look on their faces. They were surprised, impressed, *and* a little annoyed that Tawni was holding her own among these seasoned investigators and experts.

"You two *have* to come over and give this presentation to Scotland Yard," one of the UK detectives said. "As far as we knew, we didn't have an issue with Volksfront in the UK." His cohort added, "No, this goes beyond the UK." They were unassuming and matter-of-fact with the new realities. VF was an "American crew," so it made sense UK law enforcement didn't know the group was present in the UK at the level they were. These two were *great* cops; they just didn't know about VF's reach. They were just like me the first time I'd visited The Nile and met the National Alliance—waking up to a problem that had been right in front of me all along.

We got the call a few weeks later. We were headed to teach at Scotland Yard. I was excited to be able to teach one of the oldest police agencies in the world and to tell them what was going on in their own back yard.

Tawni and I waited for the trip, excited about what the new year might bring. Excited for the future.

We were not, however, yet done with the past.

———

The product of an extramarital tryst, Jason had been adopted by his grandfather and passed around to other family members throughout his childhood. At fifteen, he made his way back to his mother only to be abused by her new husband. A teenager, Jason is now known by family and friends as a "hot head," and one night, he chases after a fellow student in his car and runs the other teen's car off the road, then attacks the car and student with a baseball bat. He is arrested, but when his parole sentence is completed, he enlists in the U.S. Marine Corps with the publicly stated goal of wanting to "kill some Arabs." Jason is quickly dismissed from the elite Reconnaissance Company, and as the rest of his company boards the USS *Anchorage* for a tour overseas, he is left behind to tend a bad knee and his ballooning weight. Jason is court-martialed twice (for going AWOL and stealing), demoted back to private, and imprisoned by the Marines for three months. Following the second court martial, he is discharged. Now a trained killer, if even an insubordinate one, he is loose again on our streets and soon finds work and purpose as a telephone fundraiser for Christian and pro-life groups. Jason shoots a Mexican American "in self-defense" and is exonerated. He begins attending the local community college and becomes the new president of his college's Republican Club. He eventually joins, organizes, and founds multiple border militia groups and runs for public office multiple times—winning a position with the local Republican party. He gets in an argument with his Latino girlfriend and kills her with a 9-millimeter handgun. He also shoots and kills his girlfriend's daughter (twenty-three), her daughter's fiancé (a twenty-four-year-old Afghan vet), and her granddaughter (fifteen months). He then shoots himself. After the murders, authorities search his home and find AR-15-style rifles, two dozen military ordnance/40-millimeter grenades, Nazi flags, and police and Nazi uniforms.

———

JT Ready was dead.

For years, I'd told anyone who'd listen—and even those who wouldn't—this guy was a dangerous killer. What good had it done?

All the abuses and frustrations and injustices came to mind.

Tawni and I were at a little locally owned and grown nursery that we frequent, laughing and goofing off and looking at plants. It was one of those days when it seemed all was going well in the world. Then my phone rang. It was a number I recognized, Mesa Police Department. Feeling my nerves and anxiety starting, I answered the call. I knew something was up.

"Hey, Matt. It's Kevin." Kevin was the homicide sergeant in Mesa at the time, a good friend, and a great cop. I'd helped train him in patrol. We'd worked Gangs together and on the Major Felon Squad, and we've been friends for over twenty years.

"It's about JT Ready..." he said.

"What now?" I asked.

"He's dead."

I said nothing.

"Apparently, he killed everyone at his house, including a baby. Just thought you'd like to know. Anyhow, unless you want to chase a ghost, you can stop with JT Ready."

Neither one of us was much for small talk. I'm sure I asked a few questions, but it was a brief call. I hung up, kind of in shock. Tawni turned and saw I looked odd. "What's going on?" she asked. I told her what I knew, and her face dropped. "We should go home..."

"Nah," I said. "Just give me a moment."

But within five minutes, my phone was inundated with calls

from law enforcement and different people wanting to know what I knew, my thoughts, or if they could give my name to comment. The news hadn't even hit the media yet. I called some of the civilian agencies I'd worked with, letting them hear it from me first, and then I stopped taking calls altogether.

I really didn't know what to say. I was angry and devastated for the family, but I think most of all, I was confused. I got home and walked into the office and made a call; it was the same old phone number I'd been assigned while on the FBI Joint Terrorist Task Force. It now belonged to the guy who'd taken my place. I'd warned these guys over and over...

I could hardly speak. "Timmy," I said, "these murders are on *your* heads, not mine. I *told* you guys, I *warned* you...I pleaded." I was caught somewhere between being overcome with emotion and feeling rage and I think Timmy knew it, because he didn't even try to reply. "This family is on your guys' head, whether or not he was working with you. I told you he was bad news, that he was hurting immigrants and would kill again. I just didn't think it would be this..."

"Come on, Matt," he finally responded. "You can't put this thing on us."

"I just did," I said. "You knew."

I hung up, held Tawni, and wept.

I still believe, and always will, that JT Ready was an informant for a federal agency, either the ATF or FBI.

Honestly, there is no other way in this world a person could get away with all he did and not work for a federal agency. Three days later, the FBI claimed it had been in the midst of conducting a domestic terrorism investigation on JT *before* he killed that family. But if that was true, why did federal prosecutors decline to bring charges against him even when they had more than enough to do so? Why did the ATF refuse to pursue my leads, even when they were seemingly excited and invested to do so?

The call didn't make me feel any better, but at least I had said my piece.

Russell Pearce and the Minuteman Project wouldn't acknowledge they'd ever associated with JT. But his latest militia, the U.S. Border Guard, plastered the news on their website: "We lament the untimely death of JT Ready." And a local veterans' newspaper reported that JT and his family had been killed by two carloads of Narco Terrorists, that "all news stories in the mainstream media were false"—that JT was actually, in fact, a "National Hero."[ii]

Nobody claimed JT's body for weeks. All his time put into hate, all his time put into politics left him dead and alone in an ice box in Phoenix, with no one to claim him. His grandmother did finally come forward and buried him in an unknown location.

JT's death haunted me.

He was the one guy in my career whom I was not able to put into jail. The one I'd tracked relentlessly, even on my own time, but was still unable to nab. *Why?* I was struck with the helplessness of knowing I might have saved an entire family if I'd done something more.

JT Ready was finally gone. I still, to this day, fight thoughts about all he did, making it hard to move on with my own journey.

But I had to. How exactly, I yet had no idea.

Fortunately, there was a plane heading to England.

ENGLAND

The UK has been battling White supremacy groups for over one hundred years: Blood & Honour, National Front, British National

Party, Combat 18, Order of Nine Angels, Patriotic Alternative, the Sonnenkrieg Division... Volksfront was merely the newest addition and not one they'd yet truly noticed.

We met with a group from Scotland Yard, the U.S. FBI legal attaché or legat, Europol, Holland Interpol, and others. To their credit, they hung on our every word.

We showed them how Kirk Barker, the leader of VF UK, was building an empire separate from—and even more ambitious than—the original American group. Barker is one of England's oldest known skinheads, whose reputation had landed him a gig as security chief for the Blood & Honour crew and its leaders. He'd also been a member of the ultraright British National Party (BNP) and one of those first arrested during London's infamous Battle of Waterloo in 1992, a major riot at the Waterloo train station between the neo-Nazis and antifascists.

Now, years later, he was using the UK as home base for the founding of a worldwide unified Volksfront—one separate from the squalling VFers in America. To do so, he'd opened direct lines of communication with the other chapters and members in Spain, Germany, Australia, and Portugal and the newly established prospective Slovakian and Polish chapters. Their main focus had become increasing means of money and staying involved in punk and oi gigs, because as Barker stressed to our sources, "That's where the youngsters are."

In Europe and the UK, VF was tight with other organizations including the Racial Volunteer Force (RVF) and the British Movement (BM). The RVF is a militaristic organization that openly endorses the notion of armed conflict with "the establishment," touting the importance of firearms training and admiration for the Russian nationalists because of their emphasis on combat and survivalist training. And the British Movement is the largest and most powerful White nationalist entity in the UK—a network of "semi-autonomous units" engaged primarily in the production of nationalist literature (both hard copy and online) and a presence at various nationalist functions via public marches and demonstrations.

Scotland Yard proved the most genial, most interested cops we've yet been able to work with. We were treated "smashingly" and given the royal treatment, so very grateful for the years' worth of information in an afternoon. There was zero ego. Only *"Let's get it done"* and *"Thanks for bringing this to our attention* and *How are we going to combat this?"*

"How about a visit to the Smugglers Inn?" I asked.

———

Nestled in the small seaside town of Minehead, north of Cornwall—where Jesus supposedly stayed, according to Aryan fable—is the Smugglers Inn, a three-story, four-hundred-year-old pub owned and operated by Simon Curtis.

Curtis is a weathered Englishman with a large scar on the right side of his face who'd recently leased his property to Afghans Heroes, a nonprofit formed in 2009 by Denise Harris, who'd lost her soldier son in the war; in 2012, its focus had changed from providing care packages to halfway houses to rehousing and reassimilating British solders suffering from PTSD.

Afghan Heroes planned ten or twelve "retreats for solders." Curtis's place was the second. There were five bedrooms over the tavern and an adjoining cottage. Wristbands were sold to help raise awareness and money for the retreat (Prince Harry was photographed wearing one), and there was even a Charity Single Song by Tony Christie and the Band of Her Majesty's Royal Marines called "Steal the Sun." A member of Parliament, Dr. Liam Fox MP was a trustee, and Afghan Heroes had support from the highest reaches in the UK military.

No one seemed to realize Simon Curtis was a full-patched member of Volksfront UK, one with a leadership position. In fact, he was their "Sergeant in Arms"—which meant he was basically a bouncer and head thumper for the group. In his younger years, Curtis had worked security for the band Skrewdriver—one of the original and premier hate bands in the racist skinhead movement. He'd been an active skinhead member for decades, openly referenced by his Facebook page, which showcased VF work, pictures, and a moniker of "simoncurtiEs88"—"88" of course meaning "Heil Hitler."

The Smugglers Inn, in fact, was *still* the location for VF's meetings and national gatherings. A major outpost in an extended global VF network.

Curtis had, at first, been reluctant about the whole deal, but Kirk Barker convinced him they could use the charity as a feeder entity for potential prospects. The idea was that soldiers returning from a hostile, non-White environment would now see England's growing foreign populations as enemies; they'd likely already possessed a somewhat nationalistic mindset and likely were missing the fraternal connection they'd shared while in the service. One, Kirk Barker argued, Volksfront could provide.

As part of the agreement, Simon would continue to run the establishment for a set salary and would continue to reside on the third floor of the building. He was also in charge of hiring the staff. Most were Volksfront members, including the newest team member to the Smugglers Inn retreat staff: Kirk Barker himself. Yes, the leader of UK Volksfront.

Most troubling, Tawni had learned that Kirk Barker and Simon Curtis were also to act as mentors to the soldiers, and Simon Curtis had been tapped to begin assisting with the establishment of other properties around the country toward the same goals. Needless to say, it was an enormous recruiting opportunity for Volksfront's UK chapter for prized military-trained personnel.

Clearly, nobody had any idea what was going on with the soldiers, except for us and those in Volksfront, and the last thing we wanted was for these guys who were seeking help to get wrapped up in a supremacy cult.

———

Not coincidentally, Volksfront was holding its European *Althing* (an Icelandic word for "assembly" that White power groups often use for special gatherings) the same week we were there. *At* the Smugglers Inn.

It was time to crash another party uninvited. A retired officer from the Southern Poverty Law Center had come with us.

But things were different this year. Usually, according to multiple sources who'd been the years before, there'd be a chock-full pub in attendance, guests and members spilling upstairs, outside, and everywhere in between, while hate and oi bands played.

This year, there were fewer than twenty people in attendance. A handful of patched jackets with supremacy gangs and tattoos that ran up necks and onto faces.

That night, we learned Simon Curtis had essentially called the whole event off after he'd recently gotten phone calls from a few local customers wondering why skinheads were drinking at his place. Dozens of would-be attendees were called and told not to come, two bands canceled, and the only people who attended were those already there or who'd not been reached by phone. Thus, the "event" amounted to little more than a gathering of a dozen skinheads who simply drank and shot pool all night, and a couple of locals who didn't know any better.

We mixed in with that group. Just two Americans and their UK pal grabbing a pint and listening to some hard rock on a Friday night.

We also, of course, slipped upstairs for a quick look and a bunch of photos to share later with our UK guests at Scotland Yard. Racist décor (Nazi flags along with VF Banners) was hung in plain sight—as well as the guns and weapons, illegal in the UK without the proper licenses (and according to the UK guys, almost impossible for a guy in Simon's position to ever get).

While it was fair to assume no one with the Afghan Heroes charity knew these hooligans' backgrounds, a simple visual inspection would make it obvious *something* was up.

We were able to identify those guys and gals who *did* show up, while we hung out and watched, nursing our drafts. But more intel wasn't really our goal that night. We already knew who most of these people were; it was time to do something more.

Tonight was just a chance to say goodbye.

The Smugglers Inn was on borrowed time.

———

Everyone knew we had to stop this situation of veterans being sent to a known VF command center before it went any further.

Days after our visit, the SPLC contacted Afghan Heroes directly, the charity seemingly floored by the revelation. They claimed to have no idea about Simon Curtis's past and what his program had been.

The Charity Commission told Afghan Heroes to cease any future endeavors and issued a formal investigation.[iii] Then, UK police showed up at the charity asking why they were employing White supremacists. They also showed up at some VF supporters' and members' homes for a variety of reasons—raiding homes and arresting one for a prior infraction. Basically, they hammered everybody, and the investigation opened the door to *other* investigations that looked into other organizations with associations to VF.

Plainly put, UK law enforcement wasn't having it.

The police and media had visited Simon Curtis and had been on it all immediately.

Simon Curtis and Kirk Barker went completely quiet, only saying there was some "real weird shit" going on but not elaborating to others, and they were worried that their phones and emails had been tapped by the "reds." They closed down VF and deleted their Facebook pages "to weather the storm" and "try to help the charity."

———

The UK was not alone in their fight against Volksfront.

With the fall of the charity in the UK, the rest of the European VF chapters soon followed. It's hard to have a group when there are no leaders, and nobody wanted to be a leader with all the media attention.

Germany, in particular, now saw what was happening, and

their law enforcement had already paid a visit to several VF members. Within weeks, Germany's VF chapter folded and went silent.

Once Germany knew of VF's presence there, they didn't hesitate and also didn't care or question where the info originated—even if from a married couple from Arizona.

They were just happy to have it.

If only others felt the same.

"THIS ISN'T AMERICA!"

We had new information on one of the older, more established VF members, a man responsible for most of the funding throughout the world. This guy loved to travel to far-off lands to set up rogue governments in small villages. He was from Germany but lived in Australia.

I called Geoff, a member of SIN, and our first international member from the New South Wales Police. Once we let him know this guy was living in Sydney, Geoff started gathering intel on him. Geoff also thought it'd be great if people back home knew more about it all and suggested that Tawni, Laurie from the SPLC (a great friend and incredibly knowledgeable investigator in her own right; a driving force behind the scenes of SIN), and I all come over to Australia to help him with a multi-agency, country-wide conference. "Geoff," I said, "you tell us when and we will be there."

About six months later, he called. "Pack ya bags, mate," he said in his thick Australian accent.

After the longest flight of my life and a few days speaking to various outreach and media personnel, we were taken to the main training location where we were guests at the New South Wales Police Department's discussion on bias-motivated hate crimes and more than well received and respected. The event was open to all law enforcement and political leaders in Australia. I spoke on organized hate groups and their international ties, while Tawni spoke on ways to escape radicalization and her experiences with *Escaping Polygamy* and how they tied into so much of what we'd seen in the White nationalist movement—"same dudes, different pants" is how she phrased it.

After, we then went to the National Forum. This was the elite of the bunch and held in a beautiful venue, the Australian Institute of Police Management in Manly, New South Wales. Tawni, Laurie, Geoff, Judy (an amazing Australian police psychologist), and I sat at the table to the right of the huge grease board and PowerPoint screen. My topic was the role and function of the Skinhead Intelligence Network and what part it had already played, and might play ongoing, in Australian operations.

It was probably one of my best presentations on hate music (which, at the time, Australia was leading the world in) and the organizational White supremacy links between Australia and the United States. I noted that, at the time, the Australian Blood & Honour organization was producing the most hate music in the world—and I had the sources to back it up.

But, at the table smack dab in the middle of the room, was an older woman with dark hair and a blue-and-white striped shirt who began shaking her head. You could feel the tension. I looked at my slide, nothing offensive there; I figured I was imagining it and quickly flipped through a few more slides to show a clearer connection to Australia, our German VF financier, and—

I again got the shaking head and some grumbles. *Tough crowd*, I thought. *OK, let's try this one...* Earlier, Geoff had played a video of American Jon Ritzheimer, a former U.S. Marine and Iraqi vet,

Three Percenter, and Oath Keeper, with a Quran in his hand (which he shoots at the end of the video), calling for a "United Global Protest for Humanity," specifically referencing "Our boys down in Australia" and "all you other [sic] countries in Europe." He went on to state, "We here in America are honored to stand next to you in defense of a common enemy." I referenced that video as another example—I was hoping a stronger one—that linked us all globally.

"With all due respect," the influential woman in stripes called out. "This *isn't* America."

I was kind of taken aback. *You've been here before, Matt.* I thought, *This is new to them, it's important they get it, so do your thing.* I looked over at Tawni, who gave me her "what-the" look, Geoff looked furious, and Laurie was half out of her chair. All three were ready to come to my defense with facts, but I was OK for now. "Well," I said, "you are right.... It isn't the U.S. But I tell you what... You're pretty close to *passing* us on the number of hits on Stormfront, the U.S.-based hate website. And you're now producing more hate music than any other Western nation. So, something's going on..."

I should have kept my mouth shut, because all I heard next was a montage of very professional but patronizing *"And who told you that? You think you really know what's happening here? You have a lot of problems back home...shouldn't you be more concerned with what's happening there?"* And my favorite: *We don't have guns, so we just don't have the same problems.* I politely rephrased, "America definitely has problems that are unique to America. But other problems are more common. You *do* have a problem here. A real one. And one you share with us in the States and a lot of other countries. And, if we don't address it together...we'll have a bigger one."

I finished my presentation, promised that SIN and our team

were here to help them if they ever needed it. I had made my case and wasn't going to make a stronger one, so I was done.

In a few years, the prominent woman in the center of the room would be proven wrong in front of the entire world. I would find no satisfaction in this.

I still wish she'd been right.

BACK HOME

By the end of summer, Volksfront, specifically in the United States, began imploding. First, there were the ongoing Hammers battle, infighting across European VFs crews, and then in August, a man walked into a Sikh temple in Wisconsin and killed six people.[iv] He'd been tied to the Hammerskins, but his girlfriend, Misty Cook, was connected to Volksfront, the only patched American woman in the group. VF would try to deny she'd ever been a member, but somehow *her* crew and not the Hammerskins became the focus. All law enforcement and public eyes had turned on Volksfront as a breeding ground for killers. So much for going "legitimate."

With the extra attention, many of VF's key players walked off and infighting grew even more. Through various sources, we remained privy to their top tier communications from around the world. And it wasn't atypical for Randall Krager to tell people to shut up, but he did now: "Regarding the current bullshit...," Randy implored, "nothing should be said publicly because of reds and police monitoring everything."

I don't know about the "reds" but can't deny the rest.

There were a retired cop and a "housewife" in Arizona with ears all over the world now. And Randall Lee Krager and American Volksfront were about to find this out firsthand.

———

Volksfront was planning its annual U.S. *Althing* party, scheduled for October. For security reasons—fearing the police and, mostly, Hammers—Randy Krager changed the event's location at the last minute from their "secret lair" in Fredericktown, Missouri, to a member's home some three and a half hours away.

Thanks to our sources, Tawni and I had already been out to the original hideout—a tin shed on a small piece of land in the middle of nowhere. We'd toured it and taken some pictures.

We called the state police, local police, sheriff's departments, and even the FBI with our info. This was all great intel with potentially more to be had *at* the actual gathering. A win all around. But, for whatever reason, frustratingly so, nobody took the time to actually act on our intel. Despite the extra attention Volksfront was now garnering, they still weren't on anyone's genuine "radar in the States." Eighteen calls and *nobody* was willing to do anything about it. (I had info from the group itself that a couple local cops "sympathized" with VF, but a couple local cops didn't have enough pull to cancel investigations at the state or federal level; this was merely folk having other, more pressing priorities.)

Side note: the same happened in Charlottesville, Virginia, leading up to the Unite the Right rally, rioting, and three deaths. A cop, supervisor, and member of SIN had intel on who was coming, how big the event would become, and warned multiple local departments, yet few plans were made as five hundred mostly armed protesters and a thousand counterprotesters descended on Charlottesville.

"Who else can I call?" I asked Tawni. There was no one else.

"Just call *them*," she said.

"Volksfront?"

"Yes. Call and say, 'Hi, it's Matt, and I'd like you to shut down your event. Thank you.'"

"OK, Tawni. Right."

"No, really," she said. "Like you always say: Be direct. Tell them who you are and do your thing."

It wasn't that absurd, of course. Hadn't a couple of random phone calls from locals in the UK gotten the Smugglers Inn to cancel *their* event?

But I didn't want to. I still wanted law enforcement to do *their* thing.

"You're not getting anywhere anyway, Matt. Call them."

The day of the *Althing* came, and I was still waiting for someone in Missouri law enforcement to call me back. I had no more arguments to make, so I made the call.

The new event location was a house owned by Richie Graves, a loose cannon and former member of the Aryan Nations. He'd also owned a gym, bought with the use of VF money, to train himself and others for MMA fights. He was one of the three most violent VF members we knew in America. I called the first number I had for Richie. It rang twice and a woman answered. "Hello?"

"Hey, is Richie there?"

"Well, he's just a little busy right now," she said. "Can I take a message?"

"I can imagine how busy you guys are… With everyone coming to your place tonight instead of the VF base in Fredricktown. Really must be chaotic. I know if I were having a gathering like that at *my* house… Hello? Are you there?"

"Who is this?"

"Maybe best if you got either Richie or Randy so I can talk to them."

"Hold on."

I waited a couple of minutes before someone angrily picked up the phone.

"Who the fuck is this?" the voice asked.

"Hi, Richie..."

"Fuck you! Who is this?"

"OK. So, this is Matt Browning, and I'm with the Skinhead Intelligence Network. We know you're having a little event and I'm just calling to—"

"Fuck you! Do you want... Ahhh, what *do* you want? Who the hell gave you my number, anyway? And how do you know where we are?"

"As I was saying... This is just a courtesy call, sir, to let you know law enforcement will—"

"Seriously, what the fuck?"

"I suggest you cancel, Richie."

"Fuck you." Click.

Tawni had heard the whole thing. "Well?" I asked. We discussed some, figured that was the end of it. Worth a shot, right?

Then my phone rang. The number was from Missouri.

"Hi, Richie," I answered.

"Fuck you! You motherfuckin' piece of shit! I don't know what you want... But I looked up SIN and I know where you live. I *will* come to Phoenix, to your address, and beat the fuck out of you."

"Richie... If you think I'm irresponsible enough to use my real address on the stuff you just looked up, you really are a moron."

"Fuck you, you pussy-ass motherfucking piece of garbage."

"Listen, you idiot," I said. "We know you're having the *Althing* at your place and I obviously know where *you* live. You have a choice. Either cancel it all now, or we'll have every available cop within fifty miles sitting outside your property, waiting to write as many tickets as possible for anyone coming and going. Then VF can have a glorious time paying off all those fines while *you* sit around and talk about me. Choice is yours; I suggest you call it."

It was my turn to hang up. *I'd like to thank the Academy…*

Late that same night, I got the call from a source close to the situation and then a Missouri police officer who confirmed everything.

Apparently, after Richie and I spoke, he'd gotten in a fight with some skinhead who'd come in from California for the event. The local police showed up, broke up the fight, and started writing tickets, which caused more infighting. Randy got tired of all the squabbling and drama and called it all off.

He even threw all the VF patches they'd purchased for new recruits into a fire, then told everyone to cut the patches off their jackets and burn them. He'd cut his own off and tossed it on the ground.

As a cop, I'd had to wait until someone committed a crime before I could act.

As a private citizen, I could somehow affect the environment where such crimes are first born.

Did those guys have the right to gather and drink beer and say repugnant things? Absolutely. And we had the right to make a phone call.

There was no anniversary party that year—or the next.

In America, Volksfront crawled back into the shadows. How long they'd stay there, I couldn't say. But there is zero doubt that one call and a whole lot of work prior to it played a major part.

———

A month or so later, we got the word that Afghan Heroes had officially broken all ties and ended its relationship with the Smugglers Inn and Simon Curtis. Publicly, they saved face by claiming a random ordinance had "prevented housing on the upper levels of the pub" and thus the break.

The mother who'd first started the charity proved more forthcoming: "I wasn't aware of any of this," she told the SPLC. "Thank you for raising this matter with us. It came as a complete shock, and our decision will involve the charity in some considerable disruption, but we believe it is the right action to take." And Simon Curtis was devastated according to our sources but publicly maintained, "It's no good crying over spilt milk."

Volksfront's military recruiting center was no more. I hadn't stopped JT Ready. But we'd gotten out ahead of something that might have been a hundred times worse. We'd done… *something*.

Over the next year and a half, Volksfront would collapse across the world. Chapters folded. Patches burned. Businesses closed.

I'd like to think we had something to do with that.

Truth is, I know we did.

POLYGAMY

Tawni's been fighting polygamy for years just like I've been fighting hate for years.

She'd started back in 2014 when asked to help another producer build a new show, *Escaping Polygamy*. The producer had previously met with me several times long before, with interest in forming a show or documentary or something about supremacy groups, and she and Tawni had hit it off.

Months later, while the supremacy idea lay fallow, an idea

for a program about modern American polygamists and helping women escape had gotten the greenlight from A&E. However, most polygamists' communities openly find themselves superior to all people and routinely call Black people slurs with no shame. This other producer was biracial and having difficulty making headway into these closed circles.

To help, she'd brought Tawni on as an Investigative Producer and then, shortly after, as the Supervising Field Producer. Just as she'd worked beside me for years, Tawni put her heart into it all, and that proved successful for the show.

Over time, Tawni learned the men and women within these polygamous communities. Many she'd grown to genuinely like or sympathize with. Their stories were infinite and often heartbreaking and, hopefully, to be shared someday. However, something always bothered her about these groups...

Besides the fact that many are pedophiles and rapists, she'd also quickly learned they are, like many polygamist sects, White supremacists.

While the church's founder, Joseph Smith, spoke out against slavery and ordained Black priests, his influential successor, Brigham Young, had other views: he declared Black people as cursed with dark skin as punishment for Cain's murder and regarded intermarriage as a sin worthy of a man having "his head cut off" and spilling "his blood upon the ground" to atone. While efforts had been made over the ensuing one hundred years to overhaul such thinking, alike viewpoints persist throughout the church to this very day.

Those viewpoints were especially ingrained within the Kingstons, a powerful Mormon splinter group whose ten thousand members maintain a prevailing presence in Utah's Salt Lake

Valley despite not being affiliated with the mainstream church. Tawni learned firsthand working within this specific group.

Ethnic jokes and stereotypes were commonly repeated. Chinese people were "stupid," and Mexicans were "dirty." Tawni once called an Uber for a young member who, upon seeing the driver, openly called him a "nigger." When the teenage polygamist saw Tawni's reaction, she innocently asked, "Well, what do *you* call them?" She genuinely hadn't known the word was bad and was eighteen years old.

One Sunday school teacher entered class with a bucket of water and a vial of black food coloring, added a drop of dye to the water, and the children watched as the blackness slowly spread. "You can never get that out," the teacher warned, then taught they shouldn't associate with Black people or anybody of a different race or they would "turn Black" as well.

Black people, the group claimed, suffered from multiple scriptural curses, from the mark of Cain to Noah's curse on Ham. Black blood was "the worst thing you can have," children were taught, particularly since the Kingstons consider themselves to be the whitest of the White, descended directly from White Jesus Christ and White King David.

Obsessed with the purity of their bloodline, the Kingstons have made incest the cornerstone of an apocalyptic vision that foresees a bloody race war. From that perspective, the Kingstons would be the ultimate victors, chosen by their Heavenly Father to rule the world for a millennium. Members see intermarriage as a way to "keep the bloodline pure"—pure White.

The cult's justification for its racism goes back to early Mormon teachings about a war in heaven between the forces of Satan and those of Jesus. The battle took place in the spiritual pre-existence that Mormons teach all souls come from. Black people were "the less valiant people in heaven" who sat on the sidelines while others took sides, according to the Kingstons. Their punishment? Dark skin. (The Main LDS church has disavowed such teachings[v]).

Another of the Kingstons' teachings: Adolf Hitler had the right idea about creating a master race but didn't have the Lord's help, so he failed. Ortell, a Kingston prophet, warns there is a movement that wants to "homogenize the people" and "make one race." Members are warned about marrying "Ham's kids," a reference to the aforementioned biblical curse. "If you have as much as one drop of that blood in your veins," says Carl, a Kingston lawyer, "you're cursed from holding the priesthood."[vi]

The lawyer's words call to mind another heavenly curse, described in 2 Nephi, Chapter 5 of the Book of Mormon, where God caused a "skin of blackness" to come upon a group called the Lamanites, supposed ancestors of Native Americans. Modern interpretations of this passage are quite different, especially among the mainstream church, but The Order apparently takes quite literally this idea of "blackness" being a sign of iniquity.

Former members have called the group "White supremacists" and "ten times more racist" than your run-of-the-mill skinhead. During work on the show, we'd identified a full-blown secret militia organization, complete with their own patches, as part of the polygamist group's private security detail. This militia was being trained by veterans, purchasing guns, silencers, explosives, and ammunition and learning things like vehicle assaults, building searches, and urban warfare to be used against the government in the end-of-the-world war.

While the A&E program focused on polygamy and helping young women get out of that world, Tawni had gathered enough info on White supremacy to get the SPLC involved.

They ultimately labeled the Kingstons a hate group.

The cost to the cult was immediate—they lost millions in business partnerships, and banks stopped doing business with many of the Kingston elite. Added pressure and exposure turned up the heat on all the Kingstons. The Law Center cited "available evidence, including the accounts of numerous former [Kingston] members."

Exactly how they'd been introduced to these former members was left out of the report.

———

I have been a member of the Church of Jesus Christ of Latter-Day Saints my entire life. It's the tradition of my family and all I've ever known. I have found peace within its walls, comfort when needed, and I owe a lot of what is good in my life to the blessings of its membership.

Yet the more we delved into the White nationalist movement within my own communities, the more I saw connected to the Mormon church. And the more it pained me to have to look at what I never wanted to admit or know.

My church had always been a refuge, but that had quickly changed.

THERE AND BACK AGAIN...

Hate, we confirmed, is the same all over the world.

Warped notions of supremacy. Of fearing, then dehumanizing, The Other.

Give it a different flag, different language or accent, drive on the different side of the road... haters are haters. And these individuals have reach far beyond just an email or phone call.

We tracked one Arizona Hammerskin across Europe, starting in the UK and ending in Italy, who wasn't paying for one meal or night's lodging. Another skinhead, in the U.S. military, used his weekend passes to hang out with his German and Italian brothers in various hate music events across Europe. We know an Australian Volksfront member who spends more time touring the U.S. at White-pride events and festivals than he does in his home country. Hate bands from the U.S. travel to the UK for packed concerts, and hate-crime suspects can contact members of the same organization anywhere in the world whenever it's time to run and hide from justice.

We also learned that law enforcement is the same everywhere. As we discussed the politics of policing in the U.S. with cops from the UK, they had all the same gripes, same concerns, same headaches that we have.

Of course, some issues *are* uniquely American.

We were about to enter the world of 21st-century American politics. Not a world, surely, we'd ever wanted to be part of.

But that's where the White supremacists had gone.

A man named Brenton Harrison Tarrant, twenty-eight years old, from New South Wales, enters two mosques in suburban New Zealand. A neighbor describes him as a "friendly loner." After Tarrant's parents separated when he was young, his mother's subsequent boyfriend abused her and the children; the doctors have treated Brenton for steroid abuse. As Tarrant approaches, a worshipper greets him with "Hello, brother," and Tarrant kills him with a shotgun. He then opens fire on people inside with an AR-15-style rifle, which includes a strobe light to disorient victims. He live-streams the shooting on Facebook. During the attack he plays "military music" from a portable speaker attached to a tactical vest he wears. In preparation, he had visited the mosques multiple times dressed in traditional Pakistani clothing, filmed the sites with a drone, and studied the interiors carefully via the internet. He had come into contact with far-right organizations only two years before while visiting other European nations. He'd donated funds to Identitäre Bewegung Österreich (IBÖ), the Austrian branch of Generation Identity, and to Génération Identitaire, the French branch of the group, and interacted with IBÖ leader Martin Sellner via email. He has posted Balkan nationalist material on social media platforms. After his arrest, he tells investigators he frequented right-wing discussion boards on 4chan and 8chan and found YouTube "a significant source of information and inspiration." His 74-page manifesto titled "The Great Replacement" discusses concerns with "White genocide." The guns and magazines he uses are covered in white writing naming historical events, people, and motifs related to historical conflicts, wars, and battles between Muslims and European Christians, as well as the names of recent Islamic terrorist attack victims and White supremacist slogans such as the anti-Muslim phrase "Remove Kebab," which originated from Serbia, and the Fourteen Words. On his pack are two dog tags: one with a Celtic cross, and one with a Slavic swastika design. He murders fifty-one people.

---

*Brenton: Graham Macklin, "The Christchurch Attacks: Livestream Terror in the Viral Video Age," *Combating Terrorism Center Sentinel* Vol 12, no. 6 (July 2019), https://ctc.westpoint.edu/christchurch-attacks-livestream-terror-viral-video-age/; Jason Wilson, "Christchurch Shooter's Links to Austrian Far Right 'Thought More Extensive than Thought'," *The Guardian*, May 15, 2019, www.theguardian.com/world/2019/may/16/christchurch-shooters-links-to-austrian-far-right-more-extensive-than-thought; Max Walden, "New Zealand Mosque Attacks: Who is Brenton Tarrant?" *Alajazeera*, March 19, 2019, www.aljazeera.com/news/2019/3/18/new-zealand-mosque-attacks-who-is-brenton-tarrant.

EXTREMISM ON MAIN STREET

White supremacy has moved into mainstream political groups and agendas as an opportunity to increase numbers, awareness, and power.

This chapter is about all of us—just not skinheads in some other town or camouflaged men down on a border thousands of miles away. Anger over pandemic constraints, perceived religious attacks, a shaken economy, and the felt threat of partial news and a "radical left government" have become umbrellas under which old and terrible ideas have found a new and fruitful breeding ground.

Charlottesville *began* as a protest against removing Confederate statues. (Polls at the time suggested only 26% of Americans believed such statues should be taken down.[i] To argue that the other 73% "are racist" is a discussion beyond the scope of this book.)

Those who showed up for the planned protest, however, soon included a who's who of extremism: neo-Confederates like the League of the South and Identity Dixie, neo-Nazi groups Identity Evropa (now called the American Identity Movement), the Traditionalist Worker Party, Vanguard America, and the National Socialist Movement; the Ku Klux Klan, Loyal White Knights and Confederate White Knights; Fraternal Order of Alt-Knights; the Southern California–based fight club Rise Above Movement;

militias such as the American Guard, the Detroit *Right* Wings, True Cascadia; the Canada-based Alt-Right Montreal, Hammer Brothers, and Anti-Communist Action.

The organizer, Jason Kessler, who'd supported Obama twice and had Black apartment mates and friends for years, is today labeled everywhere as a "racist neo-Nazi."[ii] That's not for me to say or argue. He, at first, was no doubt just happy someone was showing up to his political rally about problematic statues. What followed, of course, was utter chaos and testimony to how easily White hate groups can infiltrate and even hijack conservative politics.

The partisan divide in America has created dangerous bedfellows.

In the past ten years, I have been called in by local law departments to infiltrate and consult on multiple such political rallies. At each, most of the people in attendance are merely citizens representing one side of the political aisle.

But then, there are also those people with sniper rifles aimed at cops and protesters from *both* sides for "if" a skirmish breaks out, literally tracking the other side all day through the targeted scope of a high-powered rifle. Those people with explosives, Molotovs, pre-planted stacks of bricks to throw at police, and disguises to costume as the opposing side when an opportunity to create a false narrative presents itself.

Scary, indeed.

And, as America grows more divided politically—as sensationalized 24/7 new programming is the norm, and each side is fed only the information that supports and amplifies its worldview leanings—it's only going to get worse.

———

We are still—and may forever be—determining and arguing over who, exactly, was part of the Capitol storming in January of 2021. Militias? Oath Keepers? Proud Boys? Neo-Nazis? Yes, likely, to all.

From all accounts, more than a dozen far-right organizations were represented that day, and I personally recognized familiar Oath Keepers as well as Three Percenters, Proud Boys, various members of many militias, and Arizona stars of the extreme right including the QAnon Shaman and members of the Arizona Patriots.

I watched the videos from the "March to Save America" and the ensuing Capitol riot with everyone else. I watched to spot specific patches, tattoos, flags, and mannerisms of all those involved. And, based upon their clothing and tattoos—from a sweatshirt that read "Camp Auschwitz" to Confederate flags and a Totenkopf-head tattoo, a symbol for Hitler's security branch—there absolutely *were* racialists and White supremacists there that day.

But Women for America First and Tea Party members *also* helped organize the event. And thousands more in attendance that day were citizens concerned the vote had been stolen. Of 221 defendants arrested, researchers determined 198 had no known links to militias or other far-right groups.

No, we will likely never know the true makeup of this event. But, if there was one takeaway for the context of this book, it was this:

Militant and radical groups have emerged to stand shoulder-to-shoulder beside traditional conservative- and liberal leaning citizens. And sifting out who is who—unraveling violent radicals from those with opposing political views—is challenging, onerous, harrowing…and necessary.

THE POLITICAL RALLIES

My first Trump rally was in 2017. I'd been asked to attend by an international anti-hate organization. I spent most of my time on the protester side to better observe all the militia and pro-Trump individuals standing directly opposite. There was a lot to see.

One guy, not too smart, had dressed in total skinhead attire, all the way to his red braces and ox-blood-colored boots. He stood across the walkway no more than ten yards away from a dozen Antifa guys. He was "monitoring them" and taking their pictures— basically, the same thing Antifa does to the far right.

On the third floor of a four-story parking garage, catty-corner from the Trump event were men dressed in full camouflage tactical gear. Three older guys, gray hair, and gray full beards, and one kid no more than sixteen. Sitting on a tripod next to the teen was a .50-caliber rifle manufactured for the military and to fire at lightly armored vehicles, boats, and planes. It was now aimed at the crowd of anti-Trump protesters.

Guns were *everywhere*. On both "sides." AK-47s, AR-15s, shotguns, and handguns. Full tactical gear: extra magazines in front pouches, zip tie handcuffs, metal plate breast shields. One shot from a single person would have set everyone off: mass shoot- ing with numerous deaths.

One family had just arrived with their kids who were, clearly, excited to see the president of the United States. The kids' political beliefs had surely not formed much beyond that. The protesters hurled profanities at the parents and then focused on their six- year-old boy: "Look at the little Nazi!" "Your parents are racists!" I remember thinking: *Have we really come to this?*

But it was the guns that most concerned me. Armed anti- Trump protesters walking in groups, two by two, throughout the crowd, while anti-immigration and pro-Trump supporters stood in armed groups of four and six. All at strategic points, just monitoring the other side.

When the rally ended, Phoenix PD had the attendees exit through doors behind the building, away from the protesters, hoping to disperse the crowd quickly and peacefully. When protesters discovered the switcheroo, it only made them angrier. Anti-cop chants began instead. Barricades crashed down, and rocks and firecrackers were thrown at the police. Bottles and bricks. The riot squad appeared. And when riot squads appear, and tear gas starts flying…I'm out.

Sill, I'd seen firsthand that some in the crowd were far more right-leaning than typical voters. The legacy of JT Ready—fanatical racism metastasizing *within* mainstream politics—was undeniable.

———

A year later, another Trump rally proved to be a really non-eventful event. Trump spoke in a huge hangar at one of our local airports while protesters yelled "Nazi" and threw garbage at Trump supporters.

This is where I got my first good look at the Proud Boys.

A "radical White supremacist" group, say some. Or homo-phobes. Misogynists. Racists. (The fact that many of its members are Black, Latino, Asian, gay, including major leaders, may throw some of that narrative off; beyond the scope of this book.) Or, perhaps, just the world's worst adult fraternity—guys who get together to drink and complain about PC culture and the machi-nations of an ever more progressive world. Five thousand to thir-ty-five thousand members depending on who's counting and why.

I also recognized that mixed in within or around or only near the Proud Boys were several grown-up skinheads. Hair grown out, no boots or braces, tattoos covered. Just like Jerry Harbin had wanted all those years before; it'd finally come to pass.

They claimed they were there to "trash Antifa." Unfortunately for them, Antifa never showed up. There were many left protesters but none that day who identified as Antifa.

Guns, again, were everywhere. Guns, guns, and more guns. In Arizona, we're an open-carry state. Extremists make effective use of that stance. But why had so many Americans brought an arsenal to the tarmac of Williams Gateway Airport (now the Phoenix-Mesa Gateway Airport) to hear some guy give a speech?

That same year, we'd attended a Tax Protest meeting, a huge protest with my old pal, state senator Russell Pearce (the GIITEM guy) as the keynote speaker. Along with tax concerns, there were "Constitution" booths, an AZ Patriots booth (for immigration concerns), a gun rights booth, and a bunch of other right leaning booths selling T-shirts and flags. All the groups had come out for this one: the Proud Boys again (who were there to "fight Antifa," who again hadn't shown up to counter-protest), the American Guard (a border militia), the AZ Patriots, and various other border and state's rights militia members.

As far as White supremacy, in the traditional sense, this wasn't really the event for it. Until…

Russell Pearce finally spoke. He *still* sounded like JT Ready. The incendiary language. The anti-Latino rhetoric. Crime, disease, jobs. An America that would be forever changed and destroyed. "It's time we start replacing those [politicians] that refuse to stand up for those values," he warned. "It may take the shedding of blood to keep this republic."

———

A local journalist had asked Tawni and me to go undercover for an Elizabeth Warren rally as his private security and to help point out key players on both sides—knowing full well they'd show up.

I'd soon spotted a group I recognized as very active members of AZ Patriots—a group of anti-immigration, pro-Trump, anti-Muslim agitators who often, now, carry guns. Not necessarily known for violence, more for vocal and disturbing demonstrations against Muslims and undocumented immigrants, they often use Trump events to amplify their own agendas and rhetoric.

Legitimizing their own more radical ideals by latching on to, and fading *into*, mainstream politics.

The primary tactic of White power in the 2020s: to stand *beside* more conventional Tax Protesters or citizens who don't care for big government. To make your group of twenty appear larger and more important, stand directly beside a group of a thousand. Both groups feel encouraged by the appearance of greater numbers and support.

I acted like I was taking a phone call, secretly recording while Tawni was "texting" as we both took candid photos of the group.

Their leader was Jen Harrison, who'd become nationally known for her live-stream confrontations with city councils, churches, ICE, democratic politicians such as Bernie Sanders and Elizabeth Warren, law enforcement, even undocumented schoolchildren—yelling "American Dreams are for *American* children!" at Latino students walking in line at an outing at the state capitol.[iii]

She'd become—just like JT Ready—a precinct committee member, an official position within the Arizona Republican Party, in April 2019. Shortly after, at Black Lives Matter (BLM) protests she'd be yelling "Pants up, don't loot!" and "Black rifles matter!" She claimed she was willing "to run over protesters if she felt threatened" and said she had told police she'd "start shooting" if they didn't help her leave a protest area. She wears a side arm while attending and sponsoring protests.[iv] She seemed the perfect activist to stand near this day, and we found spots directly behind the AZ Patriots for the event. Our journalist friend couldn't be happier.

Waiting for Warren to speak, off came the overshirts to show bright red T-shirts with white lettering that read "AZ Patriots." The group began walking around the theater, bumping anyone they could in the crowd as they did. When Warren came on stage, the group chanted: "USA, USA, USA" and then "Close the border, close the border now!"

From somewhere came a large cardboard sign: "TRUMP 2020." And the others pulled out their MAGA hats and flags. Warren continued to give her talk, and the AZ Patriots broke into two groups on either side of the room, now heckling Warren: "Go back to the reservation!", "Hey, Pocahontas!" Whenever Warren spoke of growing up, Jen Harrison would add and yell, "On the rez!"

By now, event security had arrived and said Harrison and her crew needed to leave. The typical "freedom-of-speech" arguments started, but security was dead set on forcing them out.

I started arguing in *defense* of the AZ Patriots. "They have the right to be here!" Tawni, taking my lead, jumped in also. This is a simple tactic we use, when it presents itself, to get in good with… just about anyone. Most people need support and seek to be noticed, listened to. Our journalist friend was overjoyed.

"You can go too!" security shouted at us now.

The AZ Patriots were led from the theater, and we followed closely behind. Outside, Tawni suggested we go over and just talk with them, but before we figured out how to make that happen, whether we even wanted to, they walked up to us. "Appreciate you guys speaking out for us," one guy said.

After a lengthy conversation about who they were and what they stood for, cards were given, and then we had a discussion about how they knew we couldn't be Warren supporters. Hecklers yelled at all of us the whole time we talked.

In January, several AZ Patriots helped storm the Capitol.

BOOGALOOS AND QANON

After the 2020 election, we got a call from a law enforcement contact who wanted us to check out the local Count the Vote rally.

Count the Vote was like many of the rallies we'd seen before except, this time, it'd been broadcast on the national news in the days prior. The crowd was bigger than we'd expected, and we had to park a few blocks away and walk to the county building where the pro-Trump people were marching around the parking lot. The crowd consisted of *mostly* White people but also had a substantial showing from Latinos, Native Americans, and Black protestors. Entire families were there.

A beautiful November night. Armored cars and county SWAT guys stood at the ready, while Boogaloos, Three Percenters and other various armed and tactical-armored out—backpacks, load-bearing vests, more mags than ever needed, ARs and AKs, and one guy had a Steyr Aug assault rifle. There were handguns everywhere. I had my typical two guns on me and Tawni had one, and we were definitely outgunned.

Boogaloo Boys are a loosely organized group who found their start on the 4chan message board. Their membership is a wide variety of racists, neo-Nazi, pro-gun, pro-Trump, and race-war theorists. They've been present at nearly every rally and protest since 2019 and are easily recognized by their camouflage pants, load-bearing vests, open-carry weapons, and, most especially, their Hawaiian shirts.

Just like other far-right radical activists, the Boogaloos had started with an online presence to prepare for the race war and spread into action. Numerous members have been arrested on crimes ranging from explosives possession to murder with a few inciting a riot along the way. They are legit and they are violent, well armed and well trained. They are definitely people to be aware of because of their online recruiting firepower (they are extreme pro Second Amendment and they come to the rallies clearly showing off their firepower), and with their race war prep, they can easily fit into any White nationalist association.

By June 2020, there were more than 2 million views on their hashtag.

It is reported that the plot to kidnap Michigan governor Gretchen Whitmer was planned, and training for the crime was conducted, by either possible Boogaloo members or their associates.

Here in Arizona, they were now marching and praying in earnest with other "patriots" for then-President Trump and the country. Music blasted, everything from Def Leppard to the Lee Greenwood classic "God Bless the USA" (with its "I'm proud to be an American" lyrics), which must have played a hundred times. Each time, everyone stopped what they were doing and sang along like it was the National Anthem.

We continued to monitor the crowd—I watched the guns and

Tawni watched the people. She got more and better information that night than I did, truthfully. While I watched the Boogaloos with their hideous Hawaiian shirts with ARs strapped to their chests, Tawni made a new friend.

It was a guy wearing leather pants, no shirt, a Q flag, and a fluffy horned buffalo hat. He was a cross between a mountain man and one of the singers in the Village People. Kind of a goof. But, over the next few months, this guy became a staple at these events.

By the time we were done, she had a full conversation with the guy who would become known as the QAnon Shaman, but he told Tawni he was simply Jake. A guy almost childlike with a gruff voice. We learned where Jake (Jacob Chansley) had gone to high school, learned a bit more about his beliefs and background and then a whole lot more about "Q."

———

The ideas of QAnon have been around in one form or another in the far-right realm for an awfully long time. When Tawni and I first got into all this, many skins were already discussing the "New World Order," "deep state," and the Illuminati, which included American presidents, the richest of the rich, Masonic symbology, and ancient rituals that all fed into these theories. They'd even provided Tawni with "proof" and videos to watch. I wish we'd saved these videos because they are ridiculously similar to what is now being taught by Q today.

Q, in and of itself, is a conspiracy theory. A far-right loose organization of devotees who believe in a battle of good and evil. The evil being "Satan-worshipping pedophiles" of the deep-state government. QAnon adherents are waiting for "The Storm," the capture and arrest of people in high-powered positions who will have to face the "great awakening," ushering in an age of utopia when all the world will realize that Q was right. QAnon believers proclaim Trump is the chosen one to save the country from the "pedophilia Democrats" and are chief devotees of the theory that the 2020 vote was stolen.

At the head of the Q conspiracy is only more conspiracy. "Q" is, perhaps, merely a father-son team spreading outlandish conspiracy theories over 8Kun, or *one* person on the 4 and 8chan networks who has now springboarded from the fringe to the mainstream social media platforms, pouring gasoline on already-flaming anti-government and anti-big-business conspiracy theories and rhetoric; or a high-ranking government insider committed to exposing the truth of the "international bureaucracy," Satan worshippers, New World Order, etc.

The net result is that QAnon now numbers in the thousands, if not millions by association, of individuals who believe conspiracies from Pizzagate (which led to a shooting with an AR-15-style rifle at a pizza place) to the recent Californian father who murdered his two infant children with a speargun after concluding, from another Q story, that his children were filled with "serpent blood." (Familiar from anything you read in Chapter 4?)

On May 30, 2019, an FBI "Intelligence Bulletin" memo from the Phoenix Field Office identified QAnon-driven extremists as a domestic terrorism threat.

———

At Count the Vote, I met some of the artillery guys. I marveled at the *ten* Antifa guys standing on the corner and was invited to volunteer at the Count the Vote organizational meeting.

While Tawni and I began discussing where to have dinner, her new pal with the horns shouted through his bullhorn to the protesters across the street: "Hey, Antifa." There were only ten of them at most, none of whom I was convinced were Antifa, despite claims from everyone else. "Let's have a dance off! You get your best dancers, and we will get ours; winner stays, loser goes home."

Tawni and I looked at each other. "Dinner," she said.

I typed the expected report and gave it to a friend of mine with the FBI.

Two months later, Jake was the face of the Capitol riot.

WHAT NOW?

Tawni and I, and the country for the most part, had survived the 2020 election and all that followed.

And it was now perfectly clear that White supremacy had both retreated and come out more into the open at the same time. Its leaders had gone quiet, individual clubs and websites shut down. Those interested in such thinking had found others they could march beside and behind.

Maybe their views weren't in perfect alliance. But, close enough.

Close enough to feel part of something. Something significant.

Something worth fighting for.

As the country splits more into "us" and "them," White suprem-acists are *not* going to join the side marching for BLM, open borders, reparations, affirmative action—or those who advocate introducing concepts of "White privilege" in public elementary schools.

No swastika pins. Or crossed-hammer tattoos on necks. Not even the shaved heads or Doc Marten boots that'd become part of my world.

Camos, maybe. A rifle slung over one shoulder. More likely flannel shirts. Jeans. Nike sweatshirts and sneakers. A ball cap from the local team.

Spotting the White supremacist in the crowd would prove harder than ever.

There's still work to be done with SIN.

We'd evolved with the changing face of hate in America. But part of our evolution was learning to see and solve the problem from multiple sides.

Over two decades, we'd learned to expose and combat White supremacists. To catch racist criminals. But working so closely with these individuals—often lost and wounded and lonely—we'd come to understand that to make the greatest effect on White supremacy, we needed to reach these people *before* such a life path even began.

There *are* solutions to hate.

We started talking about maybe writing of our experiences in the White power world and ending our hypothetical book with solutions *everyone* could be part of. Solutions that could end hate and racism before they even started.

This next chapter, the last, offers paths both to escape a world of hate *and* to avoid it altogether. Paths we can all be a part of.

A young boy named Anders and his mother spend a month in the National Centre for Child and Adolescent Psychiatry as outpatients, resulting in several reports showing concern about the boy's mental health, and the conclusion that he ought to be removed from his mother, who has "sexualized" him, hits him, and frequently says she wishes "he were dead." He is not removed from his mother. He is remembered by classmates as intelligent and a bigger boy who often took care of other students who were bullied. In his teens, Anders spends his time weight training and starts using anabolic steroids. He also begins criticizing his parents for supporting the policies of the Norwegian Labour Party and his mother for being, in his opinion, a feminist. He has also developed critical views on Islam and socialism, worldviews echoed and amplified by an increase in "counterjihad blogs" now spreading across Europe. Now in his twenties, he saves money to purchase a farm so that he can legally obtain artificial fertilizers and other chemicals for the manufacturing of explosives. After seventy-five years of planning, he is ready. The first attack is a car bomb next to the office of the then Prime Minister, an explosion that kills eight and injures another two hundred. An hour later, Anders arrives at the island of Utøya dressed as a police officer. The island is the location of the Norwegian Labour Party's annual AUF youth camp—a summer camp, basically, for the children of liberals—attended by approximately six hundred teenagers. He calls campers closer to talk, begins shooting, and it is an hour before police arrive. He murders sixty-seven by gunfire, mostly teenagers. In an emailed fifteen-hundred-page manifesto sent to a thousand recipients, he explains white Europe now faces a Muslim invasion and multiculturalism and that the slaughter of the campers, the children of the party most responsible, is meant as a "wake-up call" to the great war.

---

*Anders: Craig Brown, "Anders Breivik's Childhood Was Unloved, Friendless, and Cruel," *Daily Mail*, February 28, 2015, www.dailymail.co.uk/home/event/article-2970411/CRAIG-BROWN-Anders -Breivik-s-childhood-unloved-friendless-cruel.html; Asbjørn Olsen, "Breivik was 'already damaged by the age of two:' The story of Anders Behring Breivik is one of a disaster in the making," April 20, 2016, https:// www.tv2.no/a/8241631/; Laura Smith-Spark, "A far-right extremist killed 77 people in Norway. A decade on, 'the hatred is still out there' but attacker's influence is seen as low," CNN, July 23, 2021, www.cnn .com/2021/07/22/europe/anders-breivik-july-22-attacks-norway-anniversary-cmd-intl/index.html.

SOLUTIONS

Lunch with a "Monster"

A leader of the Aryan Brotherhood and I were having lunch recently.

A *former* leader.

He'd been out of the movement for almost four years now.

Both his arms were sleeved in tattoos, and I knew the ones he'd had some work done on to cover the previous symbols and numbers. He still looked like he could bench 315 easy.

We knew a lot of the same people and stories. Even laughed a few times. He was only a couple years younger than me but kept calling me "Mr. Browning."

Years before, I'd gotten him a minor piece of equipment for a small business he was starting in return for some information on a case. Later, he'd reached out to me to warn me when there was a new contract on my life. Then he'd just started reaching out, letting me know how his life was going.

When we agreed to meet in person, he first shared concerns that I was going to arrest him or somehow connect him to some old crime. He was well aware of the work I'd done, the groups I'd infiltrated, friends of his I'd helped put away.

"We'll just talk," I promised.

In his twenties he'd beaten down child molesters, tracked and assaulted meth dealers, and had even been linked to a few murders. Now, he told me about his business, which was still going, and he talked about his kids. We even talked about local high school football for a little bit.

He was like a lot of these guys I meet when they're older—*repentant*. Not in a strictly religious sense but wanting to do more than move on from the life they left behind, wanting to somehow atone for it. He'd picked up the patter of self-reflection and regret as easily as he'd learned the patter of hate speech.

We spoke for a couple hours that day, promised to do it again sometime. Maybe we will. As we shook hands and walked our separate ways, I understood that part of me may forever see him as the stone-cold killer he once was. The rest of me hopes he continues down this new and better path.

———

And a very recent text we received from another former supremacist—on Mother's Day, no less:

> Something you said in an interview one time about something your son said about being scared...that has been a heavy weight I've carried for a lot of years. Fuck, it's making me tear up now just talking about it. Your son was scared and if I recall slept with a kni*f*. I always took that personal, because it was because of me and pieces of shit like me, that your little boy went through stuff like that. I can never tell you or him, or the rest of your family how truly sorry I am for putting any and all of you through that and so much more. I'll never be able to put into words how much you and a few

others have meant to me, still mean to me. I'd have never found the strength to make the positive changes I've made in my life and to maintain the path I'm on...

———

People *do* get out of this mindset, out of these organizations. Often.

Hate groups and militias, statistically, have remarkably high turnover rates. Far more than more traditional street gangs do—where issues of territory, economics, and survival play a bigger role.

Very few of those who get pulled into hate groups will spend a lifetime in the movement.

Our mission—as a society, as a parent, teacher, coach, friend—should be to help these people, usually young, out as quickly and positively as possible. And, to stop it from happening altogether.

Here are some ideas to help.

HELPING SOMEONE OUT OF HATE GROUPS

» **Don't challenge**

Every report, study, and expert tells us this will backfire.

If you tell the person you're trying to help that their ideas are wrong, dangerous, criminal, abnormal...they will only dig in more. The cliché has always been that the surest way to guarantee your son or daughter will date the "wrong person" is by demanding that they don't date that person; the more you criticize their new amore, the more they will cling to them.

Most people in hate groups aren't convinced enough by

statistics, facts, and history to change their mindset. First, their assumption will be that you're coming with biased statistics and facts and history. Second, they will be put on the defensive and will retreat to where they feel safest and most accepted—in the rhetoric and company of the world you're trying to save them from.

Confirmation bias is when you only look for information that confirms your strongly held belief. *Cognitive dissonance* occurs when you're presented with new information that contradicts your strongly held belief, and that often causes you to become *more extreme* in your original beliefs, not less.

Either way, the only way to get around confirmation bias or cognitive dissonance is by showing the person that you have their best interest at heart. You do this by spending time with them, caring about them, even having fun with them. Once they feel that close connection, then and only then will they be willing to look at alternative pieces of information that challenges their biases or work through the cognitive dissonance they may be feeling.

Instead of arguing politics or morality or social theory, first try to determine WHY they fell in with this hate group in the first place. Ask them what media post or video or news story first got them seriously interested. Then talk more about the group or movement itself.

Many members of militias and hate groups do not come for the hate. They're pulled into the life for other reasons. Ask questions to help them reflect on why they first joined. Were they seeking love? Safety? A course for their life? Acceptance? What do *they* "get" out of the group beyond the agendas and politics and hate? Set aside the talk about their agenda of "saving the White race" to focus on asking what else they're getting from this affiliation.

And then...just listen. Don't scoff at their answers or refute them, no matter how objectionable they may be. You might want to blurt out: "How could you be friends with such horrible people?!" Comments like this will accomplish almost nothing at best; at worst, they will end any chance of dialogue.

Determining what they get out the group will help you both see alternative paths to their finding love, safety, a course for their life, acceptance, etc.

Your very first conversation will not end with "You know, I'm really just doing this so I can feel like I'm important…" That conversation may never happen. It's asking a lot, from anyone, to be that reflective, that vulnerable. But you can start with baby steps.

The questions you ask can still lead both of you to a better unspoken understanding of the WHY… and that's one step closer to solutions.

» **Free them from the echo chamber**

We're all guilty of getting caught in the echo chamber. Modern media allows consumers to custom-build their worldviews—even without knowing it. In a very short time, you can be getting only "one side" of a story and each progressive rotation brings you further and further down to the most radical of ideas and, often, completely fabricated information.

The vast majority of people in hate groups or who identify as White supremacists were pulled into the movement via the internet. Most between the ages of fifteen to thirty spend three hours a day online; many spend as much as *twelve* hours a day online. Imagine your entire worldview being shaped *only* by what you read online. For many, especially those caught in hate, that's exactly the case.

The other echo chamber is their new group of friends. Are these the only people they now talk to? Beyond the web, prisons are the second greatest recruiter for hate groups. Talk about a limited worldview. Your "White brothers" are there to "explain" the news, politics, history, science, even faith. There are no dissenting voices.

TikTok, YouTube, Facebook, and other social media platforms have all been accused of using algorithms that enable *and accelerate* far-right self-radicalization. Such "rabbit holes" are custom built by these corporations to increase usage and revenues. (In 2020, TikTok classified more than a third of its daily users as fourteen or younger. [i])

Do whatever you can to expand the worldview of the person you're trying to save. Get them out with *other* friends and family. Grab dinner, go on walks with the dog, watch TV shows together. Give them novels you've loved reading. Encourage old hobbies and interests.

Sports? Playing guitar? Drawing? Travel? Career goals?

Remind them of a life and world outside these hate groups.

It may seem you're only wasting your time. They may go running back to their group as soon as the family dinner is done. Fine. Keep going.

This is not something that is solved in a week.

Keep patient, and keep the bridges to other worlds open to them. You might not talk them into going on a weeklong family vacation or starting college in the fall, but sit down and watch the game for ten minutes or say "Let's grab lunch or coffee" or "Band X is playing in town next month; wanna go?" Something, anything.

To get them unplugged from one worldview and see the larger world around them again. A world that isn't focused on "Jews in the media" and "White replacement" and "earning your red laces."

That's the smallest, and darkest, corner of a *much* larger world.

Give them a glimpse of that larger world wherever possible, and you may find that eventually, they want to see more than a glimpse of it. They might even want to return to it in full.

» **Acknowledge the whole person**

Recognize your loved one's full, rich identity. Remind them they are already valuable *outside* the ideology. It is not what defines them—only a part of a full life. Help them connect to their fuller identity by again exploring more positive activities from their past.

Let them know they are enough…because they are.

» **Address trauma and mental illness**

Most *every* person caught in hate groups suffers from previous emotional or physical trauma: poverty, physical abuse, sexual abuse, crime or violence, divorce, bullying, health issues, PTSD.

Many struggle with depression, anxiety, bipolar disorder, anger-management issues, schizophrenia, various other psychoses, and developmental disorders. Meds and counseling, where possible, must be part of the overall plan to genuine recovery.

Something happened *before* they joined a hate group. Something drove them to desire this form of intense belonging around feelings of hate. That something must be explored and addressed.

These are things that can be talked about and "worked on" that are beyond the supremacist dogma and agendas. Again, this will not happen in a week. And you likely are not equipped to do it yourself. It may take years of counseling. You may never talk them into even getting counseling.

But, also again, the discussions alone can still lead both of you to a better unspoken understanding of the why…and that's one more step closer to solutions.

» **Set up an intervention**

Build a team of trusted allies. Family and friends. People your person trusts and cares about that are outside of their new group. It may be allies you wouldn't call upon for other things, but you know this person has a particular fondness or bond with these people.

A coach or teacher? That one goofy uncle? A boss? An old friend or coworker? Family and friends do have influence, far more than any counselors or law enforcement might.

You've seen the TV shows and maybe experienced one of these yourself with family as part of a drug or alcohol intervention. This is *not* the first step but one that can be used when you feel there is no other path, and a drastic move is needed. The only goal of such interventions is to say loudly: WE ARE HERE FOR YOU.

It is not the time or place for threats or ultimatums. It is the time and place to say, collectively and simply, that a room full of people who love them is "worried" about this person and has their back. It is another reminder of a bigger world and support within reach. When Dad cries and says he's worried about you and is there for you is one thing. When a room with seven or ten once-trusted allies does the same…many people take notice.

» **Provide a pathway back**

The intervention may have taken a turn toward tough love. "You're out! We won't have that in this house…" Understood. This happens—it is a natural human reaction to a loved one who refuses to do the right thing. And it is the wake-up call that some need.

But if you take this route, you must always leave a clear path back. If you shut this person completely off, they will feel they have no choice but to go deeper with their newfound "family."

Remember: most people caught in hate groups eventually

leave. Some in a matter of a few years. Make it as easy as possible for them to do so. Leave obvious breadcrumbs home. Make sure they understand the door back *is* always open.

» **Commit to being a work in progress**

This is a journey—a long one. One conversation or one month will not "fix" someone who is on this path. It may take years coming back again and again to steps described above. Most pulled into hate groups are in their teens and twenties; they are still discovering who they are as people. Allow that to happen with support and light touches toward the right direction.

» **Engage in some "deep canvassing"**

In the film *American History X,* the main character loses his hate after being sent to prison and is forced to spend months working beside a Black inmate who shares his life story, eventually becoming a legitimate friend to the White supremacist.

Fine, write it off as a cookie-cutter Hollywood ending—but multiple studies have proven that real people sharing real stories and narratives with others outside their worldview is a legitimate path to new understanding and changing mindsets. Not burying each other in facts of history, but asking open-ended questions, just talking about the experiences we've had as human beings.

"Deep canvassing" (being used very effectively in politics right now) works like this:

- Share your experience and get the conversation started
- Listen, get the other person thinking and sharing
- Highlight common humanity, common ground

A cofounder of Life After Hate, a nonprofit organization created to help extremists and supremacists out of the life, was a Hammerskin who'd opened a record store in Chicago to sell hate music and promote White Pride bands. To keep the store afloat, he also sold punk, metal, and ska music, which attracted a diverse clientele—many of whom were in racial and ethnic groups hated by the Hammerskins. But he began to "bond" with these customers over music and neighborhood issues. Before long, he quit the Hammerskins and started helping others to do the same.

Sports, music, work, church, a neighbor… Where are the paths to meet and get to know those outside of a White supremacist's worldview. In discussing real-life stories with each other, people become humans, not "the other." In sharing personal stories, we are humanized.

Humanize each other.

» **Examine your own relationship with White supremacy**

If you are White, it is important you become more aware of your own language and actions. Become more aware of your history.

Do you use racial statements or openly express concerns for the "future of America" at home? Are there microaggressions you use that you're not even aware of (subtle statements or actions that indirectly discriminate or hurt those in marginalized groups).

Before you dismiss those who might be pointing out your "White privilege," try to put yourself in *their* shoes. Try to see things through their eyes and ears. What are they hearing and seeing when they interact with you? What can you learn from their perspectives? If you feel defensive, what does your defensiveness say about you, rather than about what they are saying? How might you reframe discussions and comments to better encourage discussion, learning, and genuine critical thinking together?

HOW TO GET OUT AHEAD OF IT

How do we (community, teachers, parents) help our kids avoid all of this to begin with? Any of these can be applied to those already heading into or trapped within the movement, but the earlier the better...

Those most at risk include young people with:

- unprocessed trauma
- lack of economic/educational opportunities
- absence of alternative social networks

What can we do as parents and communities to address these issues while our kids are still young? What clubs can be added at a school? What is worth going into your local school board about and fighting for? Where can we best allocate our resources? How can we volunteer our time in the most effective way? What grants or charities can be started in your community?

» **Make kids seen and heard**

Give our young people a genuine voice with agency. Are your children or students merely expected to spit back *your* worldview? Are their paths—discussion, journaling, the arts—for them to share their opinions and reactions to the world? If such paths are not given, they will find them online or standing around firepits with others who hold only one, ugly view. Many supremacists are quite bright and want, as young people, to "deeply engage and grapple with big ideas."

Where are they being encouraged to do so? At school? At the dinner table? After practice? Where will such discussion be met otherwise?

» **Establish loving, meaningful connections**

Life is hard and busy. At the top of the list of things to do is make sure our children have meaningful connections. With parents, siblings, coaches, teachers, religious, bosses, friends. Otherwise, they *will* seek them anywhere they can find them. Human beings need connections—no matter what the cost. We are biologically programmed to connect.

» **Introduce complexity in worldviews**

Our various TV channels would have us all believe the world is either black or white—it's tough to get ratings when promoting a messy gray world. But it *is* a messy gray world—something we all know deep down despite the fact that we defriended all those people on "Side X" on our social media—family or friends we'd had for twenty years who are now "evil" because they believe Thing A or B.

Adults are now guilty of extreme black/white worldviews; what chance do young minds have? Our children must learn to consider opposing voices and points of view.

Encourage questions. Don't hide politics and social discussion from the dining room table. Explore the different view without name calling or declaring a "winner."

You: Some people believe X. Some believe Y.

Child: What do *we* believe?

You: Dad and I believe Y. But your Uncle Steve believes X.

Child: <thinking> OK…

Do this for twenty years, the chances of your child ending up in a hate group are slim. They will have learned that the world is not a zero-sum gain with no "middle ground" or filled with "evil people" on the opposing side.

» **Discuss where information comes from**

Explore with your child (or student or player, etc.): How is information given to us? By whom? Why? We are indeed in the "Information Age," but do we have informed consumers of the information? Do they understand algorithms and how social media and websites and chat boards work and use data? Are they aware of how supremacy and hate groups openly recruit on such sites? Are they aware of the bias in marketing and media, and do they have tools to sort out the truth from the hype, to understand the need for fact-checking before buying into something? How legitimate are the sources we take as truth? How "Explore this for yourself" is really often code for "We're bending the truth as far as we might, but below are links to proof of those lies—have at it."

Neither mass media nor hyper-targeted media are going anywhere.

We need informed and savvy children of the Information Age who understand where our information comes from, are always open to multiple sources of information, and seek primary sourcing and fact-checking of what they are fed online and in other information outletsEncourage friendships and participation in the community

» **Encourage friendships and participation in the community**

How cliché is the "quiet loner" who... Not saying you should force every introvert out into the big world but, whenever possible, encourage hobbies, sports, clubs, programs in the community and at church, school clubs, music, art, reading, fishing, and a list that could go on for ten pages. As community members, we must support local programs, volunteer when we can, hold school boards more accountable for programs being cut to "punish" communities for not approving tax hikes.

Many supremacists went from three hours online to twelve to violent action in less than a year… because they had nothing else.

Let's make sure every child has something else.

» **Continue to learn**

If you've read this far, you already know more than 95% of the country about hate groups. Well done! Keep going. Keep an eye on the latest news, names, and groups.

In the back of the book are the symbols, terms, and signs you should know to recognize when a problem may exist so you can get out ahead of it. These symbols, and another dozen like them, can just as easily appear on notebook covers, license plates, or snuck into the name of a fantasy-football team. Be aware and be prepared to start the tough conversation.

Quite recently, a suburban twenty something we know in the Midwest (the kind with a full ride to college for academics) changed his fantasy football name to "88StormFront." (You now know what "88" means, and Stormfront was once the largest neo-Nazi Internet forum in the world.) No one in the family league (all "educated and well-read" adults) knew what it meant or even thought to question it. Just two years later, he was arrested for punching his mother unconscious when she wouldn't watch a video mocking Kamala Harris, the U.S.'s first VP of color.

» **Eliminate meritocracy**

Help our children understand they matter. Their "worth" is not connected to financial success or social expectations of "making it." Dispense with the notion that our "worth" is determined by the car we drive, the clothes we wear, the job we have. Many who are pulled into hate movements do so for a sense of identity and progress—they are accomplishing something in a world in which they've been made to feel they weren't otherwise.

Most in hate groups feel they are now "working toward something," replacing the often-unreachable expectations of working toward the "amazing careers and lives" society teaches us to reach for.

» **Save the labels for when they're truly deserved**

Collectively, we must all be very careful not to lump everyone with a conservative, or different political viewpoint, as a "White supremacist" or "separatist" or, on the other side, "radical liberal" etc. Today's rhetoric, often used fallaciously as a means to weaken political rivals and movements, is only creating *more* extremists… on all sides.

Many were quick to connect Kyle Rittenhouse (famous from the contentious 2020 shooting case in Kenosha, Wisconsin) to "White supremacy," but there's been no evidence, at the writing of this book, that the teen has *any* connection to supremacy groups. It was just a convenient label for his detractors.

"The Boy Who Cried Wolf" is such a simple and relevant story. If everything is "racist" and becomes shorthand to dismiss or attack someone with opposing views, how does a community know when, and *how*, to respond when something truly is?

Writing off all self-proclaimed conservatives (37% of the country—a long-standing majority over self-proclaimed moderates and also liberals; finally matched in 2022 by moderates[ii]) only *allows the real supremacists to hide.* They get lost in the noise and shuffle, as opposed to being held truly accountable for racist words, ideas, and actions.

Further, such rhetoric often draws those on the right *more* right. Attacking someone as "racist" for being a Trump supporter or not being keen on the idea of reparations guarantees they will seek, and even embrace, backing or political comradeship from those more/most in their camp—*some* with ideals and agendas far more aggressive than they would have ever tolerated otherwise.

IF YOU ARE LOOKING TO ESCAPE HATE

If you are reading this section, maybe you, yourself, are looking to get out of a hate group or the supremacist mindset. Hopefully, you've read the above on how we're hoping to help; no secrets here. Here are some more specifics you might consider.

» **Discover yourself—other interests/friendships**

Your involvement in a hate group or militia or political movement is not the sum total of who you are as a person. You have/had other goals, hobbies, friends, interests. Pursue one, then two. No one is *only* one thing. (Being a detective was important to me, my life's work…but less than half of who I *am*—it was that other half that ultimately saved me.)

» **Establish support**

You know your trusted crew. Family and friends *outside* the supremacy community. A trusted teacher or coach? A religious leader? A neighbor or old friend? Put your team together…don't be afraid or embarrassed to reach out. Rebuild those bridges so that when it's time to leave, it's easy to cross back over.

» **Educate yourself**

Recruitment into these organizations is systematic and methodical. Websites and blogs are designed with algorithms to pull you in deeper into the movement. Recruiters will always appeal to your love for your race (understandable) and your need for acceptance and affirmation (universal)—they will not come at you talking about "hate." That comes later. Read more about cults and the history of supremacy movements and the manipulation that occurs. If it's too close to home, read more about cults like Heaven's Gate and Jonestown. Discover how quickly "brotherhood" flies out the window, how ideals give away to everything from missing funds to violence.

» **Cut ties**

You can't be a "little bit" pregnant. When you're ready to leave, leave. Don't attend events anymore. If cutting them in half at first is necessary to "feel safe," do so. But you're still "half pregnant." I was an undercover cop and routinely got phone calls from guys I'd met years before inviting me out to have beers or to go "hunting" on a Saturday night. Change your email and phone. Get off the message boards. Cold turkey, full stop. Of those I know who've gotten out of the movement, this is how they ultimately did it.

PTSD AND LAW ENFORCEMENT

Allow a short moment here at the very end for those in law enforcement and their families. (Skip if neither.) While this is not the focus of the book, I wanted to let folks know they are not alone. It doesn't have to be a death sentence to your career to admit limitations and ask for that help. Every year, more cops die by suicide than are killed in the line of duty. That's not some urban legend. The risk of suicide among cops is 54% greater than for the average American.[iii] And, the average years of service for those suicides is *sixteen years* on the job.[iv]

Medical professionals have concluded police officers are five times more likely to have PTSD than other Americans. There's a reason these few paragraphs are the last in this book. Until the last few years, this topic was taboo and one that would cost you your career. Yet, I could have been one of those statistics. When I finally was forced to admit things, Johnny Meza was once again the guy who showed up making sure in those final days my family and I were taken care of.

I will keep my solutions brief and simple:

» **Departments must take care of their officers**

Provide mental health personnel to work beside your whole crew. Someone, ideally, who's been a cop, experienced the traumas… and can be trusted. The greatest barriers to cops asking for help are ego, fear of losing your job or promotions, of being taken off the street and not allowed to work your cases, and the shame. In all of those, total confidentiality is key.

» **Cops, it's time to talk**

The risk of suicide, depression, anxiety, schizophrenia is real. *You really think that you can get through this alone?* No one has before. Talk to those you love…not those who you brag to. It's OK to say how much it hurts to have a kid die in your lap, how much you were scared during your first fight as a cop, the nightmares. Congratulations—you're human. Now, talk about it.

» **Get out of the garbage**

Police officers who hang out with police officers on their days off, pushing everything down and feeding the ego…you're just looking for trouble. Days off should be time away from the job and getting outside that cop mentality and back into real life where everyone's not a "dirtball" or "druggie" or "neo-Nazi." Most people aren't. Build a full life and identity outside of law enforcement.

» **Supervisors must recognize the problem**

You. Are. The. Problem. I have been blessed with some outstanding supervisors. However, I've also had supervisors who could never get it. There's already enough pressure externally. Believe in your people and let them do their jobs.

» **Undercover work takes its toll**

Never in my wildest dreams did I think I'd do undercover work for as long as I did. From my experience, and the studies support the idea, there *is* a physical transformation in the brain when a person is exposed to that much hate and violence and danger. Clear your mind daily: sleep, exercise, diet, practice mindfulness, hug your loved ones—and not in that order.

» **"Informed Consent"—know what you're getting into**

For lack of a better word. It's important cops know what they're getting into, from experienced veterans who've been there—and not just one guy, but several willing and encouraged to talk. If they're anything like I was back in the day, the rookies won't listen then…but, as things start happening a few years down the line, they can draw on what we once told them and maybe even reach out for a talk later on.

A story... A teen named Tommy goes to a private high school thanks to his mom, who volunteers in the main office. His parents divorced recently, and sometimes his father, who is loving, doesn't make it as promised for fishing-trip plans. Tommy plays on the high school base-ball team and has a wide circle of friends. He is arrested on his six-teenth birthday for drugs, and when he's in jail for six months, killers become his role models. After high school and jail, he bounces around entry-level jobs for a few years. He and a coworker share talk about immigration concerns and all the new gang violence in town and the coworker invites Tommy to a party. There, he meets a group who likes good music, beer, and understands how the whole world is trying to take down the White race. He makes friends easily here, especially with the girls. A year later, he's practically running the group. They're called 88 Skins. He helps with recruiting and is the liaison when working with, or beefing with, other White pride groups. He earns his red boot laces by firing a gun eight times into the passing car of a Latino gangbanger. He is arrested twice more and ultimately spends eleven years in and out of jail. In his midthirties now, he is talked into getting "some help" and agrees to take a single welding class. Something he'd thought about in high school but never got around to; he is afraid to try. Two years later, he's an apprentice. He is filled with dread and anxiety about his life. Another three years and he's a certified instructor and making six figures, traveling the country. He hasn't attended a supremacist outing in six years now, and when he hears talk leaning that direction, he tries warning people to head the other way. Yet, he still has passing feelings of anger toward other races and fear for the future of his own. And, he is working on this also. He knows his story is only beginning.

WHERE ARE THEY NOW...

Casey Nethercott: *founder of Ranch Rescue, supremacist with the ranch on the border*

For years, Nethercott continued to host "security guards" for the ranchers along the U.S.-Mexico border. Ironically, he lost his ranch in a lawsuit to two Salvadorian immigrants who'd been assaulted and threatened by Casey and other Ranch Rescue members on his property. Nethercott went missing in 2017 in Black Canyon City, Arizona. His vehicles, credit cards, cash, keys were all in his home. He has still never been found.

Jason Stafford: *the skinhead who first tried to kill me*

Jason was released from prison in 2015 and is now living in Mesa. He'd been incarcerated in his formative years, at just twenty-two. When life was beginning for most, his was ending. Not surprisingly, a study by the *Journal of the American Academy of Pediatrics* concluded that "cumulative incarceration during early adulthood is independently associated with worse physical and mental health later." Released inmates have higher rates of fatal drug overdose, suicide, PTSD, along with other mental health struggles and stress-related illnesses such as hypertension and obesity. I have no idea what Jason is doing now and genuinely wish him the best moving forward, but I know, given these statistics, he has a long road ahead of him.

Jerry Harbin: *president of the National Alliance (Arizona Chapter)*

After I was outed at the capitol, Jerry Harbin combined forces with JT and attempted to destroy me and my career with Internal Affairs complaints and city council outbursts. However, I never talked to Jerry again. He was a coward, so I didn't expect to hear from him. But I was told by numerous sources he was working out some "revenge" behind the scenes. Perhaps he still is, but nothing ever came of those threats and rumors. Instead, the Arizona National Alliance—an organization he'd built from scratch into a hundred-plus loyal followers—slowly disappeared. Some say it was because of the failed leadership on a *national* level, but I like to think they were merely afraid of this type of infiltration happening again: law enforcement undercover as one of their most-trusted members. I know, from those in the movement, that my reveal shook Jerry and others in the White supremacy movement. After Jerry's son went to prison (see below) and the Unit 88 skins dismantled, Jerry Harbin soon ended his work for the National Alliance. (He will be just shy of eighty when this book is published.) He still works two days a week as a respiratory therapist and lives in Phoenix with his son. Though his official capacity as an organizer may be in his past, as is true of most old-timers in White supremacy, the hate ideology still runs deep. The books he touts online now are often about eugenics, nationalist, and anti-Semitic. A recent online posting: *"Just send all the Muslims, Zionists, and 3rd-World trash back to their original rat holes. And make damn sure that Zionists DO NOT control the media, banking, education, medicine, and OUR churches."*

Jeffrey Harbin: *Jerry's son and a pal of JT Ready*

Young Harbin was arrested for possession and transportation of fifteen grenade-like explosives and a pipe bomb in 2011 after a "tip" to law enforcement. He and JT Ready wanted to use these types of explosives, infused with shrapnel to do the most damage, on their "hunting trips" along the Arizona portion of the

U.S.-Mexico border. Jeffrey's extreme behavior eventually landed him a two-year sentence in prison and three years' probation with the condition that he does not associate with White nationalists or possess any kind of White nationalist materials.

Elton Hall: *older Hitler fanatic with the National Alliance*

Still alive and still denying the Holocaust ever happened, as well as protesting the border and undocumented immigrants. Fatefully, this one-time American Nazi Party Arizona organizer was hit by a car driven by an undocumented immigrant while he protested at a day labor camp with the Phoenix Patriots. The accident resulted in a broken hip. Elton currently lives in the Phoenix Valley and continues to financially support the politicians and nationalist causes that he values.

Josh Fiedler: *young, charismatic Unit 88 skinhead*

Years after I was outed, I was helping another detective track Josh down as a suspect for a recent home-invasion robbery. We ultimately arrested Josh at a traffic stop. As he was being handcuffed and put in the back of the squad car, he looked at me confused and said, "Do I know you?" I grumbled back, "Yeah, you moron." *I'd stood next to him as Packy a hundred times.* I asked Fiedler if, since he was going away for a long time, he'd give me his Doc Martens so I could use them in training. The skin who once so proudly offered *sieg heil*s in the park that sunny day years before was *still* trying to place me. His brows furrowed in defeat. "Just take them," he said. "They're no use to me now." I still have those red-laced boots. They serve as a reminder for why I do what I do.

Out of the numerous members who made up Unit 88 when I worked it, nineteen are currently incarcerated. Two, Jessica Nelson and Jeremy Johnson, served their time for the Mathes murder and are now back on the streets. I ran into them at a gas station a few years ago, and they followed me all the way home. No high-speed chase needed this time. Instinct tells me they were more curious than anything, but I continue to move around town with eyes in the back of my head.

Erich Gliebe: *former leader of the National Alliance (NA)*

Gliebe, "The Aryan Barbarian" who visited Arizona shortly before he took over NA, eventually left the movement. But not before he found his Ohio home on the auction block. Or before he sold off National Alliance's and William Pierce's personal artifacts and real estate to cover an expensive personal life—committing NA "treason." And not before he tried to expose Pierce's sexual escapades to former NA members, disgracing the organization's founding father. And not before he personally "soiled the White race" by marrying a former *Playboy* model/stripper who'd "danced for negro athletes." When Gliebe assumed leadership of the National Alliance, the group was bringing in more than a million dollars a year. Accusations of child pedophilia, paranoia, insecurity, indecision, and infighting ultimately resulted in loss of dues, bands, and followers. When my undercover persona was outed, Gliebe claimed he "always knew" I was a snitch because I hadn't spouted the ideology enough or used the N-word, and he'd apparently asked about me behind the scenes regarding why I hadn't ever taken on a larger leadership role. The National Alliance is now nearly non-existent. Gliebe has since divorced his wife—who is rumored to be an FBI informant—and currently resides quietly in Ohio.

Sammy of 88 Skins: *the kid who didn't get to carry the right flag*

Sammy was always a loose cannon. After his arrest in 2003 for the murder of Cole Bailey, Jr., he decided to act as his own attorney because his court-appointed attorney was Black. He ranted in court filings that his enemies could "suck his patriotic American penis." Oliver Wendell Holmes, he was not. Court docs suggest he suffered from "manic depression, bipolar disorder, attention deficit disorder, epilepsy, compulsion disorder, and was delusional at times." From what I saw, I agree with this assessment. He received twenty-two years for the murder and is still in prison today—far more tattooed, and lost, than the Sammy I spent time with.

Merton Pekrul: *Mesa Bible Church pastor*

Pekrul is still the pastor, and Bible study, at last check, is still on Wednesday nights. Urban warfare and weapons training, unknown; contact as needed.

Brandon Miller, Chris Whitley, Sammy Compton, Justin Larue, Cassandra Wood, and Kelly Coffman: *the skinheads who attacked and killed Cole Bailey*

One week, I had a motorcycle that needed a little work, and my brother-in-law always knows the right guy for such things. He'd called Tawni and asked if he could bring over his friend Brandon, who'd attended some mechanic school. Tawni called to let me know. Hearing the name "Brandon" and knowing that local skinheads flocked to mechanic schools, I had to ask: "Ask your brother… if his friend's last name is Miller." Even before I got the answer, somehow, I knew. This was *that* Brandon Miller—one of the kickers in the Cole Bailey murder, the one first caught who'd escaped jail time. Tawni's brother had met Brandon at church, knew he was crawling out of an unpleasant situation, and was just trying to be his friend or offer simple "fellowship" and a way back into the fold. At the risk of being judge and jury, no one needed Christ more than Brandon. But in this matter, there was, I admit, no Christian spirit in my heart at his time. It was far baser, a fiery rage. Not only did this endanger the sanctity of my home, but now the sanctuary of my faith was being exposed.

"Tawni," I said, panicked, "do not under *any* circumstances allow them to come over. Not only will I kill Brandon, but I will kill your brother if they come anywhere near the house." A little over the top, but I was still working out some things at the time. My family, understandably now, ended up mad at *me*. But Tawni also by now appreciated that I knew what I was talking about. He never came around. Brandon is married now and living his best life in the Phoenix Valley, apparently a church-goin' "believer."

Chris Whitley and Sammy Compton are still in custody for the murder of Cole Bailey. Justin Larue is out of prison, roaming Phoenix last I heard, but not on my radar.

Cassandra Wood and Kelly Coffman dropped off the White pride radar years ago; whereabouts unknown.

David Bounds: *Unit 88 skinhead*

Years after escaping justice for his suspected involvement in the Chris Gromberg murder (the recruit killed under a bridge), David Bounds was finally tried for the TGIFridays armed robbery. By that time, I had already been outed in the White supremacy world and was called as a witness in the evidentiary hearing. The prosecution wanted to link Bounds to hate groups. In order to be an expert witness in court, you must first be certified by the prosecution and the defense attorneys. Then the judge looks at your résumé and other cases you've worked on and makes a decision. I was deemed suitable by all. The prosecution was quick with me. They kept me on the stand for maybe ten minutes. David, acting as his own attorney, barraged me with questions for about forty-five minutes. He asked me about things ranging from my law enforcement jobs to my police training to who I knew in the skinhead scene.

The last statement made by David, who'd been in the movement both inside and outside of prison his whole life, was, "Browning, you sure know your shit." To this day, it remains one of the best compliments I've ever been given.

Rob Strong: *murder suspect who chased my son and me after T-ball*

Strong bounced around from group to group for the next two decades—from Volksfront to Vinlander, active Tea Party member to Proud Boy.

Russell Pearce: *Arizona State senator*

After our run-in at the State House, Pearce went on to sponsor Senate Bill 1108, which would bar Arizona public schools from teachings that "denigrate American values and the teachings of Western civilization." It also came to light that Pearce received help drafting the text for the Arizona SB 1070 legislation (the law requiring all Arizona Latinos be stopped to have their papers checked) from two interesting groups: (a) the Federation for American Immigration Reform (FAIR), a group founded by eugenicist John Tanton in the 1990s that had earlier identified as a "hate group" by the SPLC and (b) officials of the company Corrections Corporation of America (CCA), later renamed CoreCivic, whose executives believed, according to NPR, "immigrant detention is their next big market." In 2011, Citizens for a Better Arizona turned in 18,315 signatures to the Arizona Secretary of State's Office to recall Pearce from office, and Arizona governor Jan Brewer (R) issued an order calling a special recall election. Pearce was the first state lawmaker in Arizona history to be recalled. He remained vice-chair of the Arizona GOP. Pearce went on to host a talk-radio show on KKNT ("The Patriot") in Phoenix on Saturday nights. In 2014, Pearce argued on his show that poor women on Medicaid should receive forced sterilization. As a result of the controversy, he resigned his position. He still, today, plays an active role in shaping Arizona politics. (As this book was heading to the publisher, Pearce was publicly calling on the states to nullify all Congressional, Executive, and Judicial acts deemed Unconstitutional in order to secure the borders against the "invasion" from Mexico and Central America.)

Randall Lee Krager: *founder of Volksfront*

Krager has, by all accounts, actually moved on from a movement of booze-soaked drunks, social philosophers, and steroid-injected racists. Still respected in supremacy circles, he's been approached many times to fire it all up again. Randy, instead, lives quietly in the Midwest, takes care of his family, and works in his orchard. He's even taken up karate with his sons. He still has the aspiration to create a safe "White homeland" for close associates (by invitation only) and has reportedly bought land in several states to that end. The ideology is clearly still there, but the desire to activism is not, at least right now. (And he's probably smart, as there are a few crimes he's yet to have to pay for.)

Chris Simcox: *Minuteman Civil Defense Corps, border militia in the red beret*

Last time I saw Chris in person, Tawni was beside me. There was also a journalist with us. The four of us met in a steak restaurant as I'd won a bet: the journalist had contended I could "never" find Simcox or get him to agree to an interview. By this point, Simcox knew I was Detective Matt Brownin—that I'd infiltrated his Minuteman Civil Defense Corps multiple times… He didn't care. At this point, Simcox was on his way out and half the man he once was. Within the border-control crowds he probably could've still brought people out, but he looked pathetic. Seeing him so frail and almost defeated looking was honestly a surprise. By this time, his wife had gotten a restraining order against him for threatening her and their three kids with a gun as well as threatening to shoot the police if they interfered. Shortly after, the Minuteman Civil Defense Corp had dissolved completely, so that may have taken a toll as well. Put it this way, he was *certainly* no longer the man who might challenge McCain for the Senate. He was instead merely, as I'd predicted, glad *someone* wanted to talk to him. The press, or me. Truly a needy guy. He still didn't want to be "seen" with me; I was still understandably the pariah in town with the folk he associated with anyway. So, we'd gathered in the darkest corner of some out-of-the-way Scottsdale restaurant. He seemed broken—*What living with all those demons and hatred will do*, I well remembered—glad to have someone buy him dinner. He gave us sound bites, everything rehearsed. All about the wall, how he was proud of the wall, how he'd "done his part." Chris also implied he'd always been concerned with those who came to the border to "hunt Mexicans" but that he couldn't control who he'd attracted to his border patrol, or who'd eventually spin off to form more aggressive groups.

He was all but admitting the border hunting trips *were* happening. I wasn't conducting the interview—this was the journalist's night—but I *really* wanted to talk to him *without* the journalist. Eventually, of course, I couldn't hold it back anymore and asked about the murders on the border and he clammed up, switched subjects entirely. During all this, Tawni attempted to swipe a quick pic of Simcox at the table beside me. We always *try* to get a picture so folk can never claim later "I don't know them," and it's nice insurance to have—ever come at us, and we'll post the picture of you "snitching to Detective Browning" all over the White pride internet. This time, Tawni was dealing with a new iPhone and, when she took the covert picture, the entire dark corner lit up with the brightest flash. It all happened so fast, and the journalist was upset, but I just laughed because that's so Tawni. "Wow, wow… wait, wait. No pictures, please. No pictures," Chris said. He still thought he was so important. Tawni was able to recover quickly, claimed she was just texting, and had no idea what happened. She'd talked her way right out of the situation and even got a hug from Simcox when we left. She was "creeped out." She actually felt sorry for him because she didn't see the tough border guy she'd expected but a mousy, truly lonely and defeated man.

Chris Simcox was arrested less than a year later. He is currently serving nineteen and a half years for child molestation and furnishing harmful and obscene material to a minor.

And the Minuteman Civil Defense Corps? Sans Simcox, one of the bigger groups around soon dissolved, stating it could no longer be held responsible for the actions of its members. In the official last email, the group stated: "It is up to each individual now, you will do what you personally feel is right. You may still go to the border, but you are either on your own or you can try to find another group to associate with—you do so at your own risk. I hope you continue as independent Minutemen; you are needed; we are needed to save this country." This was just months after the call to come to the border "locked, loaded and ready to stop each and every individual we encounter along the frontier that is now more dangerous than the frontier of Afghanistan." Strife with infighting, litigation, leadership, and money issues—it was all bound to happen. It always does.

Matson and Tawni Browning:

The book is now done, but our efforts continue. In the past year, we've gone undercover, documented members of hate groups, uncovered some *new* groups, identified members getting out of prison, consulted law enforcement, and given information both behind the scenes and as expert witnesses in court to assist in putting criminals away. We've also sat and talked to sources both new and old to continue our understanding of the White supremacy world and how to erase it once and for all. Time doesn't stop, and neither does the work. In words that, to this day, continue to echo in my mind, words Tawni has made a priority in our lives: "Truth is truth." And we continue to seek after that truth in all that we do whether it's Tawni helping young girls escape polygamist cults or the two of us going undercover to another anti-immigration meeting to learn the new names, faces, and directions in the movement. SIN continues to grow with more conferences coming in the future as new members continue to share information, teach new officers, track violent offenders, and educate community leaders on what we can do to put a stop to hate. Tawni continues to develop close relationships with women and girls involved in cult religions, and helping them "Escape Polygamy" is a full-time calling, which has gone far beyond a TV show. To Tawni, it has become personal. We've also been involved in an investigation and podcast that brings to light an even more evil side of man, seeking justice for victims of an organization that preys on children and women. With our kids growing up, and with their own lives and families, we spend as much time with them as we can. Family will always be a priority for us; when one Browning succeeds, we all succeed.

TERMS AND SYMBOLS TO RECOGNIZE

100%: "100% White." Often combined with alphanumeric variations to proclaim solidarity with a particular White supremacist group or gang, such as "112%" to mean "100% Aryan Brotherhood" (*A* first letter of alphabet, *B* second).

109/110: The number of countries Jews have been expelled from is allegedly 109. The U.S. is to be the 110th.

12: Aryan Brotherhood (as *A* is the first letter of alphabet, *B* The second). Many/most gangs use this same alphanumeric system.

13/52 or 13/90: White supremacists claim Black people make up only 13% of the U.S. population but also commit 52% of all murders and 90% of all violent interracial crime.

14 or 14 Words: The White supremacist slogan known as the "14 Words"—*"We must secure the existence of our people and a future for White children."*

1488: An alphanumeric combination of two common White supremacist numeric symbols—14 (shorthand for the "14 Words" slogan and 88 (standing for "Heil Hitler").

18: Alphanumeric code for Adolf Hitler (1 = *A* and 8 = *H*).

2083: The title of Anders Breivik's (2011 Norway attacks) manifesto, *2083: European Declaration of Independence,* about driving Muslims and non-Whites from Europe.

23 or 23 (hand sign): Alphanumeric symbol for *W* ("White")— the 23rd letter. White supremacists may also use a two-handed hand sign consisting of one hand showing or flashing two fingers and the other hand showing or flashing three fingers. Together, they signify 23.

23/16: Alphanumeric for *W/P* or "White Power." Sometimes the combination is rendered as 16/23, in which case it's intended to mean *P/W* for "peckerwood" (foot soldier White supremacists).

28: Alphanumeric for *B*lood & *H*onour (letters 2 and 8 in the alphabet)

311: Alphanumeric code for the Ku Klux Klan. The 11th letter of the alphabet is the letter *K*; thus 3 times 11 equals "KKK."

33/6: Three (3) *K*s signify "KKK" or the Ku Klux Klan. Klan members will frequently follow this with the number 6, to indicate the "historical era" of the Klan they think the Klan currently is in.

38: The number 38 is used as a numeric symbol by members of the Hammerskins, a racist skinhead group. Substituting letters for numbers, 38 stands for *CH* or "Crossed Hammers," a reference to the group's logo.

5 Words/5: "I have nothing to say." The 5 words used when White supremacists are invoking their "code of silence." (Funny how quickly that code falls apart when you buy them some beer or get one in the interrogation room.)

6 Words/6: "Never Date Outside of Your Race"

83: Alphanumeric code for "Heil Christ" or "Hail Christ," typically used by adherents of the Christian Identity movement.

88: Alphanumeric code for "Heil Hitler." *H* is the 8th letter of the alphabet, so 88 = HH = Heil Hitler.

9%: The purported percentage of the world's current White population or the projected percentage by 2060.

ACAB: "All Cops Are Bastards"

AKIA: "A Klansman I Am"

Anudda Shoah: A phrase mocking Jewish people, whom White supremacists claim bring up the Holocaust when confronted with anything they don't like. "Another Shoah." (*Shoah* is the term Judaism uses for the Holocaust.)

Aryan Brotherhood: The oldest and most notorious White supremacy prison gang in the United States. Its most common symbol is a shamrock, often in combination with a swastika.

Aryan Fist: A White supremacist symbol adopted from the "Black power fist" used by Black nationalist groups in the 1960s and 1970s.

Aryan Nations: A decades-old American neo-Nazi group with a long history of criminal activity. Its logo consists of a Wolfsangel symbol ᛣ in which the vertical line is replaced by a sword.

Aryan Terror Brigade: The Aryan Terror Brigade (ATB) is a racist skinhead group with members in the United States and Europe. The group's logo is in the form of a Waffen SS divisional insignia outline, with a man's head and a gun, a wreath, and the initials *ATB* inside the outline. The shield has black, white, and red stripes (the colors of the Nazi flag).

Atomwaffen Division: A neo-Nazi group that emerged in 2016. *Atomwaffen* is the German word for atomic weapons and the group's logo features a radiation warning symbol on a Waffen SS divisional insignia shield.

AYAK: "Are You A Klansman?"

Blood & Honour: An international neo-Nazi/racist skinhead group started by British White supremacist and singer Ian Stuart.

Blood Drop Cross: The primary insignia of Ku Klux Klan groups is the MIOAK (or "Mystic Insignia of a Klansman"), commonly referred to as the "blood drop" cross.

Blue Eyed Devils: A racial epithet originating in Asia and later used by Black Americans directed against White people of European ancestry; a term since appropriated by White supremacists as a positive.

Blut und Ehre: *Blut und Ehre* is a German phrase that translates into "Blood and Honor,"; the Nazi Party (as a Hitler Youth slogan) popularized it. Since World War II, this German phrase (and even more so for its English translation) has commonly been used by White supremacists in Europe, the United States, and elsewhere.

Boots and Laces: Racist skinheads prefer wearing steel-toed work boots, typically with red or white shoelaces laced a certain way.

Bowlcut/Dylann Roof: The "Bowlcut" is an image of a bowl-shaped haircut resembling the one sported by White supremacist mass killer Dylann Roof. People who use the "bowlcut" image or other "bowl" references admire Roof and call for others to emulate his racist murders.

Burning: Neo-Nazis have adopted the Ku Klux Klan practice of symbolic burnings, substituting swastikas, othala and life runes, triskeles, and the Celtic cross for the traditional cross burned by Klan members.

Celtic Cross: The White supremacist version of the Celtic Cross, (or Odin's Cross), which consists of a square cross interlocking with or surrounded by a circle, is one of the most popular White supremacist symbols.

Confederate Flag: The Confederate flag is one of the more common White supremacist symbols. Although still used by non-extremists, especially in the South, as a symbol of Southern heritage or history, it's still recognized by a growing number of people as a hate symbol.

Crazy White Boy or CWB: A phrase used generically by some White supremacists (often as a tattoo) but also commonly used as the name for various White gangs. Although it's commonly used by White supremacists, others may also use the term, so it should be carefully judged in its context.

Creativity Movement: A White supremacist group that claims to be a religion for White people. Its symbol is a crown on top of a large *W* (for "White").

Crucified Skinhead: The crucified skinhead is a common symbol used by racist and non-racist skinheads alike, typically to express a perceived sense that society is opposed to them. Racist skinheads often adorn the symbol with additional hate symbols or replace the cross itself with a hate symbol.

Daily Stormer Book Club: Informal groups of supporters of White supremacist propagandist Andrew Anglin, who runs the *Daily Stormer* website.

Day of the Rope: A White supremacist slogan referring to mass murders of "race traitors" that occur in *The Turner Diaries*, an infamous novel written by neo-Nazi William Pierce. The slogan is typically used to urge or promise a similar scenario in the real world.

"Diversity = White Genocide": A White supremacist slogan intended to suggest that multiculturalism will mean the death of the White race.

Echo: The "echo" is an online term used for multiple parentheses around a person's name to indicate they are Jewish or, when used around a phrase or term, such as (((banker))) or (((professor))), to imply that the word "Jewish" should be added to it.

Fasces: An ancient Roman symbol for authority and government co-opted by Mussolini's Fascist movement in Italy. Some White supremacists in the USA have adopted the symbol both because it has fascist connections and because it is more publicly acceptable than the swastika.

Featherwood: Deriving from the related term "peckerwood," refers to a woman belonging to or associating with the racist prison gang subculture.

FFF: "Faith, Folk, Family"

FGRN: "For God, Race and Nation," a common Klan slogan.

Firm 22: The name used by the Vinlanders Social Club, a racist skinhead group, for supporters and associates of the group who are not actually members. The number 22 stands for the letter *V*.

Free America Rally: A loosely coordinated network of White supremacists who hold protests and rallies.

German Phrases: Many White supremacists, especially neo-Nazis and racist skinheads, may use various German (or German-like) words or phrases, often derived from Nazi Germany or earlier German ultranationalists, but also sometimes more modern (such as *Weiss Macht* for "White power").

German Soldier: The image of a World War II-era German soldier, especially a Waffen SS soldier, has become a common symbol used by neo-Nazis and other White supremacists.

The Goyim Know/Shut It Down: An anti-Semitic phrase portraying the ostensible reaction of Jewish people when their supposedly conspiratorial or manipulative misdeeds are revealed to the public. Often combined with "Shut It Down."

GTKRWN: "Gas the Kikes; Race War Now."

H8: White supremacists use the letter/number combination *H8* to mean "hate." Common motifs for the word include playing cards and billiards balls.

Hammerskins: A considerable racist skinhead gang with a history of violence. Their logo consists of two crossed hammers, typically superimposed over a cogwheel.

The Happy Merchant: A common anti-Semitic meme featuring a man with exaggerated stereotypically Jewish features grasping hands, meant to convey a "greedy Jew."

Hate: Commonly used as a White supremacist symbol for tattoos and clothing. (See H8 above.) Many White supremacists use the word to openly proclaim their hatred of people unlike them.

HFFH or HSN: Acronyms used by the Hammerskins, standing for "Hammerskins Forever, Forever Hammerskins" or "Hammerskin Nation."

Hitler Salute (hand sign): The Nazi or Hitler salute debuted in Nazi Germany in the 1930s as a way to pay homage to Adolf Hitler. In Nazi Germany, it was often accompanied by chanting or shouting *"Heil Hitler"* or *"Sieg heil."* Since World War II, neo-Nazis and other White supremacists have continued to use the salute, making it the most common White supremacist hand sign in the world.

Ian Stuart Donaldson/ISD: Front man and founder of White supremacy bands such as Screwdriver (perhaps the biggest), The Klansmen, and White Diamond. Died in a car crash in 1993.

Imperial German Flag: Because Germany banned use of the swastika and other Nazi imagery, some German neo-Nazis use an older flag, taken from Imperial Germany, as a substitute for the Nazi flag. Nazis elsewhere sometimes do the same.

Iron Cross: A famous German military medal that became a common White supremacist symbol after World War II. Today, it is also used in many non-racist/extremist situations and cannot be assumed to be used as a hate symbol alone.

It's Okay to Be White: A slogan popularized on the website 4chan for trolling purposes and that was soon adopted by White supremacists (who had occasionally used the phrase themselves in the past).

ITSUB: A Ku Klux Klan acronym for "In the Sacred Unfailing Being," a reference to God.

Jera Rune: An ancient European runic symbol and part of the runic alphabet that White supremacists have appropriated; but is also commonly used by non-racist modern Norse pagans, so care needs to be taken in its evaluation.

KIGY: Shorthand for "Klansman I Greet You."

KLASP: Acronym for "Klannish Loyalty, A Sacred Principle."

Ku Klux Klan (hand sign): Some Ku Klux Klan members use a hand sign that consists of angling the index and middle fingers out to the side in order to look vaguely like the letter *K*.

Life Rune: An ancient runic symbol appropriated by the Nazis to help create an idealized "Aryan/Norse" heritage, which led to its later adoption by White supremacists. Because the life rune is also used by many non-racists, it should carefully be judged in context.

LOTIE: Abbreviation for a "Lady of the Invisible Empire," i.e., a woman Klan member.

Love Your Race: A White supremacist slogan originally

popularized by the neo-Nazi National Alliance. The phrase is often accompanied by an idealized image of a beautiful and maternal White woman.

Meine Ehre Heisst Treue: A German phrase that translates roughly to "My Honor Is Loyalty." A motto of the Waffen SS in Nazi Germany; as a result, many neo-Nazis and other White supremacists around the world use this German phrase, or English equivalent.

Moon Man: A meme derived from a character in 1980s McDonald's restaurant commercials that was appropriated by White supremacists who attach it to racist songs, language, and imagery.

Muh Holocaust: An anti-Semitic phrase used to convey the notion that Jewish people routinely bring up the Holocaust to gain attention or to deflect negative attention.

Nazi Eagle: The Nazi Eagle—an eagle clutching a swastika— emerged as a symbol during the Nazi era in Germany and since the end of that regime has been adopted by White supremacists and neo-Nazis worldwide.

Nazi Flag: The flag of Nazi Germany remains one of the most potent hate symbols worldwide.

No Race Mixing: A fairly common White supremacist symbol depicts a multiracial couple or family, with a red circle/ bar superimposed over the depiction, indicating that such relationships ought to be prohibited.

Noose: The hangman's noose, a symbol connected to lynching, is one of the most powerful visual symbols directed primarily at African Americans.

Northwest American Republic: A fictional land/group based on the so-called "Northwest Imperative," a long-standing call by some White supremacists for White people to move to the Pacific Northwest and establish their own country.

Not Equal: A symbol to proclaim that different races are not equal (and to imply that the White race is superior).

OK (hand gesture): A common hand gesture that a 4chan trolling campaign claimed in 2017 had been appropriated as a symbol meaning "White power." Used now by many on the right, not just extremists, for the purpose of trolling liberals, the symbol eventually came to be used by actual White supremacists. Caution must be used in evaluating instances of this symbol's use.

The Order: An American White supremacist terrorist group from the early to mid-1980s that committed assassinations, armored-car robberies, and bombings for several years before being brought down by law enforcement.

ORION: "Our Race Is Our Nation," or "ORION," is a racist slogan proclaiming that racial ties are paramount to all else, transcending national borders or boundaries.

Othala Rune: The Nazis adopted this ancient European rune, among others, into their symbology, causing it to be a favorite symbol among White supremacists ever since.

Peckerwood: Derived from an old racial epithet aimed at Whites; has evolved to become a term used to refer to White prisoners, particularly White prisoners belonging to the racist prison gang subculture. Often the term is shortened to "wood," and all such prisoners in a particular prison might be referred to as the "woodpile."

Peckerwood (hand sign): The hand sign for "peckerwood" consists of forming the thumb, index finger, and middle finger of one hand to form the letter *P*, and the four fingers of the other hand to form the letter *W*.

Pepe the Frog: A popular Internet meme used in a variety of contexts. In recent years it has also been appropriated by White supremacists.

Phineas Priesthood: The Phineas Priesthood (or Phinehas Priesthood) is a concept created by the racist and anti-Semitic religious sect known as Christian Identity and refers to self-appointed "holy warriors" in the Christian Identity cause.

Pit Bull: The favorite dogs of many White supremacists because they are perceived as savage fighters. One particular graphic has become a common supremacist symbol.

RAHOWA: Acronym for "Racial Holy War," a rallying cry for the White supremacist movement.

ROA: Acronym for "Race Over All," popularized by the neo-Nazi/racist skinhead gang Volksfront.

Sieg Heil: *Sieg heil* is a German phrase that translates to "Hail Victory." The Nazi Party in Germany adopted the phrase, which became one of its most widely used and notorious slogans. As a result, after World War II, White supremacists in Europe, North America, and elsewhere adopted the phrase as well.

SS (hand sign): A hand sign intended to memorialize the Schutzstaffel, or SS, of Nazi Germany. The hand sign utilizes both hands to make a lightning bolt symbol, as a pair of lightning bolts was the main symbol of the SS.

SS Bolts: Derived from the Nazi-era symbol for the Schutzstaffel (SS), whose members ranged from Gestapo agents to concentration camp guards.

SS Divisional Insignia: During World War II, the SS fielded a private army of nearly forty divisions that fought on every front. Neo-Nazis and other White supremacists often use the various divisional insignia of these military formations as hate symbols.

St. Michael's Cross: A White supremacist symbol that originated in Romania in the years before World War II as the symbol of the fascist Iron Guard movement.

Stormfront: The oldest and largest White supremacist website. Its logo consists of a squarish Celtic cross encircled by the phrase "White Pride Worldwide."

Swastika: An ancient symbol used in many cultures that was adopted by Adolf Hitler and turned into a symbol of hatred. Since then, the swastika has become perhaps the most notorious hate symbol in Western culture.

SWP: "Supreme White Power."

Thor's Hammer: An ancient Norse symbol used today primarily in neo-pagan religions such as Ásatrú. White supremacist Norse pagans have appropriated this symbol to use in a White supremacist context. However, because it continues to be used by many non-racists, one should carefully judge it in the context in which it appears.

Totenkopf: The "Death's Head" was a symbol used by Hitler's SS that has been adopted by neo-Nazis and White supremacists.

Triangular Klan Symbol: This Ku Klux Klan symbol consists of what looks like a triangle *within* a triangle but actually represents three letter *K*s aligned *into* a triangle and facing inward. A variation on this symbol has the *K*s facing.

Triskele: An ancient symbol with three curved or jointed segments emanating from a single point that has been adopted by White supremacists.

Tyr/Tiwaz Rune: An ancient runic symbol appropriated by the Nazis and subsequently popular among White supremacists. The rune signifies sacrifice, justice, and success in all efforts that are righteous. Note: folk who are NOT White supremacists also use this image; take in with all available information.

Valknot: The "knot of the slain" is an old Norse symbol associated with the afterlife that has been appropriated by White supremacists. As with all Norse runes, nonracist pagans may *also* use this symbol, so it should be examined in context.

Vinland Flag: The "Vinland Flag" was designed in the 1990s by goth metal musician Peter Steele for an album cover. "Vinland" was the name given by Viking explorers to the area of North America. In the early 2000s, White supremacists began to appropriate the "flag" as a White supremacist symbol.

Volksfront: A hybrid racist skinhead gang/neo-Nazi group that started in the Pacific Northwest in the 1990s but all but disbanded in the 2010s. Members of the group used several hand signs to represent their gang: A common one-handed sign features the fingers of the right hand divided into a *V* shape, often held over the chest. A two-handed sign uses one hand to make a *V* shape (using two or four fingers) and the other hand to make the shape of the letter *F*.

We Wuz Kangs: Phrase used to taunt African Americans by racist mockery of Afrocentric theories about Egyptian connections to sub-Saharan Africa.

White Aryan Resistance (WAR): A loosely organized racist skinhead movement in the late 1980s and early 1990s centered on White supremacist Tom Metzger. Now used as a general hate symbol.

White Lives Matter: Slogan adopted after the rise of the Black Lives Matter movement as well as a loose movement of White supremacists who hold events to popularize the phrase.

White Power (hand sign): Some White supremacists, particularly in California, may use a two-handed hand sign in which one hand forms the letter *W* and the other hand forms the letter *P*, to represent WP, or "White Power."

Wolfsangel: An ancient runic symbol that was believed to be able to ward off wolves. Today, thanks to its appropriation by Nazi Germany, the Wolfsangel is one of the more popular White supremacist symbols.

Women for Aryan Unity: A long-standing White supremacist group for women. Its logo is a diamond featuring red and white stripes and stylized letters spelling "WAU."

WP: "White Power" or "White Pride."

WPWW: "White Pride World Wide."

You Will Not Replace Us or YWNRU: A slogan referring to the common White supremacist belief that the White race is in danger of going extinct due to rising numbers of non-Whites who are controlled and manipulated by Jewish people.

ZOG: "Zionist Occupied Government." Reflects the common White supremacist belief that the U.S. government, or entire world, is "controlled by Jews."

Zyklon B: Zyklon B was the name of the gas used to kill over a million victims, most of them Jewish, in the death camps during the Holocaust. Because of its connection to the Nazis, Zyklon B has been adopted as a symbol by modern-day White supremacists.

NOTE ON THE LANGUAGE USED

Language is constantly evolving, especially words related to race and identity. Great care was taken with this book to use language that is current and culturally sensitive.

For instance, the trend to capitalize both White and Black (while there *are* different opinions and editorial styles regarding currently) is, of the writing, mostly leaning toward capitalizing both. When in doubt, we settled upon the most-used standards in publishing and for textual/written consistency. These are used with the understanding, and apology, if necessary, that what is "standard" two years from now may be completely different.

We also recognize that some of the language in the book—especially words and ideas expressed by those within the White supremacy movement—will be offensive to most readers. The decision was made not to soften these words or ideas, which would be akin to me calling these dangerous people "goofballs." The real language used reveals the real problem.

Finally, a "sensitivity reader" was part of the publishing team to help question, advocate, and inform. Thanks to Manu for this important role.

The best way to solve this issue is for us to actually talk about it. And those language slips and adjustments that may come along the way are an important part of that ongoing discussion.

READING GROUP GUIDE

1. The FBI restricts undercover assignments to two years or fewer. Based on Matt's experiences of almost twenty years undercover, why do you think those limits are imposed?

2. What, according to Matt, is the danger of thinking of the White supremacist movement as a small movement filled with "morons" and "clowns?" How did they become so easy to dismiss when they are still so numerous and active?

3. "Packy's" PO Box and voicemail quickly overflow with literature and invites from the various skinhead groups in town. For someone who is truly connecting to these groups for the first time, what effect do you think this sort of information-bombing has?

4. Why is "brother" such an important designation for members of White supremacist hate groups?

5. Completely against protocol, Tawni eventually joined Matt on undercover jaunts. What drove her to get involved, and why did she and Matt take the risk when it could have cost Matt his job or even their lives?

6. How does the structure of American law enforcement discourage information-sharing and complicate investigations that have far-reaching consequences across state lines?

7. Matt points to the "'us against them' mentality" that cops are trained with as one of the reasons police officers are likely to hold extremist views. What do you think of this analysis?

8. The relationship between Volksfront and Afghan Heroes showcases a key recruitment tactic for White supremacist groups. How can that type of recruitment be prevented in veteran support organizations? What did you think of the response of UK law enforcement?

9. How did you feel reading the final chapter of potential solutions to the problem of White supremacy? What strategies stood out to you?

ACKNOWLEDGMENTS

You have probably already picked up on this, but it can't be said enough: I could not have done this job, or book, without the help, support, and love of my wife, Tawni.

In no way does this book come close to capturing all she has done, and still does, for me and our family. When I was off fighting hate, she kept us intact and made sure there was love. When I was working way too much, she'd meet me at parks with the kids so I might see them for a few minutes, drop by while I was on patrol, and show me the kids in their Halloween costumes. She always made them, and sometimes me, believe I was a superhero, but the superhero was never me. Tawni has always been my rock, my soft place, and my sounding board for both the good and bad. She's walked through my pain *with* me, even to her own detriment. There during my darkest moments. There for all the death contracts and threats to our family. There when I was literally dodging bullets, and for so many trauma-related stories that are not even part of this book, ones I may never share with anyone else. I am having a hard time finding the right words. Simply: Without her, there is no me. Tawni always brought me back and helped me remember who I was and what was important. She is the love in an often hate-filled world. As for the book, she worked beside me throughout. Research, editing, writing, remembering, encouraging, and helping me get through some of the tougher memories and feelings. It's her story and book, also. Her name isn't beside mine by accident.

This project took years to complete and adopted many forms and stages before finding its finished shape. I'm not going to list everyone else who made it possible because, honestly, we'd forget so many. But here are a few to start...

Thanks to Susy Buchanan, who began it all with the original article for the SPLC, finally convincing me to take our story in another direction when no one else wanted to listen. To Lori Golden-Stryer and all our friends at RIVR Media. To Peter McGuigan of Ultra Literary, for getting a book started, never being able to "get the story out of your head," always taking my calls, and introducing us to such talented people; you are a wise, and good, man. To Nikki Braendlin and Scarlette Bennet Tapp, who first helped us begin to collect and capture our story. To our wonderful and gracious literary agent, Gillian MacKenzie, for taking on this project, and to Anna Michels, our editor at Sourcebooks. Thank you both for seeing the importance in sharing this story and for believing in it and us. You are part of the solution. (To Luke Dempsey of HarperCollins, who introduced us to Gillian.) To the whole Sourcebooks team of behind-the-scenes editors, designers, etc., especially the astute and diligent Marian Perales and Emily Proano. And for Geoffrey, a talented writer and friend. Thank you for never giving up, for understanding, and for making it personal. Don't know how you do it, but you nailed it. Never have I been able to trust enough to put my thoughts to words. You inspired me to talk to my kids about PTSD, and I knew I could trust you in a way that is not natural for me; I knew you'd take care of us.

To my friends and partners in law enforcement, G-34, G-47, G-33, G-32, S95, G17, Chief and the original Major Felon Squad—you always had my back. Bob and Chris, you guys brought me back from the craziness of life and reminded me that there are friendships outside of law enforcement. And to Rachel Jeffs—thank you. To Laurie Wood for putting so much of your life and time into SIN, for being on the front lines, and for your friendship. Thank you also to Joe Roy and Heidi Berich and all the good people at the Southern Poverty Law Center for backing the work and giving SIN a home. Michelle...what can be said for all the work you did to make the Southwest a safer place? You are a mentor and example to so many. To all the hard-working men and women of SIN who put their hearts and lives on the line to fight hate and for all those in law enforcement who keep us safe—keep fighting the good fight.

Finally...through all the chaos, threats from bad people, late nights, paranoia, anxiety, good times and bad, thanks to our five kids who didn't have a choice but to ride it out with us. Each of you has your own memories and stories of how life is/was to be raised as a cop's kid. Thank you for always believing in what we are doing, not rolling your eyes when Mom and Dad ran from the dinner table to some secret task without warning. We love you more than any written acknowledgment could ever hope to capture. May our family and yours be stronger for your sacrifices, and may the next generation not have to suffer the hate that still today lives "next door." Someday, yes? As Mom always says: "Love Wins."

NOTES

CHAPTER 1: AMERICAN NAZIS

i   Christopher Thompson, "In Defense of Skinheads," *Time*, May 03, 2007, http://content.time.com/time/arts/article/0,8599,1617295,00.html.

ii   Thompson.

iii   "Racist Markings Spur Target Recall," *Washington Post*, August 29, 2002. https://www.washingtonpost.com/archive/business/2002/08/29/racist-markings-spur-target-recall/93db618b-896c-4b35-9bc3-1578b50f0ac5/.

CHAPTER 2: GOING UNDERCOVER

i   Romano, Aja. "How a dystopian neo-Nazi novel helped fuel decades of white supremacist terrorism," *Vox*, January 28, 2021, https://www.vox.com/22232779/the-turner-diaries-novel-links-to-terrorism-william-luther-pierce.

CHAPTER 3: HATE GROUPS

i   *Connor v. Tilton* No. 3:2007cv04965—Document 37, https://law.justia.com/cases/federal/district-courts/california/candce/3:2007cv04965/196250/37/.

ii   "Aryan Nations," SPLC Southern Poverty Law Center, https://www.splcenter.org/fighting-hate/extremist-files/group/aryan-nations.

iii   "Aryan Nations," SPLC Southern Poverty Law Center, https://www.splcenter.org/fighting-hate/extremist-files/group/aryan-nations.

iv   Heidi Beirich and Mark Potok, "Two Faces of Volksfront," *Intelligence Report* 114 (Summer 2004): 28–36, https://www.ojp.gov/ncjrs/virtual-library/abstracts/two-faces-volksfront.

CHAPTER 4: A QUESTION OF FAITH

i   "Washitaw Nation Comes Under Investigation," *Intelligence Report* (June 15, 1999), SPLC Southern Poverty Law Center, https://www.splcenter.org/fighting-hate/intelligence-report/1999/washitaw-nation-comes-under-investigation.

ii   Danny Lewis, "Twenty Years Ago Today, the Montana Freemen Started Its 81-Day Standoff," *Smithsonian Magazine*, March 25, 2016, https://www.smithsonianmag .com/smart-news/twenty-years-ago-today-the-montana-freeman-started-its-81 -day-standoff-180958568/.

iii   Michael McFarland and Glenn Gottfried, "The Chosen Ones: A Mythic Analysis of the Theological and Political Self-Justification of Christian Identity," *Journal for the Study of Religion* 15, no. 1 (2002):125–145, https://www.jstor.org /stable/24764349.

iv   E. Ann Carson, "Prisoners in 2020—Statistical Tables," U.S. Dept. of Justice, Office of Justice Programs, Bureau of Justice Statistics (December 2021), https:// bjs.ojp.gov/content/pub/pdf/p20st.pdf.

v   "The Doctrine of Discovery, 1493: A Spotlight on a Primary Source by Pope Alexander VI," History Resources, The Gilder Lehhrman Institute of American History, www.gilderlehrman.org/history-resources/spotlight-primary-source/doctrine -discovery-1493.

vi   "Summer Unrest over Racial Justice Moves the Country, But Not Republicans or White Evangelicals," PRRI, August 21, 2020, https://www.prri.org/research /racial-justice-2020-george-floyd/.

vii   "Summer Unrest," PRRI..

viii   Robert K. Vischer, "Racial Segregation in American Churches and Its Implications for School Vouchers," *Florida Law Review* 53, no. 2 (April 2001), 193.

ix   Richard Butler, the founder of the Aryan Nations, maybe said it best: "The cornerstone for any society is faith. Once a man believes his fight is for God and country, he becomes invincible."—*The Silent Brotherhood* by Kevin Flynn and Gary Gerhardt Free Press (July 14, 2018).

x   Matt Hale: adl.org/learn/ext_us/Hale.asp; Stephen Braun, "Did Racist's Hatred for Judge Lead to Murder?" *Los Angeles Times*, March 5, 2005, latimes.com/archives /la-xpm-2005-mar-05-na-judge5-story.html; Heidi Beirich and Mark Potok, "World Church of the Creator in Turmoil After Leader Matt Hale Imprisoned," *Intelligence Report* (April 15, 2003), SPLC Southern Poverty Law Center, splcenter.org/fighting -hate/intelligence-report/2003/world-church-creator-turmoil-after-leader-matt-hale -imprisoned (recruiting children); *A Different Breed of Terrorist: Hate Group Leader Convicted of Plotting Federal Judge's Murder*, Federal Bureau of Investigation, https:// archives.fbi.gov/archives/news/stories/2004/june/hale060904; "White Supremacist Church Leader Arrested on Charges of Soliciting Murder of U.S. Judge Presiding over Trademark Case," U.S. Department of Justice Press Release, January 8, 2003, http:// justice.gov/archive/usao/iln/chicago/2003/pr010803_01.pdf; chicagotribune.com/news /ct-xpm-2005-04-07-0504070253-story.html (convicted); *Hale v. Fed. Bureau of Prisons*, No. 18–1141 (10th Cir. Jan. 7, 2019), https://casetext.com/case/hale-v-fed-bureau -of-prisons-3 (2019 case); *Hale v. Marques*, Civil Action No. 19-cv-0752-WJM-SKC (D. Colo. Mar. 30, 2020), https://casetext.com/case/hale-v-marques-1 (2020 case)

CHAPTER 5: SKINBYRDS AND DRAGONS

i   Stephen Lemons, "Rusty's World: The Secret Life of PHX Kia Peddler and Anti-Mexican A-hole Rusty Childress," *Phoenix New Times*, April 18, 2007, https://www.phoenixnewtimes.com/news/rustys-world-the-secret-life-of-phx-kia-peddler-and-anti-mexican-a-hole-rusty-childress-6502257.

ii   "New Brand of Racist Odinist Religion on the March," *Intelligence Report* (March 15, 1998), SPLC Southern https://www.splcenter.org/fighting-hate/intelligence-report/1998/new-brand-racist-odinist-religion-march.

iii FBI"PROJECT MEGIDDO: A strategic assessment of the potential for domestic terrorism in the United States undertaken in anticipation of or response to the arrival of the new millennium," 1999, https://irp.fas.org/eprint/megiddo.pdf.

iv Shannon Weber, "White Supremacy's Old Gods: The Far Right and Neopaganism," *The Public Eye* (Winter 2018), February 1, 2018. https://politicalresearch.org/2018/02/01/white-supremacys-old-gods-the-far-right-and-neopaganism.

v   Gina Holland, "Supreme Court Sides with Inmates," Recordnet.com, June 4, 2005, https://www.recordnet.com/story/lifestyle/2005/06/04/supreme-court-sides-with-inmates/50670822007/.

vi "Religion Roundup," *Savannah Morning News*, July 28, 2006, https://www.savannahnow.com/story/news/2006/07/28/religion-roundup/13831135007/.

CHAPTER 6: QUIS CUSTODIET IPSOS CUSTODES

i   Alice Speri, "Unredacted FBI Documents Shed Light on White Supremacist Infiltration of Law Enforcement," *The Intercept*, September 29, 2020, https://theintercept.com/2020/09/29/police-white-supremacist-infiltration-fbi/.

ii   Neil MacFarquhar and Adam Goldman, "A New Face of White Supremacy: Plots Expose the Dangers of the 'The Base,'" *The New York Times*, January 25, 2020, https://www.nytimes.com/2020/01/22/us/white-supremacy-the-base.html.

iii Major Andrew T. Vandor, "Manifestation of Hateful Conduct to Radical Extremism as a Threat to the Canadian Armed Forces" (master's thesis, Canadian Forces College, 2021), www.cfc.forces.gc.ca/259/290/23/286/Vandor.pdf.

iv Mack Lamoureux and Ben Makuch, "Canadian Military Confirms Neo-Nazi Group Atomwaffen Was Within Its Ranks," Vice.com, May 28, 2019, www.vice.com/en/article/a3xndb/canadian-military-confirms-neo-nazi-group-atomwaffen-was-within-its-ranks.

v   Anne Marie O'Conner and TinaDuant, "The Secret Society Among Lawmen," *Los Angeles Times*, March 24, 1999, www.latimes.com/archives/la-xpm-1999-mar-24-mn-20461-story.html.

vi Josh Wood, "Louisville's Forgotten History of Police Officers in the KKK," *LEO Weekly*, December 15, 2021, www.leoweekly.com/2021/12/louisvilles-forgotten-history-of-police-officers-in-the-kkk/.

vii Rebecca Entralgo, "Border Patrol Agent Reportedly Called Migrants 'Subhuman' Before Hitting One with His Truck," *Think Progress*, May 20, 2019, https://

archive.thinkprogress.org/border-patrol-agent-migrants-subhuman-before
-hitting-truck-matthew-bowen-afa4d2ae2812/.

viii Tanasia Kenney, "Virginia Officer David Morley Suspended After Being Outed as White Nationalist Organizer," *Atlanta Black Star*, March 21, 2019, https://
atlantablackstar.com/2019/03/21/virginia-officer-david-morley-suspended-after
-being-outed-as-white-nationalist-organizer/.

ix "Portland Cop Disciplined for Nazi Shrine," KGW8, November 17, 2010, www
.kgw.com/article/news/portland-cop-disciplined-for-nazi-shrine/283–89750003.

x www.washingtonpost.com/nation/2019/08/09/black-man-michigan-cop-kkk
-house-suspension/.

xi Good Ole Boy Roundup Report, Executive Summary, March 1996, https://
oig.justice.gov/sites/default/files/legacy/special/9603/exec.htm.

xii "U.S. Coast Guard officer accused of plotting attacks gets 13 years in prison," *Re-
uters*, January 31, 2020, https://www.reuters.com/article/us-maryland-coast-guard
/u-s-coast-guard-officer-accused-of-plotting-attacks-gets-13-years-in-prison
-idUSKBN1ZU1EF.

xiii "Sovereign Citizen Kane," *Intelligence Report*, August 1, 2010, https://www
.splcenter.org/fighting-hate/intelligence-report/2010/sovereign-citizen-kane.

xiv "Sovereign Citizen: A Growing Threat to Law Enforcement," LEB, September
1, 2011, https://leb.fbi.gov/articles/featured-articles/sovereign-citizens-a-growing
-domestic-threat-to-law-enforcement.

xv Derek Hawkins, "'Boomer antifa': White supremacists rip into paramilitary Oath
Keepers for not being racist enough," *The Washington Post*, June 16, 2017, https://
www.washingtonpost.com/news/morning-mix/wp/2017/06/16/boomer-antifa
-white-supremacists-rip-into-paramilitary-oath-keepers-for-not-being-racist-enough/.

xvi "The Constitutional Sheriffs and Peace Officers Association (CSPOA) and Richard Mack: How Extremists Are Successfully Infiltrating Law Enforcement," ADL
Report, September 20, 2021, https://www.adl.org/resources/report/constitutional
-sheriffs-and-peace-officers-association-cspoa-and-richard-mack-how.

CHAPTER 8: MR. HITLER GOES TO WASHINGTON

i "Russell Pearce Endorsed JT Ready," https://m.youtube.com/watch?v=vqSSL
j5C_C0.

ii Michael Kiefer, "Sheriff Joe Arpaio has always done it his way," *The Arizona
Republic*, November 11, 2015, https://www.azcentral.com/story/news/arizona
/investigations/2015/09/11/sheriff-joe-arpaio-legacy/71888720/.

iii Tim Steller, "Militias in Arizona thrive despite lack of authorizing law," *Arizona Daily Star*, May 27, 2012, https://tucson.com/news/local/border/militias
-in-arizona-thrive-despite-lack-of-authorizing-law/article_087e98b6–5d8e-5e65
-ba98-ec918a309875.html.

iv "Arizona State Rep. Candidate Russell Pearce Distributes Article from Neo-Nazi
National Alliance Website," *Intelligence Report*, January 16, 2007, SPLC, https://

www.splcenter.org/fighting-hate/intelligence-report/2007/arizona-state
-rep-candidate-russell-pearce-distributes-article-neo-nazi-national-alliance.

v   "Russell Pearce Endorsed JT Ready," https://m.youtube.com/watch?v=vqSSLj5C_C0.

vi Ian Millhiser, "Reported Neo-Nazi Spree Killer Called SB 1070 Sponsor Russell
    Pearce His 'Surrogate Father,'" *Think Progress*, May 3, 2012, Thinkprogress.org,
    https://archive.thinkprogress.org/reported-neo-nazi-spree-killer-called-sb-1070
    -sponsor-russell-pearce-his-surrogate-father-ec37c031b2b2/.

vii "JT Ready," Southern Poverty Law Center, https://www.splcenter.org/fighting
    -hate/extremist-files/individual/jt-ready.

viii "JT Ready," Southern Poverty Law Center, https://www.splcenter.org/fighting
    -hate/extremist-files/individual/jt-ready.

ix Michael Hoefer, Nancy Rytina, and Christopher Campbell, "Estimates of the Unau-
    thorized Immigrant Population Residing in the United States: January 2006," Popu-
    lation Estimates (August 2007), Homeland Security, Office of Immigration Statistics,
    https://www.dhs.gov/xlibrary/assets/statistics/publications/ill_pe_2006.pdf.

CHAPTER 10: SMALL WORLD

i   Abby Rogers, "Meet the Leaders of America's Twisted White Power Movement,"
     Insider August 8, 2012, https://www.businessinsider.com/meet-the-leaders-of
     -americas-twisted-white-power-movement-2012-8.

ii   Amanda Lee Myers, "Leader Dead, But Group Says Border Patrol to Go On,"
     Associated Press, May 5, 2012, https://www.nydailynews.com/sdut-leader-dead-but
     -group-says-border-patrol-to-go-on-2012may05-story.html.

iii "Charity Inquiry: Afghan Heroes," Charity Commission for England and Wales,
     March 25, 2021, https://www.gov.uk/government/publications/charity-inquiry
     -afghan-heroes/charity-inquiry-afghan-heroes.

iv   Chuck Quirmbach, "Remembering 6 Shooting Deaths at Wisconsin Sikh Tem-
     ple," Codeswitch, August 5, 2013, https://www.npr.org/sections/codeswitch
     /2013/08/05/209097979/remembering-6-shooting-deaths-at-wis-sikh-temple.

v   Max Perry Mueller, "An Evolving Mormon Church Finally Addresses a Racist Past,"
     The Daily Progress, December 12, 2013, https://religionandpolitics.org/2013/12/12
     /an-evolving-mormon-church-finally-addresses-a-racist-past/.

vi   Stephen Lemons, "Blood Cult: Utah's polygamous Kingston clan mixes incest and
     white supremacy with old-fashioned capitalism," *Intelligence Report*, August 8, 2017,
     https://www.splcenter.org/fighting-hate/intelligence-report/2017/blood-cult.

CHAPTER 11: EXTREMISM ON MAIN STREET

i   Cameron Easley, "Taking Down Confederate Statues Is Still Relatively Unpopular,
     but Opinion Is Shifting," *Morning Consult*, June 10, 2020, https://morningconsult
     .com/2020/06/10/confederate-statue-flag-polling/.

ii   Chris Suarez, "Organizer of Charlottesville's Unite the Right rally described as
     onetime wannabe liberal activist," *The Daily Progress*, August 17, 2017, https://

richmond.com/news/virginia/organizer-of-charlottesvilles-unite-the-right-rally
-described-as-onetime-wannabe-liberal-activist/article_c0acb07f-873d-5a9b
-87dc-4f912824ad12.html.

iii Richard Ruelas and Rob O'Dell, "2 women became stars of Arizona's Patriot movement by antagonizing foes. Then they clashed," *Arizona Republic*, October 1, 2020, https://www.azcentral.com/in-depth/news/local/arizona-investigations/2020/10/01/how
-jennifer-harrison-lesa-antone-became-stars-azs-patriot-movement/5799435002/.

iv Jerod MacDonald-Evoy, "Extremist says she used 'bear spray' on a protester, threatens to 'start shooting'," *AZ Mirror*, June 3, 2020, www.azmirror.com/blog/extremist
-says-she-used-bear-spray-on-a-protester-threatens-to-start-shooting/.

CHAPTER 12: SOLUTIONS

i Morgan Keith, "From Transphobia to Ted Kaczynski: How TikTok's Algorithm Enables Far-Right Self-Radicalization," *Insider*, December 12, 2021, https://www.businessinsider.com/transphobia-ted-kaczynski-tiktok-algorithm-right
-wing-self-radicalization-2021-11.

ii Lydia Saad, "U.S. Political Ideology Steady; Conservatives, Moderates Tie," *Gallup*, January 17, 2022, https://news.gallup.com/poll/388988/political-ideology-steady
-conservatives-moderates-tie.aspx.

iii "An Occupational Risk: What Every Police Agency Should Do to Prevent Suicide Among Its Officers," *Police Executive Research Forum*, October 2019, www.policeforum.org, October, 2019, https://www.policeforum.org/assets/Prevent
OfficerSuicide.pdf.

iv Silverii, Scott. *Broken and Blue: A Policeman's Guide to Health, Hope, and Healing.* (Dallas: Five Stones, 2019).

ABOUT THE AUTHOR

Matt Browning works undercover to identify White supremacists. He and his wife, Tawni, founded the Skinhead Intelligence Network, a global information-sharing network for law enforcement.